A MILLION VACATIONS

The Max Webster Story

MARTIN POPOFF

A MILLION VACATIONS

The Max Webster Story

MARTIN POPOFF

WP
WYMER
PUBLISHING
Bedford, England

First published in Canada by Power Chord Press in July 2014
under the title *Live Magnetic Air: The Unlikely Saga of the Superlatie Max Webster.*
This revised edition published in 2025 by Wymer Publishing, Bedford, England
www.wymerpublishing.co.uk Tel: 01234 326691
Wymer Publishing is a trading name of Wymer (UK) Ltd.

Copyright © 2025 Martin Popoff / Wymer Publishing.

Print edition (fully illustrated): **ISBN: 978-1-915246-84-4**

Edited by Jerry Bloom.

The Author hereby asserts his rights to be identified
as the author of this work in accordance with sections
77 to 78 of the Copyright, Designs & Patents Act 1988.

All rights reserved. No part of this publication may be
reproduced or transmitted in any form or by any means,
electronic or mechanical, including photocopying, or any
information storage and retrieval system, without written
permission from the publisher.

This publication is sold subject to the condition that it shall not,
by way of trade or otherwise, be lent, re-sold, hired out or
otherwise circulated without the publisher's prior consent in any
form of binding or cover other than that in which it is published
and without a similar condition including this condition
being imposed on the subsequent purchaser.

A catalogue record for this book is available from the British Library.

eBook formatting by Lin White at Coinlea Services.
Typeset/Design by Andy Bishop / Tusseheia Creative.
Cover design: Tusseheia Creative.
Front cover photo: Scott Feeney.

CONTENTS

Testimony Up My Sleeve	7
Foreword I	15
Foreword II	17
Preface	19
Early Years – "Family at Macs"	25
Max Webster – "We don't dig the blockhead thing"	49
High Class in Borrowed Shoes – "What, do you mean the clown suits?"	81
Mutiny Up My Sleeve – "Fix it?! I got fired from that band!"	113
A Million Vacations – "I mean, how many moon songs are there?"	147
Live Magnetic Air – "We delivered the pizza, right?"	175
Universal Juveniles – "Are the drums loud enough for everybody?"	193
Maxed Out – "Everything's yellow"	225
Epilogue	249
Discography	251
Interviews with the Author	256
Additional Sources	257
Image Credits	258
Acknowledgements	258
About the Author	258
Martin Popoff – A Complete Bibliography	259

TESTIMONY UP MY SLEEVE

"Although I first saw (and was blown away by) Max Webster when they played at our high school, I first met Mike Tilka in my 20s after I sent him a demo tape when he was A&R guy at Anthem Records. He liked it. I liked him. I said, 'Do you want to play bass with us?' As I was soon to discover, Mike always says yes to any new musical adventure. In 1990, we needed a new keyboard player. Mike asked Terry Watkinson over and that was that. We formed Antlers. The band was a side-project in our busy lives, but we made a lot of great original music and have had a lot of fun on and off for the past 25 years. Mike Tilka is one of the most enthusiastic and adventurous musicians I have met. He is always up for a new challenge.

Mike loves different types of music. Eventually, we even attended jazz workshops together. Now he's rocking his stand-up bass in Mo Vista with authority and verve. Mike is never bored. He is always positive about music and life.

It goes without saying that Terry Watkinson is an incredible musician and songwriter. When he joined Antlers he wrote one or two great songs a week! He is as comfortable on saxophone and accordion as he is on keyboards. I have had a blast playing and singing with him on various projects over the years including his great Teratology CD. Most importantly, I am happy for the great friendship that has developed between the three of us over the years. The music is a bonus."
Sam Boutzouvis, *The Antlers*

"They played our high school dance in grade 10 (Erindale). We all had to kick in an extra 50 cents on our student cards to cover the 500 bucks they charged. We thought they were rich."
Mike Bullard, *Comedian*

"Cheap Trick was the Max Webster of the USA."
Bun E. Carlos, *Cheap Trick*

"As an aspiring young musician in Canada, I found the arrival of Max Webster on the scene bewildering at first. Where on earth could music like this have come from? Then the discovery that it was a Canadian group jolted my sense of what is possible. The sound of Max was the sound of technical proficiency at a high level married to a probing intellect. These were things I could admire. Max Webster stood out from the pack as a ferocious musical force. They made me and my fellow musicians proud of also being Canadian rockers. 'I'd like to be as cool as them' sums up the impression they made on us."
Carl Dixon, *Coney Hatch*

"I toured across Canada about three times, drumming with Kim, and I enjoyed that. It was probably one of the most challenging and satisfying gigs I've ever done, ever, in my career, was working for Kim. I respected him so much to begin with, from Max Webster in the early days of when I was in Streetheart and we came to Toronto to cut our first record in '77 and came out and saw a lot of the different groups. And when I saw Max Webster, that was like the second coming of Christ for me. And between them and Goddo and the whole eastern side of things of the music business, it was a real eye-opener for me. But when he called me to play in his band, it was a great, great honour.

Brilliant songwriter, guitar player, and he's always had a very high calibre of drummers in his bands, and I think that's pretty much a prerequisite for his music. Because he's got some challenging stuff. Even though it's within a pop music frame, there's a lot of musicality going on. Nice challenging parts, and I really enjoyed it.

I missed the reunion when they came through a few years back, when they put the band together again. Because I always wondered what Gary McCracken was doing, because he was a pretty big influence on me, coming to Toronto from the prairies, and hearing the old eastern swing, the songs out here. And when I saw Max, I added a couple of drums to my drum kit. I wanted to get that kind of melodic thing he had going.

He was a big influence on me and I really enjoyed his playing. He came from a bit of the fusion stuff that was going on in the '70s—Lenny White, Chick Corea, Cobham, Mahavishnu—and he had that kind of drumming and that kind of energy, and he added that to pop

music. And that was something that really caught my attention."
Matt Frenette, *Loverboy*

"I think the fact that so many people still talk about this band and crave their music speaks volumes for their legacy. They were quirky in appearance and even quirkier musically. I still remember seeing Kim in his band Zooom at the old Electric Circus on Queen Street in the late '60s. I thought he was a good guitar player even then, but it was the chaps he had on made from shag carpet that I remember most. Because we (Goddo) were coming up at the same time we played quite a few dates with them. We were quite close for a while with Mitchell even braving my fledgling culinary skills for dinner at my place. I always found Kim to run hot and cold, so you never really knew where you stood with him. That was cool, I had enough friends. Tilka was a sweetheart all the time and even handed me his bass at a Brampton Arena gig once to finish 'Hangover' with the band. I screwed up that funny bit at the very end, but no one seemed to mind. We called them Wax Lobster."
Greg Godovitz, *Goddo*

"I always enjoyed sharing the stage with Kim and Peter and the boys over the years."
Brian Greenway, *April Wine*

"Despite their quirky nature, bizarre name and tightrope-walking lyrics, these 'universal juveniles' stuck out in Canada's heavy rock scene with a fun-loving personality and humour with no borders."
"Metal" Tim Henderson, *BraveWords*

"Max Webster was one of the joys of Canadian music as the music industry in Canada was moving from its cottage roots to being an international force. Songs like 'Let Go the Line,' 'A Million Vacations' and 'Paradise Skies' broadened the scope and the vocabulary of Canadian music. Max Webster paved the way for acts like Cowboy Junkies, The Pursuit of Happiness and The Tragically Hip that followed. And there is indeed a Pye Dubois. Very much so. I met the revered Max Webster/Rush lyricist in the '70s when Kim Mitchell guested on CBC Radio's *Morningside* where I was senior music producer."
Larry LeBlanc, Senior Editor, *CelebrityAccess*

"I like the way Kim sings, from Max. I think he's a good vocalist, underrated; he's got a lot of expression and a nice tone."
Geddy Lee, *Rush*

"There was a scrim that went across the stage. Max was out there. Neil's kit was directly behind Sticksy (Gary McCracken), and he'd go up and that was his warm-up. He'd go up and play the last few songs with them. This happened mostly with Max. I think he might have done it a couple times with Primus, but it was a nightly thing with Max. We did so many dates with them. In fact, we were on tour when Kim had had enough and decided to go home. I remember pulling into that gig and all the guys were sitting on the grass and they looked so despondent. Kim's had enough. He can't take it anymore. He went home. He was on a flight this morning and went home. So, they were stuck there. And we took them to Europe and all over America. They were really starting to catch on in the States too. They were really developing a following where people were becoming familiar with their music. They were starting to develop a fan base. But I think Kim, it's a little much for him, to travel that much and be away, a lot of pressure, and I don't think he dealt with pressure that well. I think he was much happier to be here where everything was a given. At least, that was my impression then."
Alex Lifeson, *Rush*

"One of the most underrated Max Webster songs—'Sun Voices'—got me through some depressing times."
Mike Allan MacDonald, *Comedian*

"They were awesome uncles and teachers, plus they were good buds. Three thumbs up! (two thumbs and a boner, ha ha)."
Chris MacFarlane, *Max Webster crew*

"Everything about Max Webster was so wrong yet so right. The quirkiness invaded every aspect of the band's existence and it was totally magnetic from the first chord of any song from any of their albums. Play this shit to a youngster now and they'd probably laugh at you. In fact, they used to laugh at them back in the day but that's only because nobody understood what the hell was going on in their music or their minds. I loved them. British prog was so much more melodramatic and considered, but Max took the same mind-expanding blueprint and pumped up the pomposity to hitherto unprecedented proportions. It was complex and highfalutin' for sure, but Kim's searing heavy metal guitar riffs and ripping solos rooted the music to a place that the hard rockers in our neighbourhood could easily identify with.

Plus, the lyrics were so off-the-wall that they actually started to have meaning in the most perverse sense. Plus, I loved the fact that nobody in the band was actually called Max or Webster and that the words were written by a totally invisible third party with the unfeasibly exotic name of Pye Dubois. And what breathtaking style sense. Pantaloons were never so hip as when Max trod the boards on that Rush tour of the UK. Make no mistake, Rush were good but Max were way better."
Derek Oliver, *Rock Candy Records*

"Male pattern baldness hoser geek hockey rink glam rock. Max Webster. Only in Canada."
Geoff Pevere, *The Globe and Mail*

"Max Webster was a band which in their near ten-year existence spawned a library of amazing music. No two songs were the same and there was not a bad song on any of their albums in my view. It seemed as though despite the fact that they possessed equal talent, they pretty much basked in the shadow of Rush and I say this not to insult the community of Rush fans as I too am a Rush fan but that they lacked the amount of promotion which would have been needed to expand their horizons.

Mike Tilka had an ability to create a mood for songs which pulled you in and demanded your interest. I loved him in songs such as 'High Class in Borrowed Shoes' and 'On the Road.' Terry Watkinson was a very innovative player in that he utilised the keyboard in ways we had not before heard and a prime example of this would be songs such as 'Toronto Tontos' and 'Diamonds Diamonds.' Terry then showed us he had a great vocal ability when we heard 'Let Go the Line.' Kim Mitchell was innovative in his guitar work in that he took various styles and combined them. He shows us with songs like 'Rascal Houdi' that he is capable of speed and agility, then tones down in songs like 'Words to Words' to expose a gentle more vulnerable side.

Kim has a charisma and ability to spark the energy in any size venue and injects the right amount of humour leaving the crowd pleased and wanting more... I know I always did."
Steven "Dr. Flippy" Richard, *DJ*

"Max Webster was one of those bands at the time that 'broke the mould' and were clearly thinking outside of the box! Their musical ideas were, and still are, very inspiring."
Michael Sadler, *Saga*

"Max Webster was one of the musically and lyrically more intelligent Canadian rock bands. Pros who by the time I worked a CBC television special with them had done a lot of tours, festivals and bars. They were really easy and able to turn on the heat for rehearsals, like for the show. I had met Kim Mitchell prior to this event. Our first conversation was about our fave guitar players. We both zoomed in on Jimi Hendrix as the greatest innovator and influence of our era. I was not surprised. Good people, Kim."
Reiner W. Schwarz, *CBC Producer*

"I've been a Max Webster fan ever since my older brother brought home their debut record (the one with the weird heads on the cover). Even before I was able to articulate what it was about them, I liked, I could hear it on that first record. I loved how they could be 'rocking' one minute and then switch to an almost Beach Boy-ish type number like 'Summer Turning Blue' without losing themselves. There was humour, mystery and something rebellious going on in there.

As much as I loved that first record, when my brother came home with *High Class in Borrowed Shoes* the following year or so… a life was changed. I still believe it to be one of the best rock albums that ever came out of this country. The range of songs, the musicianship… the album cover! I could probably write a whole paragraph on Kim and Terry's incredible and original playing but then I'm a song guy and that's what ultimately draws me to Max Webster.

In the poetry of Pye Dubois, I think Kim found the perfect writing partner and I've loved all of Terry's song contributions as well ('Rain Child,' 'Let Go the Line,' 'Blowing the Blues Away'… amazing!). In fact, all of their other records were wonderful! (I'm currently on a huge *A Million Vacations* kick at the moment—it just might be their *Pet Sounds*). So anyway, I feel I've gone on a bit here so I'll end by saying that as a fan, I'm truly grateful for all the music they made together—but I sure hope they make some more. God Bless Max Webster!"
Ron "Climbing a Cloud" Sexsmith, *Solo Artist*

"Our first concert gig ever was with Max Webster and B.B. Gabor at the Kitchener arena. Our second was the next night at London Gardens with Max Webster and Goddo. Did one tour with Kim as well."
Brian Vollmer, *Helix*

"Max Webster occupies a unique place in the history of Canadian rock. In addition, it was a major statement in the career of my friend, Kim Mitchell, along with his band mates."
David Wilcox, *guitarist*

FOREWORD I

Max Webster and Ian Thomas Band Concert.

Dateline, April 28, 1978 (coincidentally, Popoff's 15th birthday), we were eagerly anticipating the upcoming concert with Max Webster touring their *Mutiny Up My Sleeve* album. As many concert-goers did back in the day, we had our supplies of various music-enhancing elements in tow.

We arrived early at the University of Calgary's MacEwan Hall in order to snag front row seats, as it was festival seating in those days and grabbed our spot at the entrance. As we were the first to arrive (about six of us) we had time on our hands to kill and the buzz was starting to set in. A few friends went adventuring while we held their cherished spots in line. A while later they arrived carrying two tubs of Labatt Blue stubbies, on ice! (for you younger folk, that was the beer bottle style back in the day).

When asked where they found this excellent haul, they merely stated, "It was in some room over there." Well, dry mouth was also setting in along with the buzz, so ice-cold beer was a godsend, and we started downing them to our delight. A while later a couple of older dudes approached us and asked where we got the beer from. We told them our story and discovered they were roadies for the Ian Thomas Band, who was opening that night. They were pissed-off. Apparently, we'd drank all of the band's beer. How were we to know?!

Fast forward, Ian Thomas is on stage and he is none to pleased about his lack of beer. During his set he would cast a few angry glances in our direction, as we were seated in the front row, over where Kim would later occupy the stage. Oh well...

When The Max machine took the stage, Kim was directly in front of us. At one point he was leering down over his mic, holding a disposable lighter. He asked a few of us if we were the owners of it, to which we shook our heads no. Kim then announced (as he threw it back towards his amps), "Take it away, as it is chock-full of LSD," accompanied by some weird guitar noodling with Terry joining in on keys. That was way too cool and set the tone for a wild ride the rest of the show. Needless to say, we were "beyond the moon" and this party was indeed higher than the Eiffel Tower.

Brian Smolik

FOREWORD II

Canuck wordsmith at the top of the mount, Pye Dubois, writes letters, long letters, usually from his winters in Florida to escape the cold. The author has received some beauties. For this introduction to an artist that I feel is the greatest rock lyricist of all time across all genres and county lines and timelines, I thought I'd include a few bits and bobs that I feel relate directly to the process.
Martin Popoff

You have anecdotes to cobble. I have a story to tell. I didn't know I had a story to tell until you opened up a can of worms/beans/tambourines... I screwed up. I've overwritten the story, I know now, I might like to tell. Copious notes for you about a story I thought sunk. And as my memories get oxygen and the past surfaces, this boat is on tilt to the possibility you will perceive me as woefully self-indulgent. This perception by others would be fearfully realised for me: that fate would be fatal.

What to do? I am conflicted and ambivalent. Anecdotes to make your book interesting are hard to come by. I know my contributions will be qualitatively and quantitatively diametric to all others' input (regardless of the questions by the questioner!).

My worst fear might be realised here: I'm coming across as self-indulgent and hoary and self-indulgent... self-indulgent...

Martin. I'm a little tired of this stuff. Too much of this is useless. I know and I knew it while writing. So, I grabbed at random and you are getting what I grabbed. I'll try again later to come up with better material. More anecdotes. Ask about Jerry McCartney, Big Al's Band, Phil Goodwin (Uniforms), Joan Chevalier ("Kathleen"), Dave Munns/Deane Cameron, van of guitars for Ritchie Blackmore, Tempe, Arizona, Jean-Luc Ponty, Allan Holdsworth, Billy Bruford, Terry's Austrian crotch pudding.

Lately, I've put the pen and paper aside. No more begging for anecdotes and no more feeding a fate others will fuel.

Seriously, I have so much material, too much material—I need someone to say, this piece of paper goes here. This piece of paper goes there. And this little metaphor needs to go wee wee wee all the way to the bone!

Actually, I may be at this point, no use to you. You want anecdotes, I want not to get off the writing continuum. Yeah! I guess I have a story to tell, but that's not your book. Again, it's not a book if you are not talking to KJM. Again—Max live in concert, 1000's having fun. That's the book. History! Regional RNR band has regional success etc., etc.

At this point (first of March), I might be useless to you. Far too many notes. I'm overwhelmed. You cobble anecdotes. I scramble to remember but I become woefully tangential... Turns to venting rather than visiting the past. I might be useless to you.

Confession: I enjoyed talking about the lyrics. Hadn't thought of them in years. Truly, am novice at talking about 'em because in the past I wouldn't traduce—I figured (re-: lyrics) I got the painting hung in the gallery, what more do you want?! To traduce meant the song lost some dignity. Anyway: is it April (the month) in Toledo or is it April (the girl) in Toledo?

Anyway: I'll try to get some pages to you. I shall send these all allowing you to redact the good stuff... stuff you need to use in a book. Might be better and more interesting if I read journal pages and some other pages to you—yeah, might be better if I stopped. Anecdotes? Where?

Quite ill years ago. Surgery (kidney). Been great for seven or eight years. Very, very healthy now... Very healthy for an old dude! How old am I? I remember Ted Nugent in a suit... Republican 'roots' I guess (his).

Other than kindling, what am I gonna do with my odes?

Please read near fluids... Spill on these pages, decoupage the Dodge!

Had copious notes to send you. Not enclosed. Too much venting, not enough vitality! Anyway, too intimidated to write prose for someone with a BABSCMAPHDSTD in English. Best I give you me in person, i.e., affect to my adverbs.

If it's really me you want to talk with
Then get in line
Get in line behind me
'Cause it's me I wanna talk to too.

Pye Dubois

PREFACE

Please, for a few minutes, lend me your ears, fellow Canucks (because for the purpose of our time together, celebrating Max Webster, we are all hosers!), I agonised over what to say in this introduction for months, main reason being that I've been known to say in interviews, radio, online, print, whatever, depending on what mood I'm in, that my favourite band of all time is the gosh-darn superlative Max Webster.

Sure, sometimes it's ZZ Top, sometimes it's Thin Lizzy, sometimes it's even Gillan. And then, in what you might call a crazed, deluded state, I can sometimes even convince myself that Max Webster is the greatest band of all time, slightly better than Led Zeppelin, vastly superior to The Beatles. In fact, I was trying to find a way to work that into the title of the tome, but it wound up too unwieldy.

Now, stay with me here. *Physical Graffiti* is the greatest album of all time, if it's not Black Sabbath's *Sabotage*, issued the same year. But Zeppelin get there by cheating, by making a double album, and I'm a sucker for double albums. Similarly, Max is the greatest tactical rock unit ever because they cheat. Read on, cheer us on...

Yes, they cheat. Max Webster—okay, let's just say it, what the hell—is the finest rock 'n' roll band in all history (and we have this discussion all the time, me and the nerds) because they didn't stick around long enough to screw up. Heck, if the world blew up in 1981 when Max Webster blew up, candidates for favourite band of all time would be anyone from Aerosmith to Black Sabbath to Queen to Rush, and I guess, most likely not Max Webster, who would nonetheless still make the top ten, at least for many Canadians.

But there—briefly and brilliantly—flashes Max Webster, issuing five gold standard studio albums, an okay live album and a posthumous greatest hits album.

And then they're gone, nice, neat, forever young/Yonge. Now, let's not get into the discussion about that first Kim Mitchell EP, which craps all over the entire Max Webster catalogue from a height of several miles. But look, Kim, as a solo artist, supports the above supposin' premise. Although the man rebounded strong with his last two platters that matter, he indeed was around for the late '80s and early '90s and kinda sucked for a while just like everybody else did. Bloody 'ell, look at Heart: same thing, superlative up to about '83, crap for a decade, and then super-strong again with three fine studio albums in a row.

In any event, I just wanted to drive home the point—and get everybody cackling at this nut who thinks there's no finer poet in all of rock than Pye—that after doing almost 135 of these damn books, at my age, doing one on Max Webster, well, that's about as labour of love as it gets. And by the way, I first wrote that bit for the original version of this book that I stuck together back in 2014. That edition was called *Live Magnetic Air: The Unlikely Saga of the Superlative Max Webster*, and the sentiment still applies today, a dozen years later.

Really, I'm doing this just to keep me happy. As I said at the time to the delightful Rodney Bowes (the designer of the *Universal Juveniles* album cover, much to his chagrin), taking six months to play Max Webster 60% of all my playing time, which in aggregate, is a heck of a lot of Max Webster, believe me, that was no chore at all. These damn records never get old, and part of that is just the sheer exquisite detail to supreme performance and production quality, plus inscrutable lyrics that keep handing out wisdoms like them weird creativity cards Brian Eno made (wish I had a set, but Pye's hand-strewn scraps of paper will do).

Fact is, and I will definitely keep driving this home throughout the book, this is one band that I'm constantly turning people onto, because I believe the catalogue is just big enough to vault the band into that hallowed zone with the smartest of my music buddies. Gotta remark, I love Max because they ain't that heavy and they understand how proggy they need to be, in sips, because you are way more cool if you dole the prog and the heavy perfectly balanced, along with keyboards, along with humour.

And who else does this? Well, that other "thinking man's heavy metal band" Blue Öyster Cult. It's them and maybe Cheap Trick that are the closest comparatives I can conjure and that's a hallowed trinity. Although, come to think of it, Cheap Trick is closer to Kim solo, right?

Anyhow, I'll friggin' rant like an old lady to the hills, in driving rain, chased by goats, that you can't argue on a completely objective basis that there's ever been a greater band in all of rock 'n' roll.

In that light, or down that path, or to start the roundhouse row, the subset of reasons I would ever talk this way are as follows. Pye Dubois is one of my favourite lyricists of all time, along with... oh, who do you want to throw in there? Neil P. Fallon from Clutch? Don van Vliet? The army of conspiracy-crazy literary types that wrote the Blue Öyster Cult canon? Certainly, all of those guys. But Pye, I just love the density, the playfulness, the hope, even though Kim Mitchell manager Tom Berry has kind of disagreed, figuring there was considerable darkness in his lyrics. I guess, being a lifelong metalhead, maybe my meter on darkness is a lot darker than his, I don't know.

And then there's the production. As I do prattle on about, I really don't think on an objective basis, you can say there is a single record from all of the '70s that sounds better than Max's second, third and fourth albums, especially the fourth, *A Million Vacations*. Sure, it gets a bit stupid. It's almost like yelling about what's the greatest song of all time. Forsooth, the song is just too small a sample of art to make the discussion meaningful. And so is production. Or it's ethereal, subjective, pretty arcane, like trying to pick the best guitar tone or snare sound or even guitar solo.

My point is, in all the areas that go to make up which group of long-haired miscreants might be called the greatest rock 'n' roll band of all time, production may as well be one of those boxes that needs to be ticked. Take that, Jimmy Page, who made one barely good sounding record, called *In Through the Out Door*. Without really studying it, I figure *Dark Side of the Moon*, in 1973, is the first perfect sounding record. And is *Rocks* as good sounding as Max? Maybe. BÖC's *Mirrors*? Sure. But part of this point is, every other Aerosmith record and every other BÖC record sounds worse than at least three of Max's, maybe four—and they only made five.

And then there's Kim Mitchell. Again, check my record over the years. Asked many times who my favourite guitarist of all time is, I'm usually blathering like some annoying fraud of an expert about three blokes: Billy Gibbons, Brian May and Kim Mitchell. Kim Mitchell is to me what Michael Schenker is to European-style power metal. Michael massages in just enough melody, accessibility, and yes, hair metal, to brighten up his Gothic European tendencies, to where there's a pretty abstract and sophisticated magic going on there.

Kim does the same thing, augmenting his impressive root arsenal with the crunch of Frank Zappa (who solos as if he is playing a parody of a guitar solo) and the swirl of Robert Fripp (of the early era, of the *Red* era and yes, of the red, blue and yellow era as well). And that root arsenal? There's accessibility, humour, versatility, jazz, pop, prog and power chords.

And it continues on from there, this shouting in a wind-tunnel about how good this band is. I totally dig Gary McCracken's arch-'70s drumming, his tuned tom-tom sound. Mad scientist Terry Watkinson has all sorts of traditional and futuristic tones in his keyboard bag of tricks. The bonus is his writing, an airy, commercial foil to Kim's and Pye's sneaky subversion. Love what Dave Myles does, and yes, for all the abuse he takes for his musicianship, Mike Tilka as well. And let's not forget Paul Kersey. Even though that first Max Webster album is pretty much agreed upon as slightly rudimentary, and closer to mortal than the subsequent four immortal masterwerks, Paul does a great job on the likes of "Lily" and "Hangover." And hey, it's Max Webster, so the thing's a friggin' 9/10, at minimum.

What else do I want to say about this book? Well, here's an important one. The first edition back in 2014 probably wouldn't have happened without the financial assistance of Brian Smolik and Adrian Orso, who put up a few grand for the same reason I put up months of typing. I won't get into details but suffice to say that here's the truth on this. These two super-fans generously came through with a base of funds that allowed me to slightly transcend the possibility—or the risk, whatever you want to call it—of spending a few months on this book and losing a few thousand dollars, to at least having a guarantee of around minimum wage. And me, being Canadian (and this is something also amusing that Rodney explained to me, this Canadian tendency of not really worried about how much we get paid for anything), that was enough for me to embark on the months it took me to write the original book. Essentially, so much of what this was about was documenting the history of a rich, creative, amazing band, who, I'm patriotically proud to say, is as gosh-darn Canadian as they come.

Another thing I'd like to mention. Even though I'm positive you are really going to know quite a bit about the relationships between these highly effective people, both in the band and at the office, by the end of this considerably lively tale, I gotta tell ya, I left out quite a bit of stuff that was just too raw. It's funny, the three times anybody said "off the record" to me, it wasn't nuthin' to get up in arms about, but of course I didn't include that. But there was a whole pile of just regular stuff said that I thought, these relationships are what they are right now and mostly healing or getting better over time. Why make them turn for the worse again? Let these men live out the rest of their lives in more peace, not less. Let them continue to stay sociable with each other and maybe meet up over beers at an Antlers gig, which I did. That's the category in which everything I left out fits. No details, but there's darkness from Pye about the brief live reunion, there's way too many financial details from Gary, and there's... damn, I can't even hint at that one... frig, those two.

Actually, there's one more category on surgical omissions. Okay, here's the deal. I have a tendency to let the words stand in terms of the sometimes film-type memories of these stories. I'll even let slightly conflicting stories butt next to each other. Or let vague things stay vague. But there were quite a few times when I was sure what I was being told was plain wrong or plainly exaggerated. These have been clipped out so as not to cause even greater confusion, and, frankly, I'd rather not have these amiable chums come off like yarn-darners, liars and braggarts.

Okay, next point of business. Some of you Popoff patrons might know that I wrote a trilogy of books on a band called Thin Lizzy, who was, for all intents and purposes, over and done with by 1983. That journey spanned something like 750 pages.

Now, here's the thing. Believe it or not, I would've had no problem crafting this into two sizable books. Or one 500+ page book. I actually had the material to do it, and hey, I would've loved to have done even more interviews. But that ultimately seemed really crazy for an obscure Canadian band with five records, who broke up in 1981. As well, I'll settle for minimum wage for a few months, but it'd be dang well irresponsible to toil madly for eight months at like half of whatever benevolent Ontario's minimum wage is these days. So, I had to let go. Just like a band will tell you, a record is done when the label snatches it away from you. Put another way, "a painting is never finished; it's just abandoned." Similarly, I had to simply stop working on this book at some point, and the academic in me hates that.

An additional reason I'm telling you this is that my original plan was to include a pretty long epilogue on Kim Mitchell's post-Max Webster career. After all, some of the greatest music ever made by mankind is embedded in that catalogue as well. And some of you may not know this—well, who am I kidding? All of you know this—Kim Mitchell had a way bigger career as a solo artist than he ever did with Max.

So, bottom line, I really did run out of room (and time) with this book. I had to draw the line somewhere, another reason being, the bigger it is, the more we gotta charge and the more postage is gonna be. So, like I say, I could've gone to two books; I could've gone to one much longer book. But here's the deal. I've chopped and possibly somewhat abruptly held back on a lot of what I have about Kim's solo career, because who the heck knows, maybe there should be a Kim Mitchell book too.

It's funny (and totally expected), but when I quipped about this to Kim in our last interview, of course the reaction was basically a variation on, 'Yeah, right, why the hell would anybody read a Kim Mitchell book, much less write one?' Which is of course how he feels about a Max Webster book times two. It's quite amusing, but Tom Berry (manager) and I agree: the guy really doesn't cotton onto how incredible the music is that he's given us, such as, for example, the greatest guitar solo of all time, inside of "Rumour Has It," from *Akimbo Alogo*.

Anyway, just a few other points of business. If you've read any of my other 50-odd books that are specifically on one band, you'll know that I have a methodology where the book is essentially about the records, song by song, one chapter per album. I most definitely do that here, and I feel more strongly about it with Max than any of these other third-rate hack bands I've written about. And the reason for that is because the intellectual (!) thrust of this volume is to proselytise about this tight little gaggle of five godly records, one upon the next, until we get to the final hurrah, *Universal Juveniles*, controversial, somewhat unloved.

So, in that spirit, prepare yourself for a geeky and freaky digging-into the music of mad, mad Max Webster, and very much as importantly, the lyrics of (now) Jerry Garcia-look-alike Pye Dubois, who... all right, I'll say it right here, it's usually not even a contest. When people do dangerously ask me (the expert on these matters) who the wisest wordsmith in all of rock, for all of time, past, present and at least prophetically futuristic, is, well, there's only one smilin' Buddha of an answer to that: Pye Dubois, here to thin the thickness of your skin.

Martin Popoff
martinp@inforamp.net; martinpopoff.com

EARLY YEARS –
"Family at Macs"

Is there any reason in the world, sifted back through the tea leaves, divined through the rod of rock, that Max Webster would coalesce to become the greatest rock band that ever was? Perhaps if there was a formula to be perceived and detected deep within Ontario's B-cities in the '60s and low '70s, just maybe The Beatles could have taken that prize had they come from Sarnia. Or if they had visited the glovebox of Ontario from their home in Birmingham and hung out here among the cats, Robert Plant and John Bonham could have slaked of such exalted heights. In any event, neither The Beatles nor any of Led Zeppelin did, so they didn't, and they weren't. Ergo there goes Max Webster, the finest rock 'n' roll act in the history of the genre now 60 years on.

In deference to leaving some of the magic water in the bottle, we aren't going to go into too much detail on how this happened. But let's start with a broad generality: the guys in Max Webster most definitely paid their dues, playing in a bewildering array of micro bands addressing a number of genres, some of them well beyond rock. That's the gist of how they got so good. And look, I've never dug all of the talk of garage bands that must be there nonetheless to set the stage in rock books. Furthermore, when the records are this good, I just want to get onto them and discuss them. In that light, I'm even more bored by the formative band stuff, or at least impatient to get it over with.

But briefly, the tale of future divinity goes something like this, and I guess, given he's the oldster in the holster, let's start with mad scientist keyboardist Terry Watkinson, born in 1940 in Fort William, Ontario, now not really a thing, but part of Thunder Bay. There he lived, as well as Iroquois Falls, Ontario, 400 miles to the east and even more remote. There once was a band called Dee and the Yeomen, the Dee being a British singer named Graham Dunnett. Terry arrived in the band in the fall of 1964 from Sonny and the Sequins, and what followed would be a half dozen very collectible singles, admired variously as garage rock, proto-punk, sophisticated pop and psych. The name of the band had variants, such as Dee and the Quotum, The Yeomen and Rock Show and the Yeomen. The band was based in Toronto but did business around the Golden Horseshoe and up to Montreal.

Meanwhile, Kim Mitchell, a dozen years Terry's junior, was in a suited bunch from Sarnia, Ontario called The Grass Company, which also included among the ranks second Max Webster bassist Dave Myles. Kim had begun his journey strumming on a Stella guitar, then an acoustic/electric Kay, eventually graduating to an orange Gretsch, on which he would hone his country rock chops.

First came The Gladiators and then occasional gigs with The Volcanoes, playing bass, along with The Quotations. Dave's directly previous band was Unit Four. He took music in school, playing tuba as well as stand-up bass. Also taking music at the same time and at the same high school was future Max drummer Gary McCracken, and naturally, the two would jam together on weekends.

The Grass Company went so far as nipping over to Battle Creek, Michigan and opening for the explosive MC5 at Kellogg Community College. Due to MC5 manager Jim Sinclair's radical politics, foisted upon the band, the National Guard was there to keep an eye on things.

In 1967, when local paper *The Windsor Star* ran a piece on the band, Dave was 15 years old and Kim was all of 14. Mrs. Mitchell (mom, that is), was interviewed and seemed chuffed about Kim's hobby, pleased that they had raised money for benefits, notwithstanding the amassing of $5000 worth of noisemaking equipment in the process.

Apparently, Kim also quite liked a game of tennis. The Grass

Company was not as prolific as Terry's joint, issuing one single on the Sound label out of Detroit (where it was also recorded), pairing a-side "Once a Days" (a bit of a typo; the song was actually called "Days") with "Once a Child." Highlight of the pair was the spooky flipside, which features a howling fuzz guitar solo by a then 16-year-old Kim, marking his debut as a rebellious recording artist.

"Kim was very good on guitar from day one," relates Paul "Pye Dubois" Woods, soon to be lyricist for Max Webster but at this stage, shiftless teenager with his head in the clouds. "When he got that guitar as a teenager, 13, 14, I think it was a real comfort. And even with his first time on stage, he was obviously very good. He practiced always, always, always. We didn't go to the same high school, but I remember us as hippies, operating on the fringe, Kim, myself and our friend Jimmy Chevalier. We used to hang out all the time, and our hair continued to grow over our ears, and we were really the outcasts. But there were just so many bands back then. Sarnia had three or four bands that could do the high schools, just rotate them every week. So, it was very easy, and I think one of Kim's first professional gigs was a country & western band. So yeah, he was good from the get-go." In fact, Kim's mother had sung in a country & western band, and they would rehearse at the house, giving Kim an early glimpse into the business.

"We would go to restaurants," continues Pye on those days of aimless small-town bewilderment. "We'd walk the streets and we'd skip high school and be smoking cigarettes out the back. Just typical teenage stuff. But always finding someplace to go. I can remember a couple basements we used to go to; the parents would let us go and we'd listen to Zappa's *200 Motels* or something. Someone usually had a joint."

The Grass Company soon became Big Al's Band and then after a move to Toronto, Zooom. Big city to be sure, but let's not forget that Montreal was still the big apple of Canada's eye in the late '60s, larger in population than its conservative Anglo rival plus still high on the fumes of Expo 67. Nonetheless, it had the Yonge Street strip and a growing hippie scene based in Yorkville, and it was the place to be in Canada for rock 'n' roll, if we had one at all.

Continues Pye, "Zooom came along and they all moved to Toronto. They were eating rice and peanut butter. And I remember, I had moved, a lot of us have moved to Toronto. A lot of Sarnia people lived on Howard Street in Toronto, in all those buildings now that are almost condemned. And I remember I used to take peanut butter and rice down to them because they weren't eating."

Academics quickly fizzled. "Well yes, I loved the idea of going to university, because I felt... I didn't think that I was going to learn anything, but I thought they would teach me about the library. So, in my first year at York, I was in the arts, painting and drawing, and I used to do some paintings and get high marks. But I just wasn't cut out for the academic stuff. I just couldn't read five books a week. I just couldn't do it. My mind just isn't that fast. I absolutely stopped doing art once I started writing. But I did want to paint and draw. That was my first love."

Pye did no writing for Zooom. "No, Jimmy Chevalier, he had a lot of wonderful originals, and they played his originals. And Phil Goodwin's originals. They were very good songs." Kim credits Jim as a major influence on his formative years, which were at this point still very formative. Mitchell was all of 17 years old when he moved to Toronto, leaving high school early to stake his claim.

Triumph drummer and co-vocalist Gil Moore, a big admirer of Max, remembers these formative years as well. "The first time I saw Kim was at the Electric Circus, playing with Zooom. You know, here was this guy from Sarnia, who I've never heard of. It was the first time I saw his name. And I was mesmerized when I saw Kim for the first time. It kind of reminds me of the first time I saw Angus Young and AC/DC, and thought, wow, this guitar player is wild. Kim was like that. He just takes over the stage. He really had a presence and a style of playing that was original, really commanding. Then I saw Max Webster. Now, it seemed to me in Zooom, it was all about him; I think Zooom was a three-piece. But Max, there was more musical definition and Kim was focused probably more on singing. But yeah, the first Max Webster gig that I was around, you couldn't help but be impressed with their tightness and musicianship. There was another band in Toronto you might remember called Leigh Ashford and a lot of musicians would come and watch Leigh Ashford play, and I think Max was in that category where musicians would go and see Max Webster because of their musicianship."

"The other thing that was interesting," continues Gil, "is that Max really did have a signature sound. I don't think anybody would deny that when you heard Max Webster, you knew it was Max Webster. And it was some sort of combination of the fact that they were always musicians of a high calibre with crisp drumming and then Kim, who's got a signature vocal style. And I think also the lyrics that he and Pye wrote, again, there was a flavour there. It's like a great recipe, a combination of what the chef does in the kitchen that produces it. And I think that's true of a lot of great bands. I was reading earlier today online about Jimmy Page, and I'm a big Led Zeppelin fan, and what this was about was, well, the other things that he's been involved in, like how underwhelming the response was to all of his other efforts. And I thought about that for second and thought of the bands that had some sort of magic. If you look at how they form, generally they didn't have the magic until they came together. And played in individual bands that weren't doing that well. Suddenly this group comes together and then all of a sudden there's that special recipe thing that kicks in. And I think Max, individually, they were all great musicians, but the magic was how they played together. And that they created as a distinct sound. You hear them on the radio today, you go bang, that's Max Webster. They didn't emulate any other band. You don't get confused hearing a Max Webster track with anybody else."

Zooom was a well-respected act on the scene, playing originals when most bands played covers. They managed to get a couple of key early support gigs as well, for Alice Cooper and for Detroit's SRC.

First drummer for Max Webster, Paul Kersey cut his teeth (but not his hair) in London, Ontario in the late '60s as part of Sally and the Bluesmen, the Sally being Paul's nickname because of his long hair. They later became the Bluesmen Revue, issuing one single in 1968, "Spin the Bottle"/"Dorian's Dance," on Columbia. Highlight of the career was an opening slot with Sly & the Family Stone which took the band down to Florida and back.

Moving into the mid '70s and an era where hippies still reigned but much to their chagrin, they were becoming an anachronism, we get the scruffy and fusion-oriented Zing Dingo, notable for the fact that two-thirds of the trio was half of Max Webster V2, namely Gary McCracken and Dave Myles. Also, part of the fold was Greg Chadd, who would be part of Max for a brief spell later on. Another band featuring two future Max members, Dave and Gary, was called Jack Pine.

"Well, I'm from London," begins Paul Kersey, offering his take on hooking up with Max's lanky guitarist for the first time. "And I was in a band called The Bluesmen Revue, or Sally and the Bluesmen before that, and we were more or less, well, we were the biggest band in southern Ontario from Kitchener down, kind of thing. We were very popular in the high schools and dances and stuff. We never played bars. This is teenage stuff back in the '60s. Bars weren't the same back then (laughs). If you went to a bar, you were old. One of those deals, right? And Kim was in a band called Grass Company, and they were in Sarnia. We used to play Sarnia. We played everywhere in the area, every high school, every dance, every pavilion, every arena, everything that could happen, we played them all. And Kim had seen me a few times, and I'd heard of The Grass Company; I may have seen them once, but we knew each other kind of."

"And I moved to Toronto and he moved to Toronto," continues Paul. "And somehow we hooked up, because I was in... all the bands I went through after that band, I was in kind of a show band. They used to call them show bands or Holiday Inn bands. You'd go out, and you're musically not trying to do much; you're just trying to make a living, okay? You're just going, well, I gotta work, I'd rather play than have a job. So, whatever the gig is, I'll do it. And I was in a band, and Kim actually, I hooked up with him somewhere in Toronto, and he joined the band for a couple of weeks. The show band... we went through a lot of different names. One of the names was Crosstown Traffic, and one place we used to play a lot was a hotel on Dixon Road. And when Kim played with us, we were playing just down outside the village, actually, a club right around on Avenue Road."

"Anyway, he said, he could only do it for a couple of weeks because he was going to Greece to back up... I think the guy's name was Alex Nikolis. He had a three-month/four-month gig in Greece, on the island of Rhodes or something. And Mitchell was thinking, I don't really want to back... he was like a Tom Jones/Elvis kind of guy, showman kind of guy, and Kim wasn't really thrilled about doing it. But he's going, hey, if I could go to Greece for three or four months and be paid to be there, I'll probably never, ever go again, so why not do it, right? So, he did that. And then he said he's gonna call me when he got back and try to put a band together. And I went, oh, sure. And in the meantime, he's off enjoying the island and I'm left here with what I've got to do."

Also in the band was Kim's buddy Jim Bruton, with the connection to the Greek gig being that both of them, along with Gary McCracken, played with Nikolis in Toronto. The Greek residency was in 1972 at Club 2001, and the two of them indeed saw it as an exotic vacation, despite having to play covers and Greek music. But Kim loved the food and also gained an appreciation for the eastern scales and tricky time signatures that can be heard through the music over there. Still, despite the sun and fun, enjoyed during the day when his services weren't needed, he realised that it was a dead-end job, returning in August of 1972.

"So, Kim comes back and through the grapevine I hear he's looking for me," continues Paul. "And he's got his feelers out, I've got my feelers out, and in that time, I had moved back to London for some reason. I had joined a band called Whitehorse, because I was with a keyboard player that I had been with for more or less since we started. We grew up together in the music thing, and we were sticking together. We tried a lot of different things. We tried R&B bands, we were an R&B band at the beginning, and then we were in a psychedelic type band, and we were in show bands; we did a trio and a duo even. Did all kinds of different things together, so I tried to keep them with me. And we decided to go back to London because it was cheaper than living in Toronto, and we knew a band there for sure that we could play with, and they had gigs and so on and so forth."

"But then I hear that Mitchell is looking for me. While I'm in London. So, I think, I can't stay in London (laughs). There's no future in London. I gotta get out of here. And he was looking for a keyboard player too. So I went, well, this is it (laughs). This was big. This was do or die, move back to Toronto and take a shot at it or stick with my buddy and we'll end up playing the Holiday Inn for the rest of my life. I don't really want to do that. So, Kim was looking for me, and my girlfriend who I was living with at the time, I said okay, I gotta play, I gotta stay here. You go to Toronto and find a place to live. She worked... of course (laughs); she got a transfer to Toronto. I guess you know musicians, right? If you don't have a working wife or girlfriend you're in big trouble."

"So, I guess what I'm getting to, she came to Toronto and looked for a place, found a place, and she'd just called me in London, to say I got a place. And she told me where it was. Kim called shortly thereafter and I said, 'We just got a place in Toronto. I'm coming back.' And he says, 'Oh, where are you living?' And I said, 'At the corner of Jarvis and Isabella, an apartment building.' And he says, 'What number?' I don't remember what the number was. He was upstairs. He was two floors up. Of all the places in Toronto you could be, she coulda just walked upstairs and told him I'm coming back. Anyway, I said, that was odd. So, we hooked up and then I joined the band."

"I joined the band April Fool's Day 1973. Makes sense, doesn't it?" laughs Paul. "Kim was in the band, Mike was in the band and Jim Bruton was in the band, keyboard player; he's from Sarnia as well."

"Well, there's no recollection. I know exactly how it was named," says bassist Mike "The Whale" Tilka, on coming up with the name Max Webster. "I played in a band with my brother and Daryl Stuermer and his brother and a bunch of horn players, in Milwaukee, the summer before called Family at Mac's. And that name came from Daryl and his buddies, and when I say Daryl, he was just a kid, 17, 18 years old, and he was an amazing guitar player then. And he and his buddies used to hang around the McDonald's, and they referred to themselves as Family at Mac's: M-A-C apostrophe S. When they formed a band, everybody said they should call the band Family at Max, but they should make it M-A-X, because it sounded cooler; it sounded like a bar."

"And their bass player quit or got a gig or something. He had to leave the band right before a huge concert, 10,000 people, at Summer Fest, which is a festival that goes on to this day in Milwaukee, and they were a horn band, like Chicago, Blood, Sweat & Tears, progressive, jazzy, big, four or five horns. And my brother called me—I was a schoolteacher, I had the summer off—and he said, 'Get in your car, drive to Milwaukee, you gotta learn all these songs, you're playing bass.' So, I was living in Windsor, drove to Milwaukee, and I was in Family at Max, for the summer. And they were a real hot big bar band, concert band, in Milwaukee. And we actually recorded sometimes and everything."

"By the end of the summer," continues Mike, "the band had run its course, and Daryl and his brother and me and my brother moved back to Windsor, and formed Max Webster. And the reason we called it Max Webster was, Family at Max, and we used to end the night as Family at Max, with a song Daryl wrote, kind of a jazz-fusion rock tune called 'Song for Webster,' named for Ben Webster, the sax player. And that's where Max Webster came from."

"And a year and a half later, when Kim and I formed Max Webster, we played under a variety of names. The first name we played under was Stinky. We didn't pick that. Gord Waverly of the Abbey Road pub hired us; we played our first gig there on Christmas, the day before Christmas Eve or something—no bands wanted to play. But it was a weekend, and we said, we'll play! We played as a trio, and he said, 'If you don't give me a band name...' We didn't have a band name. He said, 'I'm going to put Stinky in the *Toronto Star*.' And the Abbey Road pub was the room to play at the time. And so, we played as Stinky. And then we played two weeks later in Bracebridge under the name Special Delivery, which we thought, this is stupid, we have to have a name."

"And then we went back home and we couldn't decide on a name. And we all loved the name Jethro Tull. And Kim liked it too; he said it was a name, it was nobody in the band, it has a certain amount of significance to the band, but really to anybody else they weren't Abraham Lincoln, they were Jethro Tull. So, he said, 'Could we use that name you and Daryl had?' And I said of course we can. We became Max Webster. We had no idea there was a Canadian horse breeder/philanthropist named Max Webster, that had a street named after him. It was nobody's name. It became... that's where it came from."

"There was no Terry and there was no Pye," continues Mike, asked about the band dynamic in its formative months. "It was me, the drummer from Max Webster, Phil Trudell, and Kim. And we were just band guys in a house that wanted to get some bar gigs. Kim was taking lessons and he practiced all day. I wanted to learn about the music business and I worked as an agent, although I had no experience as an agent, but I was a smart guy, and everybody said, 'You want to learn about the music industry? Be a middleman.' I had no intention of staying an agent. I didn't want to be a career agent. I didn't want to work for a record company. I wanted to be a bass player, maybe a producer, but I wanted to learn about the business, and I learned a lot."

And how did Mike hook up with Kim in the first place? "I remember the letter well," said Mike back in '77, speaking with Sam Charters. "It said, 'Hi, my name is Kim Mitchell. I play guitar. I hear you play bass. Would you be interested in forming a band?' He included his phone number, signed it and drew and some ducks and had a couple of 'quack quack's printed on the letter. I thought it was some kid. I called, we got together and jammed. It stunk."

"Ray Danniels, who managed Rush, hired me," continues Mike, beginning, right then, the web that tangled Max Webster with Rush through all of the rest of the band's quixotic life. "That's one reason I moved to Toronto; I had a job. So, I worked as an agent, Kim practiced all day, still hung around, and every night we practiced, and on the weekends we practiced. We loved practicing. It was fun, and we were a pretty good little trio, and Phil sang more songs than any of them. Because he was a great singer. But Phil had problems with his lungs; he had collapsed lungs a couple times and it just wasn't going to work."

"And we always had the intention of adding a keyboard player, and the person we were going to ask was in Europe. His name was

Jim Bruton. And Jim is still a dear friend of Kim and I, and Kim has known him from childhood. He's from Corunna, which is near Sarnia. And Jim got off the boat, literally started playing with us that spring. We had already done maybe three, four dates as a trio, not many. And Phil had to leave because of his lungs, and he wasn't happy, etc., and it wasn't like I'm unhappy because I'm in a band. He didn't feel well, he was away from home, and that's where Kersey came in. Kim knew Paul Kersey, and we heard him play, and he was a monster drummer, etc."

"I was only there about six months," recalls Phil Trudell. "I remember it was a tough time for musicians who moved into the Toronto area. The union was strong and musicians from out of town were not allowed to play in the city for a long time, six months or a year. So, all our gigs had to be out of town jobs which no one else wanted, i.e. far away, low pay. In spite of the hardships it was great fun playing with Kim, Mike and Sparks—Jim Bruton, a superb pianist and keyboardist. We just did cover tunes for bar gigs at first. By the time Kim started writing originals it was decided that I didn't quite fit into the vision. I was homesick for the good life in Windsor anyway and it turned out to be a great move for me. I have no regrets and nothing but respect and admiration for what Kim, Mike and Jim have accomplished."

So, Paul Kersey replaces Phil Trudell pretty much for the same reasons Neil Peart replaces John Rutsey—remarkably, including the conflicting stories about how much health enters into it. Oh, and then as we'll read later, the pressure would be on from the Rush camp for Paul to replace... John Rutsey.

Asked to sift through the years and come up with some dates, Mike offers up, "This was... hang on, I graduated from university '68, so Kim and I moved to Toronto in 1972, I guess that would've been in the fall. We played our first gig the last couple days of December of '72, and then in '73 we became Max Webster, and then Jim got off the boat, probably, late winter, early spring. There was still snow on the ground. I remember that."

So, the initial gigs as Max Webster would've been in early 1973.

"Yes. And I know that Paul Kersey posted on the internet when he started with Max, and he's off by a year. I was going to send him an email, but I thought, you know what? There's so much misinformation. And I had to call Jim Bruton and check that out. For me it's so easy. You go to high school for four years. Well, I worked for four years. So, I knew exactly when I actually quit teaching because I got a gig as a musician and I loved being a musician. And it was that summer, which would have been the summer of '72. Did I do that right again? It's when I met Kim, and I met him through Jim Bruton, the keyboard player. Kim was in Europe, Kim came back from Europe, and they were playing together, and he said, 'Look up a guy named Mike Tilka. He's a good bass player, he's a nice guy, you'll like him, I know he wants to be a full-time musician. Maybe he'll go to Toronto with you.' Kim took the train from Sarnia, or however he got to Windsor, we jammed, we had a few weeks or a couple months, and we both moved to Toronto. Didn't even know each other."

"Just a cover band," laughs Paul Kersey. "Just trying to find a direction."

This was Max Webster, again, in its formative months, a bunch of guys with over-active imaginations, with a sincere and even nerdy love of exploratory rock, guys for whom chops and their record collections meant something, possibly as much as beers, pot and girls, which were all, also important. Max... if you had to sum it up, they were late-stage original hippies.

"We did J. Geils stuff. The J. Geils tunes I remember, because Jim could sing them. We did Doobie Brothers, because Mike liked the Doobie Brothers—he sang the Doobie Brothers songs. I think we even did 'Smoke On The Water' once. What else? I think we did 'Dancing Days' by Zeppelin. Oh, we definitely did Zappa and Tull. We did a bunch of Zappa songs. I think we did more Zappa songs than any band ever in Toronto. 'Awreetus-Awrightus' on *The Grand Wazoo*, a relatively new album. This was back when *Overnight Sensation* I think was the newest album. I've got a set list around somewhere. And Jethro Tull songs as well. 'Peaches en Regalia' was the last Zappa song that we dropped. We started dropping cover songs, I think in about '74, late '74. And the last two songs to go were 'Aqualung' and then 'Peaches en Regalia' was the last one to go. And the first song we ever played was 'Aqualung.'"

Didja get that? To reiterate, Jethro Tull represented a nomenclature very much like Max Webster (and Lynyrd Skynyrd, and at a stretch—which one's Pink?). Plus, they were a heavy-rocking prog band. And Zappa? The prime influence, although... man, a whole study could be conducted on how Max did—and did not—go to Zappa-esque places. Indeed, Kim was such a big fan of Frank, that he was called onto CHUM-FM radio by FM chum Larry Wilson back in the day to review a Zappa concert.

"Kim unfortunately got pigeonholed with that label, right?" says

Pye, curiously not buying the Zappa connection, although Kim is wont to downplay it as well. "And I think it was unfair. I think there were Zappa albums that we loved. 'Peaches en Regalia,' great song. But I had trouble understanding why people hearing Kim would say, that's very Zappa-ish. I didn't hear it. Did you? You got me. You can't help but be musically... You know, I stand my ground lyrically on not having influence. But musically, when you have somebody as great as Zappa, who has such a high profile, and he wrote some pretty nice tunes, musically, I'm sure it was intriguing for Kim."

Then came originals. "First original I believe was 'Anna-Leah'— never made an album. Kim said he ripped it off from something, but it's an interesting tune. The second one I believe was 'Battle Scar.' Kim used to play that on a 12-string Hagstrom guitar, and the third one might've been 'Marmalade Mama.' That didn't make an album either."

To be sure, all the above-cited classic songs and albums were influential on the formative Max. But on a more abstract level, the DNA of rock was burned into these guys by virtue of Sarnia's proximity to the Detroit music scene.

"Yes, remember, we grew up in Sarnia," explains Pye, expounding on his lifelong hobby of deeply slaking of the live experience early and in style. "We saw Ted Nugent & the Amboy Dukes, MC5, Mitch Ryder, four, five times a summer. And we would often go to Cobo Hall to see them. MC5 is probably one of the best bands I've ever seen, and Kim would say the same thing. They were absolutely gigantic on stage. But we would go to Cobo Hall, and MC5 would open for Ted Nugent & the Amboy Dukes, and people would go wild, and two months later it would be reversed—MC5 would be backing Ted Nugent. Ted Nugent had the best bass players; I don't know where he found these guys. They were outstanding."

"So, we saw Ted Nugent with the loincloth and bow and arrow, but it was MC5 that were a major influence. They used to pull their equipment truck up to the side of the stage and be dressing in the equipment truck. And the door would fly open, and they'd come flying out onto the stage. The best concert I've ever seen was MC5 in Battle Creek, Michigan, where the riot police with the helmets and the flak jackets and the screens on the masks circled the whole crowd, when the MC5 were on stage. Which was really very sad, because the band wasn't political. It was John Sinclair and the people that were managing the band that were political."

"But I would go to Detroit and I would see Spirit and Canned Heat and Blood, Sweat & Tears and Jethro Tull. I remember going to

Battle Creek and a couple other small towns, but not Flint or Lansing. But Mitch Ryder, Bob Seger... they all had their own little regions. But MC5, that was our experience, as far as entertainment and what should a band look like on stage—it was definitely the MC5. This was 100% energy and really overwhelming. And Kim really liked the guitar player, Wayne Kramer, because he was just so good on stage. He was a great guitar player, but a great showman too. So, we were spoiled. We saw a lot of really great bands at a really young age."

Even as far back as 1974, Max were considered a quality act in and around Toronto. "A shockingly good Max Webster opened the Bachman-Turner Overdrive show at the Victory Friday night," wrote CHUM FM's Larry Wilson. "This band has been playing bars around town for some time, but little did I realise they were into material that isn't really acceptable in most clubs. By the management, anyway. Most of it is original, and to put it into some kind of category, if Pink Floyd, say, is heading in a northerly direction, Max Webster might gravitate toward the northwest. A fine band, into intricate, moving, music. A band I'd like to see again, and often."

Seconded Bruce Blackadar of *The Toronto Sun*, "There are so many rock bands in Toronto right now that it isn't difficult to expect that most of them sound exactly alike. On most nights in the city, going into a bar where a heavy metal group is playing is like going to a dentist who uses three dozen drills on your teeth: you're assaulted by the noise, which serves as a blanket to hide the fact that underneath the wall of sound lurks very little talent. Not so with Max Webster at the Piccadilly Tube, a four-man band that is probably about the best in the city right now. They're negotiating with the Nimbus 9 people now for an album, and they deserve to get it, just on the talent of their drummer alone, Paul Kersey. Prediction: they'll be Canada's next big group."

"Many in the crowd were familiar with the group and they livened up noticeably enjoying the easy-going rock style," said *The Globe and Mail*, reviewing a free park show. "Max Webster managed to establish a rapport with them, joking between numbers and exchanging shouts with the audience. The music was also original and the performance polished and professional."

Continues Paul Kersey, on the fortuitous meeting with Ray Danniels and SRO... "How'd we hook up with them? Well, Mike was an agent—Mike Tilka—he worked with Ray. Yeah, that was one of the reasons I came back, for sure, because I knew Mike was an agent at Music Shoppe, and I went, well, I don't think there'll be problems getting gigs. And I wanted to work. I definitely wanted to work. So, I thought we should be fine. And we were. We worked a lot. I think the only time we had time off was when we picked the time off."

"There was no SRO," qualifies Mike. "SRO didn't exist. It was Music Shoppe, an agency. And Ray did manage, and was the agent for Rush, at the time. I met the guys in Rush before I even moved to Toronto. I knew Ray, knew the guys in Rush, because they came to Windsor to play, and I booked talent for the college. So, SRO started later. Ray wanted me to take over Music Shoppe and run it, and I said, 'Ray, we're starting to get gigs, Max Webster is happening, I'm going to quit being an agent to play full-time.' Because we actually had work almost every week. We were starving, but you could live on 50 bucks a week."

"Mike was instrumental in getting the record deal in the first place," adds Gary McCracken, Max's second drummer, who we'll hear more from later. "See Mike kind of negotiated with Ray in the very beginning, when they did their first record. Kim didn't have much to do with any of it. He was just the guy that wrote the songs and was the weird singer. And then Mike was always the guy looking after the business. But how it started was with Kim writing a letter to Mike Tilka when Kim was in Greece. Mike was in Windsor and he was teaching at St. Clair College or whatever, and Kim didn't even know the guy. He just heard that he played bass. So, he wrote him a letter that says, I want you to play bass and get ready to set up a band, and see if we can set up a band. Because Mike was a booking agent back then. He booked bands and next thing you know, okay Mike, how about booking us in to Toronto? And then it started."

And in Toronto, Ray Danniels is of course a legend of that city's nascent rock 'n' roll industry, having managed Rush from its inception to the current day, along the way working with Van Halen, Queensrÿche, King's X and The Tea Party, among myriad others. Ray and his SRO Productions had essentially started Moon Records as an imprint for Rush and Taurus Records as an imprint for Max Webster (and a band called Liverpool), but all subsequent product eventually fell under the Anthem banner. Tom Berry, "manager" of Taurus Records would retain ties to Kim years later as a solo artist through his own imprint Alert Records.

"So, we started doing originals," continues Paul, back to the band. "'Anna-Leah' was definitely a different sounding song. Because it had a drone going through it. It was an Eastern-sounding sitar-ish thing. I don't really want to say sitar, but an Eastern sound to it. And that stimulated me, for sure, and I thought wow, that's a different kind of tune. I was really busy in that song. And I liked it."

"For some reason, the direction of the band was really... Mike was an R&B guy and Jim was a classically taught pianist who could play any chart you put in front of him. Anything. Both hands flying. He boggles me. He was great. Music, Beethoven, I don't care what you put in front of him. It looked like chicken scratch, it was so much stuff, and it was oh my God, and he was reading it and it was amazing."

"But he couldn't jam. He didn't know how to. We'd start something and say, 'Look, play.' And he goes, 'What do you mean play? What do I play?' 'Play something.' And he had trouble with that. That's a long time ago though now, but that's the way he was. And I was long-haired, gone through the drug thing. I went through an R&B thing, went through psychedelic stuff, the show stuff, and was willing to do anything. Kim was a little off-the-wall, I guess you would say. But something about his playing caught me. I just went, wow, he doesn't play solos like anybody else. I thought, this is a lot of fun. It just grabbed me. He grabbed me differently than any other guitar player so far. I just hadn't heard anybody play like Kim. And I went okay, I'm in (laughs). You got a deal. And then I don't know exactly what... I think Jim was not really happy. I don't know how that transpired. I know I wasn't involved in it. Whether he got booted or he actually just walked. I'm not sure on that to tell you the truth."

So, we arrive at the final piece of the puzzle.

"We started looking for keyboard players," says Paul. "Kim always had this thing; he wanted somebody else in the band. He tried rhythm guitar players, he tried lead singers, he tried, I think, Nash the Slash even—I think he was in a band called Breathless, right? I think we even tried him for a couple of practices or something. Kim was just looking for something else. Kim never felt confident about his singing. I don't know if I should tell you all that. Kim wasn't the most confident guy. He used to get thrown off pretty easy. I can tell you stories, things where you go, 'Come on, buddy, you got a packed house. What do you care what some asshole thinks?' One guy, we're walking into the Gasworks one day, the place is jammed, we did so good there. We did amazing there. And two guys are walking out when we're walking in, and the guy says to his buddy, 'You know, you don't walk away from Max Webster, you run.' Kim was just crushed. And I'm like, are you serious? Come on. Look at the house. You know? It's packed. I don't know (laughs). You know, you love 'em or you hate 'em right? That's a Max thing, right?"

"Yeah, never liked singing," confirms man at the mic, Kim Mitchell. "I was forced into it, at the first couple of Max Webster rehearsals. I'll always remember being in the basement, moving from... I came back from Greece, Mike Tilka moved up from Windsor, and I think we had Terry. And they were the first few rehearsals. Mike sang a couple things, Terry sang a couple things, and I'm like, ugh, this doesn't sound... so I thought, okay, I'll try yelling. And they all went, 'We like what you're doing; you can do this.' And I'm like, oh, crap, here we go. The only time I really enjoyed singing was when I was writing and I would do demos. But in the studio, it was always a challenge. I listen back to my voice and go, ooh, fuck. It's always been a challenge for me. But then again, I would think a lot of singers... it's not an easy walk in the park, right? So, I've always wanted to hire a singer, just stand there and play guitar. But Tom Berry was always like, 'You're fucking crazy.'"

"If I'm not mistaken, Ron Scribner, the guy who used to own Music Shoppe, he came up with Terry," continues Kersey, on the acquisition of Watkinson. "He knew Terry from Dee and the Yeomen, and he said, 'The keyboard player who is right at the moment out of work, you might want to try him.' Right away, he sat in, and I noticed immediately, and I'm sure Kim did, he didn't play what I would call traditional keyboard parts. I guess that sparked our interest. You go, hmm, this changes things, doesn't it? All of a sudden we have a different sound. Terry had the knack of taking minimal keyboards, of old, old keyboards, and coming up with more sounds and interesting things than guys with three times the keyboards and all brand-new stuff. We just went, this is different, this is okay. We just started writing more songs and he had songs, and away we went. I think Terry joined in '74. It must've been, because... I don't know if you know, I was offered the Rush job."

And quite a tale this is. Over in the world of a better-working version of Max Webster, namely the world-attuned Rush and all its efficiencies, being a smaller unit with more ambition to boot, Alex Lifeson and Geddy Lee found themselves with a conundrum. John Rutsey wasn't working out. He had some health issues, he partied too hard and he had an anti-social streak. That about sums it up in as few accurate words as anybody's tried. No one had heard of a Neil Peart yet, and so...

"We had opened for them," begins Paul. "I've got all this written down, the dates and everything. For some reason I kept track of every day, everywhere we played, all that stuff. It had to be '74, because that's when Rush was looking for a drummer. And Terry Watkinson was in the band. We had opened for them, and I remember Ray or Vic Wilson, the other manager at the time, saying something to me about working hard on stage or something, harder than the other guys or something. I went, what's that supposed to mean? I didn't catch what he was talking about. They were just very complimentary, and I thought, where is that coming from? Then a couple of weeks later, the onslaught started, where they started calling every day to try talk me into joining Rush. Then obviously Kim got word of it. That didn't take long, and it was a bit of a couple of uneasy weeks, maybe three weeks, where I was being bombarded by those guys. Mitchell was really getting pissed-off that they would dare to break up his band and all that stuff. Kim was saying, this is affecting our band, and this is not right, and he was getting really bummed about it. I actually was going to do it. I almost did it. I was very, very, very close, but then I said no."

Asked if he ever played with Geddy and Alex, Paul says, "No, no, but I came really close though. Came really close (laughs). I met with them, and I met with Ray and Vic."

And their pitch?

"Oh, well, you wanna be a star, boy? One of those deals. We'll guarantee you this much money, and we're going to be doing this and we're gonna be doing that, we've got this organised and on and on and on, just laying it on. They had an agent from New York calling me, they had people calling me from all over the place. I met the guys, yeah, we're gonna play here for a week, practice, and while we're playing, we're gonna get organised and tour right away. Then it got moved up a week. 'Oh, we only have this much time. We need you right now.' Again, Kim was just flipping out. It affected our gigs a little bit, because my mind gets scrambled, and it was pretty weird for a couple of weeks there."

As for Geddy and Alex... "Oh, they were just guys in the band. They were just saying, we can play. We'll be fine. Let's just go do it, so on and so forth. It was Ray and Vic that were doing the hype. The management was doing their thing."

Rush had indeed been a known entity on the scene; Kim recalling having watched them in the bars with John Rutsey drumming. Mitchell in fact was not impressed at the beginning, thinking them not much more than a baby Led Zeppelin, much the same opinion he had of Triumph. Once Neil joined, however, and Max found themselves on tour with Rush, he quickly had his big bang moment, experiencing the majesty of the band at one of those early sound checks. Kim's been a huge fan ever since, marvelling repeatedly at the band during many more sound checks—his personal favourite is "Free Will"—well up into the poppier late '80s and early '90s, being a celebrity defender of those tough-to-love records from the band.

Back to that other piece of the puzzle, Mike Tilka offers his own recollection of the hiring of Terry Watkinson. "Jim Bruton decided to leave, right before we were going to go in and record the album. Because we always talked about getting a singer. Kim talked about it more than anybody. We had a few people we tried. We auditioned, we had some ideas, there was a guy named John Unger from Windsor we talked about who played guitar and sang. Anyway, Jimmy decided that we were not going to be a career band. He loved Kim, and like I say, we're still friends—him and I are still buddies. But he went back and got his PhD and went on to teach university. He's retired now."

"When he left, we ask around, talked to people. Terry Watkinson had played in Rock Show of the Yeoman, so he had credentials. He was a wild and crazy guy, we hired him, we rehearsed, he moved into our house, we did a gig in Welland or something, in a bar, drove to Ottawa, Kim got deathly ill and ended up in the hospital and we didn't gig for a month. But Terry was in the band. Shortly thereafter, or three months later, after the first gigs we played when Kim was back, we did the first album."

So, what it sounds like is that the urge to hire on a singer sort of subsided, or was subsumed by finding Terry, who had different skills, skills that were a pleasant distraction from other shortcomings in the band.

"The idea was, we were playing bars making a living," answers Mike. "I sang some songs, Terry sang… I don't think Terry sang any songs. But then he sang some of his own. But even 'Blowing the Blues Away,' Kim ended up singing it because Kim was a better singer. The songs I did were cover tunes. I did a couple of Tull tunes, Who tunes, Stones. You know, every band did 'Jumping Jack Flash,' something like that. But we just didn't find a singer, and the chemistry got better and I thought Kim had a quirky voice, but I liked Kim's voice. He was charismatic. He was the guy. He was fine as a singer."

As Terry relayed to me in an email, on the subject of the gear at the time of his hiring, "When I joined Max Webster in the early '70s, there was very little choice for a keyboard player. I was a piano player, but there was nothing available that was portable and sounded like a piano, so I was playing a beat-up Hammond L100 organ. An okay instrument, but I liked the sound of transistor organs that I'd heard with The Animals and The Doors—nice, cutting, high frequencies that the Hammond couldn't produce. I settled on a Yamaha YC30, a transistor organ that had qualities of both Hammond and transistor organs, plus some nice bells and whistles. This was the foundation of my setup for the whole Max era, used on all the albums. It last appeared on record in "Battle Scar." Fed through an Ampeg head and a Leslie speaker, it sounded just fine for me."

So long story short, Paul Kersey stays, he doesn't join Rush, despite—and this isn't him saying this but it's out there—being offered a lot of money to jump ship. Instead, Max Webster, with the lineup firmed up, begins to take shape.

"You know, back then, nobody talked about that stuff," begins Tilka, asked if the nascent Max Webster had any sort of clear vision. "In other words, it wasn't like, oh, we want to be this, we want to be that. We just wanted to have a band. My influences and Kim's influences were similar, because he lived in Sarnia, and I had been living in Windsor, Detroit, and from Chicago. In other words, white boy rock band, and that wasn't a term back then either. Heavy metal was not a term back then either. Those terms didn't exist. CKLW played popular music and every other song was Motown and every other song was anything from Ted Nugent to Creedence Clearwater Revival. CKLW was the biggest radio station in North America at that time, and the formulas hadn't been decided. We moved to Toronto to form a band, get some work, Kim wanted to take guitar lessons from Tony Bradan who was a jazz teacher. I just wanted to be in the music business and play my bass. So, we didn't have a definition. What were we? We were somewhere a cross between Frank Zappa, 10CC and Ted Nugent. You know what I mean?"

And man, there's the rub isn't it? Mike, in fact, couldn't have nailed that off-the-cuff comment more perfectly. The Zappa was obvious, but then, sure, the riffs of Ted Nugent and most intellectually, the sardonic humour of 10CC wrapped up and practically subsumed by Godley and Creme's arch-conservative pop sensibility, bonus being their nerdy love of ear candy.

"I was not into prog rock," continues Mike, who, we're now starting to get a sense, is the adult in the room, so to speak. "Kim was, but I was into what became fusion jazz, which wasn't prog rock. In other words, I loved John McLaughlin and that sort of thing. I loved Zappa, I loved Chicago, which wasn't prog, but it was a proggy band, but it was jazzier, or different chords than just three-chord blues rock. But I think Kim had a greater appreciation of it, and it took me a while to get into it, bands like Yes and Genesis. Although I loved King Crimson, their early stuff, so absolutely, that was an influence. So, were we a bit proggy? Of course we were. When you're just a rock band, you also like to be as good as those guys who could play more than three or four chords per song and we both loved Tull. For cover tunes, we did more Jethro Tull and The Who and The Stones than anything."

Elephant in the room, or soon to be anyway, was that Max Webster, lo and behold, would feature as their prime and primo and supremo lyricist, a garrulous guru that was not, in fact, a performing member of the band. His name was Paul Woods, although playing a character of sorts, the world of Canucklehead rock would come to know him as Pye Dubois.

A precedent toward this sort of arrangement had been set with the likes of Grateful Dead and Robert Hunter, but also Elton John with Bernie Taupin and Pete Brown with Cream. No rock act would ever succeed as artistically, however, across all international and temporal borders, as Max with Pye.

As discussed, Kim Mitchell landed a bizarre gig in Greece to play guitar for a crooner named Alex Nikolis. Pye would find a weird way to tag along, and the gods of Olympus smiled on the wordsmithing Buddha and the lanky hippie with an edge.

"Well, it was a pretty terrible band he was going to do cover versions with, pop songs or whatever," laughs Pye on Kim's gig, which, it seems, both of them treated as a travel writing assignment, of sorts. "He was my friend, and he was going to Greece, and I thought oh, this is great. This is a good story, one of the reasons why I went. I was up in Thunder Bay at university, and I don't know if I can tell this story. It's a long time ago. So, the university had a contest, a raffle. You buy a ticket, and the first prize is a car, and the second prize was a stereo. I won the stereo. You had the speakers over here, and it was a console, and then it had the record player where you lift up the lid. This girl who was on the student council said to me years later, 'You know, you won the car.' Yeah, what they did is, they reversed the tickets, so somebody in the community won the car and the student won the stereo. Can you believe that? And the car was a $3400 Pontiac or something. Anyway, that money, I used to go to Greece."

"We were little kids growing up together," said Kim to *Music Express* in 1982, moving on to the Greek trip. "He started writing when he was 13, back in Sarnia. He moved to Toronto first, got a job, went to university and I screwed off to Greece. A lot of weird things have happened between Pye and myself. You have to imagine this: I'm living on one of the Greek islands—no one knows where—and Pye decides to visit me. He flies to Greece, gets a boat to the right island—all of this on instinct—takes a cab to the town and stopped in front of three or four apartment buildings. He picks the one that hasn't been finished, walks up to the third floor, down the corridor and opens the door to my room, where I'm sleeping. The guy's a bit... psychic, I think. Too many things like that have happened."

So began the partnership, explains Pye. "We started writing a song there, but all we could think of back then was, 'Oh, those would be good for Anne Murray; that would be good for Anne Murray.' So, it was this really tacky, real primitive attempt at writing what sounded like a bad country & western song. But we just had fun doing that. It did have some good moments, but it wasn't very good. And then he went back to Canada and I travelled, and when I came back, I just crashed at his place. So, there were myself, Kim, three girls, and we shared a couple of houses in Toronto. But it was on Davenport where we really started to write songs. I think we wrote 'Hangover' and 'Toronto Tontos,' all in a week, just sitting down. 'Hot Spots' and 'Overnight Sensation,' as well, were some of our first songs. I never had the idea that I was going to write songs or lyrics. I was just that guy over in the corner writing stuff on paper. I never envisioned writing a song, per se."

"I knew always I was not untalented," wrote Pye, in a letter to the author. "That said, I knew I was woefully unskilled. I went looking for art! (I glimpsed: the band with Jim Chevalier and Kim Mitchell, Phil Goodwin and Brian Mc...?). My search was half-hearted and never during the week! We rocked on the weekends, and I was never far from my select circle of buddies (in the arts). I never had an epiphany or a 'garde-malade' muse on my shoulder—I stumbled one day and wrote this 'poem' (I hate that word) causing consternation and incredulity! I wrote that? Not possible... me, I wrote that? I think from then on, I did not live vicariously—I discovered I had something to say and I would say so in my writing. I had two great gifts. One: I have a great ear. Two: I cry with the drop of a hat."

Also, Pye, again, from a hand-written letter: "Why I did okay in the arts. I refused to romanticise rock 'n' roll: a salient and invigorating stance—I was going to write lyrics with that attitude. I am anti-romantic, anti-traditionalists etc. etc. I didn't feel the need or the pressure to be like any other lyric... any other lyric! I wanted to write for the honourable mentions. The crowd! I figure(ed), fuckin' anything goes, this isn't what I do, this is what I am—I am a lyric. I am an honourable mention. The human experience of evocation and existing was no different to me than the human experience of dreaming."

"I see what I see, I write it down, I see what I hear, I write it down—I've never wavered with/from the mantra, 'This isn't what I do, it's what I am.' The mantra... a kinship to the street. An astute questioner (years ago) asked me, 'How do you keep so close to the street?' 'I don't have a drivers' license,' was my response! It is true that this enabled me to be a writer—I could see the forest through the trees and I was profoundly discouraged when I discovered others couldn't! (and, I have a great ear; this ear don't miss much doggonit—only traffic gets by me on the street). Rah rah Diaspora, from the Levant to little Etobicoke! Roads are words."

"I remember that well," says Kim, concerning the band's creative seed. "I remember where I was when I wrote all that stuff. Living in a house on Davenport and Ossington in Toronto, with three girls and Pye and myself. And it was this little semi-detached house, and what would be the living room, was where I lived. It was just very cool. Pye and I wrote most... I just had a little four-track tape recorder there, reel-to-reel, and we just cranked out 'Hangover,' 'Here Among the Cats,' 'Toronto Tontos.' The fucking girls just thought we were nuts. I think we kind of scared them. It's like, 'Are these guys okay? Are they gonna snap on us one day?' We were just peaceful little hippie boys writing some tunes in the room, you know (laughs). 'You girls are safe with us. As a matter of fact, we'll protect you against anybody bad.'"

"I had a catalogue of ideas," continues Dubois. "But I never considered then that I was going to use them, and I thought they were just not even poetry. I never saw it as poetry. I just saw them as things on paper. I just never considered myself a poet or writer. It was just something I did. I never really saw a role there or a name. But for some reason, that's a good question. How do I explain... I think it's because I just had so much material, and I would read things to Kim, and he would go oh yeah, yeah, and that's what started it. But we had that process because I was too prolific. I had so much material. So, I never really sat down with Kim at all, way until *Itch*.

And that's a long time later. I just always had a lot of material for Kim to look at and read through, and I guess inspire him."

So, in effect, the relationship did not have to be collaborative, because Kim could just read through Pye's jottings instead of needing a conference about it.

"Yeah, I might think of one or two lines to finish the song, but they were all modular. I would have an idea, something, but I didn't have to do a lot of work there. It was very easy for me to do things along the way."

I asked Pye what it was in Kim's personality that caused or allowed him not to harbour that desire to write the things he was going to sing himself.

"He had me," laughs Pye. "You know, really, I don't know. I think he might've intuitively enjoyed the humour, enjoyed the density, the levity, the dexterity, the weirdness of it—I think he enjoyed that. Because it was really challenging to sing some of those lyrics and play the guitar at the same time. It's almost magical what he did with some of those songs. To be a singing those lyrics and play that."

As for influences, Pye cautions, "Definitely not from poetry. I don't know if I was... I just was in awe of Captain Beefheart, Joni Mitchell. There were so many good songs back then, and there were so many good lyrics. Lyrics were an important part of the song, generally speaking. Some songs are music-oriented, relying on the music, but most songs rely on lyrics. I tend to think that. But definitely not poetry—I didn't like poetry."

Says rock's greatest poet. Who, for Mike Tilka's part... "As far as I'm concerned, for me personally, he didn't bring any contribution because he wasn't in the band. He was a guy who wrote stream of conscious lyrics, page after page after page of odd, sometimes incredibly interesting, clever, quirky, word poems. Kim was his editor. Kim would lift sections of this massive notebook of stuff and make them into songs. Now, does that mean he's a lyricist? Of course he's a lyricist, because those were his lyrics. But did he write, at least as far as I saw in the early stage, did I see real specific lyrics become real specific unified poems? I didn't see that, but maybe he did."

We'll learn much of Pye's and Mike's rough relationship later, but at this stage, it was all hands on deck, inventing art that would begin to replace the band's similarly eclectic covers repertoire.

"One of the first songs that we ever did live," recalls Tilka, "believe it or not, was the last song Max recorded, the one with Rush, on the album with Kim in the yellow jumpsuit on the front,

'Battle Scar.' And we played it, didn't really work, and the manager and the producers listened to it, never made the first record, never made the second record, was totally forgotten until, I guess, that record. I wasn't involved in that record. In other words, that was one of the early ones. We had some stupid little jam tunes which really weren't songs. They weren't going to get recorded; they were really Zappa-esque. But then we started doing the songs on that first album and the second album, you know. 'Hangover' was a fun, great tune. Can you get much more fun than that if you're in a rock band? It was rocky. It wasn't fun like fun-poppy, fun-cute. It ploughed and it was chunky and it was clever. It was a good tune."

Before we move on to Max Webster as recording band, we close this chapter with an early tale from the road, courtesy of Paul Kersey (and apropos of nothing except... fun).

"We used to play a place, Base Borden, by Barrie. It's an Army camp, and we used to play the dance up there. It wasn't drinking or anything. It was just a dance. We played it like, I don't know, three or four times, and we went up this time, expecting to do the same thing. They said, 'Oh no, you're over in that building.' We went oh, okay. So, we set up, and we noticed that there was a bar, for one, which, oh, that's different. The guy serving, the bartender, was in full uniform, full shiny buttons and he had a white uniform. He just looked ready to meet the Queen. I'm thinking, what? That's odd. Then the people started coming in. It's all officers with their wives, full garb, and dress, full dress, and Max Webster is playing for them. We did some quick calculations on what we had to play for songs, and we just did a lot of adjusting. We pulled out any kind of old slow songs that anybody even knew a melody to. 'Okay, we'll do that one, sure. Put it together right now (laughs). Do it.' Because we were mis-booked. But it's okay, we pulled it off. It was an interesting night. We made it through the night. We didn't die (laughs)."

MAX WEBSTER –

"We don't dig the blockhead thing"

So many bar bands, so many styles, so many eccentric hippies come and gone, so many broke Canadians trundling up and down Highway 401... finally in May of 1976, Max Webster had a record on the racks up and down Yonge Street, at Sam's, at Kelly's, at A&A.

An album so good they had to name it twice, Max Webster's *Max Webster*—all of those prog and jazz influences crowed over and notwithstanding—was a fairly heavy rocking affair, especially for the times, and especially for Canada. Forever to be known as the poor man's Rush, Max had recorded for the same boutique label as the band, shared their management and producer (the eminent Terry Brown), and then sealed the deal by perennially touring with Geddy, Alex and Neil all over North America and into Europe as well.

As was evidenced many times through the band's exploratory live gigs, proggy elements were massaged into the band's wily hard rock sound, the main brake system to this crazy train being somewhat conventional song structure, tempering an absurdist, Zappa-esque sense of humour, which emanated from lyricist Pye Dubois into the music and indeed the clown-ish hippie clothing choices of the band.

Album art as well. Keyboardist Terry Watkinson, later in life a meticulous and talented and full-time landscape painter (after a spell as a medical illustrator) and already 36 when making this record, took a stab at the cover of the band's Taurus Records debut, coming up with a tan motif with blockheads on a conveyor belt, like those found at the Ontario beer stores that fuelled the band's existence.

"I'm not sure what the exact process was. But it has something to do with double vision when the bars close down," says Terry, citing a lyric from the album's seminal lead-off track "Hangover." "People's faces start to expand and you start to see three eyes and two noses. But why the rest of it, I can't even remember now."

America, when they eventually released the album, renamed it *Hangover* and went with a whole different front cover. "They didn't like this one, I guess," says Watkinson. "I'm not sure what they didn't like about it. The US one was worse. I got out of the album cover business pretty well after that, although I did Klaatu's greatest hits album (*Peaks*, 1993) and a couple other ones for just underground CDs by people that I knew."

Terry had indeed come to this skill honestly, having actually left architectural studies at the University of Toronto after two years to ride the Max Webster wave. Once being a second-string Canuck rock star would be over, he'd return to university and obtain his Bachelor of Science degree, specializing in medical illustration, which he would teach as a prof at his old alma mater.

Adds Kim Mitchell, "I just remember the Americans going, 'We want to shoot a different cover because we don't dig the blockhead thing. It's kind of weird and stupid.' I thought it was fun. I thought it was a real serious hook. We had a blockhead on stage, and I just thought, this is a wacky thing. I always wanted to get a suit made with the blockhead guy on it. A suit jacket. That would be pretty stylin'."

"We approached Terry to just draw these things, and everybody thought it was just wonderful," recalls Pye. "And it seemed very Max Webster-ish, with these blockheads coming down the conveyor belt. And after that he actually made a papier-mâché blockhead. It travelled on tour and it was sitting on an amp for a good long time and people loved it. I think it broke, or came apart on tours, with people throwing stuff at it or wanting to touch it. But the concept... it's like a conveyor belt at a car factory. I think there's some irony there for Terry, that he would find it somewhat ironic because we are the antithesis of that. We're not a conveyor belt band for sure, but blockheads, maybe. Can't remember how it got three eyes."

"The US didn't like the blockheads," continues Pye. "Mercury didn't like us. I don't think they really put any effort into Max. I don't remember Mercury ever being out on the road and setting up interviews or anything like that. I think Kim may have done some print, but I was never approached, which was totally different from the way it was in Canada."

"Terry was an artist and he did the blockheads," says Mike. "We supported it, we loved that. He made a blockhead out of papier-mâché. We used to put it on stage with us. We loved it. But in the case of the US people, they didn't like it, they did it in green, and on the back they put a picture we liked although they edited it."

"Someone stole it out of the lobby at the Knob Hill," recalled Tilka back in '77, speaking with *Cheap Thrills* magazine. "I'm yelling, 'Hey, hey! Come back here with that head!' I leave a $20,000 synthesizer in the lobby and chase this guy out into the parking lot and almost wipe out on the ice. We got it back. It was cracked."

Once inside the record, "Hangover" kicks off with a crash and a memorable rhythm from drummer Paul Kersey, followed by a snaky, instantly classic riff from Kim.

"What I liked about Paul," muses Kim, "was that he was the kind of drummer who loved to... let me see, his favourite drummers were guys who were very stylised and would not play the same thing twice. So, he used to always say to us, 'Listen to John Bonham, listen to this fill, and then listen to the next time he goes into this part, he's always doing something different.' So, Paul strived for something different. He's a really cool presence to be around. What he brought to the band was detail. He would always stop us in rehearsals. Paul basically ran rehearsals. We would do a song and he would stop and go 'Wait a second, wait a second, how are you coming out of that part? You didn't sound like you knew what you were doing.' 'Well, I don't know what I'm doing.' Then he'd say, 'Well, find something, because I have to know what I'm doing. And when you know what you're doing...because I like to know what I'm doing, and this is going to be more powerful.' He was a really detailed guy that way, which taught me a lot. Mike Tilka, was the happy Buddha of the band. Just a laughing presence all the time, and I always felt comforted by Mike's personality. Mike always had that thing like everything is going to be okay. 'I have a business background and I'll get us the gigs. Don't worry; I'll get us booked. I'll get us the gigs. Things will run.' He was the business side of the whole thing, plus he's just this laughing presence all the time."

"Mike was one of the reasons that I joined Max Webster,"

seconds Watkinson. "Because he's very good at practicalities and taking care of getting equipment and dealing with agents and everything like that. He's a good rock bass player too. At that time Kim was pretty strange sometimes, and Mike Tilka had his feet on the ground and was shepherding the whole process along, so he was really important to the band in the early days. I wouldn't say that I was a steadying influence, except that I showed up every gig. But I was a party animal I guess, on par with the other guys in the band, except for Kim who was a little more... I wouldn't say down to earth, but a little more serious maybe. But yeah, 'Hangover,' I didn't have a synthesizer, but I think I used my keyboard in a lot of new ways there."

Mike Tilka's throbbing bass presence is a big part of "Hangover," as is Watkinson's mad scientist keyboard babbling and Kersey's memorable inverted drumbeat. The song becoming a favourite in Max Webster's live set as it was played throughout the band's five-record run up into the band's implosion in 1981. It was almost always the closing selection (sensible, given its lyric), and it had been routine live before the album at least back to June of 1975, which is also when the recording of the album was nearing completion.

"I actually changed my part a little bit in that," recalls Kersey, on laying down his tracks. "In the studio I did something I'd never done before. I don't know why. There are some shots in the song. I think I set up a cymbal different or something, and I started hitting shots in certain spots that I'd never done before. I don't know why, again. I just felt that I should do that and just did it. Nobody complained and that was that. We just did the song. It's one we had done for a long time, but again, done differently, slightly. When it came to drum fills, I tried to do odd things. I didn't want to do the standard licks because I figured Kim was a unique guitar player, so I wanted to be as unique a drummer as possible, do little silly things that you go, 'What the heck did he do that for?!' And over the years I've had guys say to me, 'What are you doing in that song? What the heck are you doing?!'"

"'Hangover,' yeah, that's just how we felt one day," says Kim. "This feeling is just disgusting. As a young kid, it doesn't last as long, but this is a disgusting feeling, and I remember it really was the sun shining through one morning, and oh God, and we start playing that riff (sings it), and that's just how that came about. Feeling crap."

"It was fairly recent stuff," continues Kim, with respect to the album's material in general. When we came back to Toronto and formed Max Webster, that's when we started to write. I guess the stuff would be about a year, because we started to write all that stuff and then Max got a record contract. Okay, about two years, because we wrote the stuff and started to play live, and then when we played it live, Ray Danniels from Taurus Records came out and said, 'Okay, let's do this.' I really love the first Max album, just because it's my first recorded album. It's the first time I heard myself on the radio, and I think there is some classic stuff on that album. 'Hangover,' 'Here Among the Cats'—my roots are right there."

"I still get chills when I hear 'Hangover,'" reflects Pye. "It's like what?! You gotta be kidding me! It was so much fun. We're sitting at the house at Ossington and Davenport, we're doing 'Toronto Tontos,' and I think we did 'Hangover' the same day. Back then I could ad-lib. I had a few ideas in my mind and a few ideas on paper. But I never really had a song in mind. But for example, when we were writing 'Hangover,' Kim was playing something on the guitar, and I made a crack to Kim like, 'That sounds like a hangover' or 'You wouldn't want to hear that if you had a hangover.' You know, so we were really laughing, and that was the start of 'Hangover:' 'Cold morning and the drums, blue eyes in the window sun.' I'm not talking about whether the sun is good or bad, I'm talking about the writing process. That's how that came to be. So, it was quite spontaneous to have the lyrics come out of me with a couple of simple ideas."

"The process is really interesting, with Kim's songs," reflects Terry, transitioning to capture these spontaneous moments on tape. "In those days, he was making demos on a two-track reel-to-reel, and it was bouncing back and forth, kind of to build up tracks. So, they always sounded pretty bad. But he used to play drums himself, kind of awkward drums, but interesting. And the bass parts he did with an Octave Divider pedal, so they had a really kind of eerie sound."

"I think his process was that Pye would give him a lot of lyrics," continues Terry," and he would do quite a bit of editing, just pieces from this page, pieces from that page, and put it all together, and yeah, the lyrics are always there, first time we would hear the song. I really love Pye's lyrics. That was one of the things that made the music develop in a not quite down the middle of the road direction, that the lyrics were a little weird, but very emotional and beautiful, and we tried to respond to that. That first album was easy to put together because we were a really hard-working band. We were doing five or six nights a week, fifty weeks a year, for the two or three years before we started to record, and we knew the songs really well before we got to record them. Mostly we learned a few songs when we were out on the road, and we were playing six nights in St. Thomas or Kingston or something like that, and we would rehearse whenever we could and work on new material. Usually by the time we were going to record again, we had most of it as we had been playing them on stage."

In fact the band were touring the whole time they were making the first record, and playing all sorts of originals that might have made the cut, including "Marmalade Mama," "X + Y," "Do You or Don't You Want to Know Me," "Blue River Liquor Shine," "Let Your Man Fly," "Research (At Beach Resorts)," "Anna Lea," "Mash Moon in Hawaii," "Lady Let Me In," "Lip Service," "Beyond the Moon," "Sunday Morning Cereal" and "Howdy Doody Boogie."

Both "Hot Spots" and "Marmalade Mama" were recorded during the Toronto Sound sessions for the album but were left off. Plus, as you can see, Max already had all sorts of songs that would pepper the remainder of the catalogue to come.

Non-originals in the set included, regularly, "Peaches en Regalia" and, occasionally, "China Grove" and "Dancing Days." All told, if a generalisation could be made about the songs that didn't make *Max Webster* or any record after it, they are proggier and wackier, with the general consensus being that cooler heads prevailed when it came to the nine picks for the first foot forward. Put another way, the songs demonstrated the band's skills across many styles, which, had more of them been chosen, would have resulted in an album in the ballpark of the debut record by The Tubes.

The guys keep it heavy for the album's second track, a grinding hard blues rocker called "Here Among the Cats," which nonetheless inverts expectations with relentless and weird art rock twists, not to mention, a keyboard solo quite quick to the draw (and later another one, or two). Kim eventually turns in a guitar solo that hints at both Fripp and Zappa, with the totality of the track somehow evoking hard and early Jethro Tull, that band's name being one of the reasons Max searched out their own odd "name name."

Lyrically, Kim says, "We wanted to write a tune about how we were never cool. That's just how that came about. How can we write a tune... because we just don't feel like we're in this cool group. We used to go to these clubs and do all this stuff as songwriters and we always felt that we were the outcast musicians. We were never the groovy guys with the fucking groovy hair and the fucking silk and the hot chicks hanging around. So, we wanted, really, to write something that dealt with that, so 'I don't have any friends here among the cats.'"

Kim's also explained that it sums up what his life was like in Sarnia, and why he quit school and moved out. It is also said that some of the inspiration comes from the fact that Pye had written the song on his Greek sojourn, stuck in a boarding house along with a bunch of cats.

Next is Terry's "Blowing the Blues Away," a thoroughly charming pop ballad blessed with naivety, sophisticated country feels and hooks for miles. Kim turns in some smart picking and lyrically, Terry, independently, sidles up to the majesty of Pye with a nice, accessible lyric tinged gaily with weirdness—for all the weight put on the Pye/Kim tunes against the Terry tunes, Watkinson's songs manage to adhere to the imagistic universe created by Pye, or at least add to the edges of it, rather than blast into outer space with a stylistic stance that doesn't fit. Having Kim sing Terry's song seemed to arrive out of a bit of a business decision, to promote Kim as front man.

"'Blowing the Blues Away' is an embarrassing song to me, now," says Terry, evidently disagreeing with my assessment! "Because there is some good stuff in it, but the structure is really stupid, especially that whole middle section. If I was to take it and rewrite it now, it would be quite a bit different. Nice chorus there though, nice ideas. But that's what happens when you're trying to learn how to write—you make mistakes and they get immortalised (laughs)."

This one's a favourite of Mike's though. If you recall, Mike has been tagged as the R&B and Doobie Brothers guy in the band. "I like 'Blowing the Blues Away,' that Terry wrote, because it was a simple, straightforward, Fleetwood Mac-like pop tune, although we never played it. It never really did much, and we probably didn't do it justice as a band either, because we weren't quite that poppy—or had that poppy thing, or even knew what to do with a poppy tune. And really, except for 'Blowing the Blues Away,' that whole album we played live. They were songs that we had arranged and worked out in the Gasworks and Piccadilly Tube and places like that. 'Here Among the Cats' was a great rocking tune; we loved it, it was fun. 'Only Your Nose Knows,' similar, not as good as 'Cats,' but it was fun; we did it, it was great. We played all those tunes live. 'Toronto Tontos' was hilarious! People loved it in the bars, and we loved playing it, and 'Summer Turning Blue' was a song we didn't play a lot, because we weren't much of a ballad band, as I was saying. But it was dramatic, it was cool, you know, I loved them."

"'Blowing the Blues Away,' that was Terry's song," recalls Kersey. "That was pretty straightforward, except for just doing a little reverse thing on the snare drum for the solo part. I just stuck that in, I think in the studio, as well, again, just to be slightly different. I just thought, try that. Nobody complained so I left it (laughs). Yeah, there was no problem with that song. We had been playing that song already."

"Blowing the Blues Away" would be issued in July '76 by Taurus as the album's only single, presented in edited form. On the B-side is "Hangover," as indicated, pretty much the band's top anthem of all time.

And why was Terry not writing with Pye? "He had his own songs," says Paul. "When Terry came in, the songs were done. He had quite a few, actually, if I remember right. I've got a few of his on tape that never made an album. I've actually got some of Kim's on tape that never made an album. I'm not sure, but there's no 'X + Y' on anything, is there? Plus, we also did a song called 'This Side of Red.'"

Also, on the subject of non-LP tracks, Paul was definitely around for the two rarities that got tacked onto the posthumous Max Webster greatest hits album, *Diamonds Diamonds*.

"'Hot Spots' and 'Overnight Sensation,' we had done. I can't remember if we did them there with Terry Brown; we must have. But we had them down. We had them recorded, so it must've been with Terry."

Paul's pretty sure that the versions on *Diamonds Diamonds* are the self-same that he performed upon. "Yeah, yeah. Kim or somebody, maybe it was Ray, Ray Danniels, somebody said, 'I don't know, get something else. Get another song.' Kim had 'Only Your Nose Knows,' so that was the newest song. But those two were completely recorded and finished, if I remember correctly. They are original songs, and somebody made the decision that they weren't good songs to... Because I remember Kim complaining at some point when I was out of the band. When I talked to him, he said, 'Okay, here are songs that weren't good enough for the first album, and now they're gonna put them on the greatest hits?! What the hell is that? It doesn't make sense.'"

Paul was wondering however, now, if they came from an earlier demo session. "'Here Among the Cats' I remember for sure. Other than that, I'm not really sure what the other songs were. It makes me wonder about 'Hot Spots' and 'Overnight Sensation.' I doubt it was there, but I'm really not sure. This was Bob Ezrin, Nimbus 9, and there was another engineer or producer; I don't recall his name. 'Here Among the Cats' was one of the songs we did. We had rearranged 'Here Among the Cats' at least four different ways—at least. It had been done over so many different ways, I don't remember which version would be on that take. I remember somebody saying to me, on headphones, tune this snare drum down, do this, do that, loosen that, do that; it was an ongoing thing. Finally the guy in the booth said to me, 'The worse it sounds out there to you, the better it sounds to me in here.' I thought to myself, 'Oh, okay, this is going to be a lot of fun.'"

"But the 'Here Among the Cats' that's on the album is all with Terry Brown," continues Paul. "There was no problem with Terry whatsoever. He said do what you do and let me do what I do, and that was it. He wasn't restricting us at all. We caught him off guard a bit; I don't think he quite grasped our music at first. I think he saw something different in the music, but he wasn't expecting it. He was fine with it, there was no problem, but I think he thought we were just a rock band, like a Led Zeppelin or whatever. He never complained about my drums. I had really large drums, 28-inch bass drums, oversized toms and stuff, and it was unusual at the time. But he didn't say anything about it. He just said let's just set it up, do your thing, don't worry about it and we recorded the album. We did it at different times. We did it on the off hours, to save money. So, we would come in after gigs or any time, and the drums we'd set up, sit looking at each other; in other words, we were not set up as on stage."

"He had the biggest bass drum," laughs Brown. "It wasn't a very long bass drum, but it was a very tall bass drum, and it was really hard to mic. I remember being miffed about that at the time. We made it work, but yeah, that was tough. I was used to getting rock kits with 22-inch bass drums. His was considerably larger. I don't remember the toms being different, but the bass drum was the key. It was just a bit difficult to dampen and get a sound."

Recalls Mike, "What was interesting was that we had done a little bit of work with Bob Ezrin for some demos. Because Bob was a brand-new guy. Jack Richardson helped set that up, because Kim and Jack were buddies when Kim had Zooom, and Jack liked him, and Jack was a really nice man, and then he liked all of us. Bob is an interesting guy, and at the time Bob was a folk singer and an assistant to Jack, who hung around the studio. Then we got Terry Brown, and Terry was a real producer, which was great, because he worked with British bands. He had tape-op'ed, and assisted and done a lot of things. Rush had become famous, or were becoming famous, and he had Toronto Sound, so we could work there at night. After playing the Gasworks, we could go and record. We didn't have a lot of money, and he taught us how to do that stuff. Terry was great—he liked the band and we liked him."

"We didn't take time to record," continues Tilka. "We recorded at night when we played in bars. We didn't take a month off like bands do. We would have the odd Monday to Wednesday off, or Sunday to Wednesday off, and we had cheaper rates at night because that was a jingle studio anyway. But I can remember going right from the Gasworks to the studio. Or just recording on weekdays or weekends, late at night after gigs, after playing a high school somewhere. As for when we did it, let's see, in '73 we played with Jim Bruton, and then he would've left some time in '74, and then Kim was sick in the fall of '74, and then Terry, we did more gigs... yeah, spring of '75 sounds about right."

"Summer Turning Blue" is another ballad, this one a little jazzier and darker, melancholic but characteristically sophisticated of both lyric and arrangement, all manner of chord change perking the ears as the song builds in richness. "Some of these obscure, folky love songs are actually quite good," reflects Pye. "'When was it I last saw you/Was it spring upon the beach?' It's a great little poem. But it's weird; some of the folky ones are gems, especially the way Kim sang them."

"I added my drumming after," remembers Kersey. "I don't know why, but they just wanted to put it down without the drums, and then I added the drums after. They said, 'Okay, put your tracks on,' and I just bashed through it. That was one take. I just played." The song goes all the way back to 1973, making it one of the band's earliest compositions, along with "Battle Scar," "Lily" and "Overnight Sensation."

"Summer Turning Blue" is in jarring contrast to side one closer "Toronto Tontos," a huge Canadian classic and perhaps the band's biggest goofball of a song from the whole catalogue. If the Mothers of Invention cared to play and record properly and entertain, this is what they might have conjured. What's more, the song's refrain of "No cigarettes, no matches" resulted in something of a stage ritual for years to come. "The crowd would throw cigarettes at him," remembers Pye. "Yeah, 'No cigarettes, no matches,' the end of 'Toronto Tontos.' And they'd be flying at the stage. Yeah, it was fun. Kim's other thing... he had this hat he pulled up, and he used to snap the hat and it would end up propped up, and people would go nuts—an orange hat."

"'Toronto Tontos' was as close as we had to a direct rip from an Arabic tune," says Kim. "When I lived on the isle of Rhodes in Greece, I had a little AM radio that I would carry around, and for some reason I locked onto this Arabic station and loved it. One afternoon, this thing was playing (sings it), and it just kept doing that, and it was in another language and all this rhythmic shit was going on. I was going holy shit, holy shit, and I had a little tape recorder too, so I was actually taping off the radio. I held the machine up to the radio and I grabbed a little bit of it. I came back, and that's where that riff came up. Somewhere, I guess some Arabic artist can sue me, but then Pye came up with the most insane thing. That's how that came about."

Reiterates Kim, on the reason for the trip to Greece, "I was playing in a show band over here in Canada, and the singer was Greek, a Greek Tom Jones, and he went, 'My family is building a nightclub in Greece. Do you guys want to come there and play for a year?' I said 'Yes, fuck, whatever, sure.'" Kim also recalls seeing the entire Pink Floyd band lounging on the beach in Greece, bemused that the band would decide to all go to the beach together.

"Who knows where a song like that came from?" adds Terry. "It's all Kim there. But how he decides to put a song together like that, I have no idea. It just happens. Then everybody adds a few ideas. But he and his songs... it's 95% Kim Mitchell, the music. Let me just say in general that I loved Kim's music. He's a real musical force to me, and he's a great player. He just has a command of what he does that struck me right from the very first time I was asked to join the band. At that time they were playing cover songs. I think they had one original, but I didn't particularly even like the songs they were doing, but I loved Kim and said, I want to work with this guy. I could really feel his musical power and charisma. And it worked out great. They were already called Max Webster then. Zooom was back in Sarnia. So, they all left to come to Toronto and make the big time, but the keyboard player decided not to come. So, they found me in Toronto."

"I think that was pretty much the way we did it live," notes Paul on the recording of "Toronto Tontos." "Although we tended to jam it live, make it longer in the solo part. Other than that, the song was the song, whatever it is. But yeah, live the solos were definitely longer—it was more of a free-for-all."

Strangest song in the Max canon this is, again, with a level of Zappa zaniness that hearkens back to the old Mothers days. Take for instance, that... "The calliope sounding-instrumental stuff in there is the four of us all playing eight wooden 'organ pipes' that Terry Watkinson made by hand," recalls Tilka. "We stood around an omni mic with two pipes each and played—blew—our notes to the part Terry wrote."

"That was interesting," recalls Brown. "'Toronto Tontos:' 'No cigarettes, no matches' (laughs). Terry Watkinson had worked out that little pan flute thing in the middle of the tune. And he had a little chart written out and he got everybody around the microphones, and everybody played according to this little chart. Everybody had a single note to play, and that's how that was put together. It was all done live. It wasn't a question of reading music as much as there was a tempo designated, a designated tempo, and everybody had these notes to play from this simplistic rotation chart."

"Beyond the Moon," "Lily," "Toronto Tontos"... again, all of these include trace elements of the trip Pye and Kim conducted over to Greece, and then Pye on to Turkey.

Remembers Pye, "In 'Toronto Tontos,' the 'Radio Moscow, US audio, bandits,' the only music we had back then, even when I was in Greece and as I travelled, the only music we could get that we could identify with was Radio Free Europe—which was Cold War; the Cold War was still very strong. But I think having that radio station and listening to it influenced Kim a bit. Because sometimes they would play Arabic music. I always believed that 'Lily' was influenced by the Arabic music he heard, although I don't know if Kim would say that. We fell in love with that."

"So, when we were writing 'Toronto Tontos,' I had a couple of these crash and clash of culture word salads, you know? Russia and radio and Moscow, and I think that became habit-forming for me. Because I always include names of towns and personal pronouns; Toledo and Rascal Houdi. It just seemed that it made it universal but also made it personal. Because I think everybody in the world, doesn't matter where you live, you have a street in your town called Walnut Avenue, you know what I'm saying? Everybody has a Walnut Avenue. So having those images and real names always appealed to me. And obviously appeal to the listener."

"We weren't struggling to write songs," continues Pye. "It's just that we weren't really good at it. But we seemed to do a really good job of a primitive understanding of getting a song together. I always thought they were very nice songs, for first attempts at writing songs. But they are definitely unique. We were writing it on Ossington and Davenport in that house where we lived with all the girls. It was a big house near Casa Loma; Kim lived there, Sue lived there, Debbie lived there, Maggie lived there and I lived there. At the end of 'Toronto Tontos,' Kim and I both smoked at the time. We ran out of matches, but we had cigarettes. I just did this Three Stooges-type pantomime, 'No cigarettes, no matches.' Well, you can have all the cigarettes you want, but if you don't have matches, it's redundant, it doesn't matter. So, we were howling over my impression of that, and that's why 'Toronto Tontos' ended with Kim doing that, 'No cigarettes, no matches.'"

"Generally speaking, I had a lot of stuff on paper, sort of modular," continues Dubois. "I always had three or four lines for one line, so there are a lot of songs that Kim wrote music for first and then picked the line he liked the most, and worked on meter and phrasing, and the song would be built that way."

It must make for a mouthful of words... "Yes, I would imagine. That might've been a wonderful challenge to Kim, and in that respect, he respected what I had on the paper and he tried to write to the word. If it didn't fit, he would tune the music, so it did fit. Because like I said before, sometimes I write lyrics the way I talk. My syntax is a bit odd and unusual, and that's why I write them down on paper. Kim had that feel for what was down on paper."

"With 'Toronto Tontos,'" I was really wanting to write a French song," continues Pye, "or have a song with French in it. But the main thing with that one, even though it's not the most popular song, it was a pivotal moment for me as a lyricist, because when I wrote the line, 'Free publicity is not free when it's public,' I had really tossed for I think two or three days, and I didn't write at all. I thought, why me? Why am I writing a line that I think is so beautiful? I couldn't figure it out. So, I thought, well, I'll just keep at this. Maybe I'm onto something here. You know, maybe I can write some nice stuff for Kim. So, I think that really is an important lyric for me."

Live, in demonstration of the band's imposing skills, any of the tricky bits that one hears on the studio version of "Toronto Tontos"—the parts one might excuse the band for leaving out upon the sweaty stage—well, the guys amplify and complicate these arrangements ten-fold. The song indeed bounds bunny rabbit-like into the kaleidoscopic world of Zappa far beyond the record, which now sounds stiff-collared by comparison. Listen to any of the Max Webster live clips on YouTube documenting this era, and it becomes obvious that the band had the chops to pull off being fully progressive. Again, the idea was to make them look more sensible on the album.

Side two opens with a killer Kim riff as "Coming Off the Moon" takes form. Again, Max work their fresh hard rock/art rock alloy, adding winks at hippie culture in its ideal form. "'Coming Off the Moon' is a little bit angry," says Pye. "I think that's the 25-year-old, 'angry at the world' thing." But it's also more than that. Kim talks about how, in actuality, it's a song about a relationship where the woman is a heroin addict who fears coming off the high, fears withdrawal, with the subtext of the song being that the man in the equation laments his helplessness at the spiralling-downward situation.

Terry Brown captures all the frequencies efficiently—Max Webster is a hi-fidelity piece of work compared to other records at the time, but it falls short of the band's next three (and arguably four), which are no less than gold standards for sound in the late '70s.

"They were pretty damn quirky," recalls Terry Brown, on twiddling the knobs for the first album. "They came in and brought a whole new thing to the studio. Because I hadn't recorded anyone like them. You don't really get a chance to work with bands like that quite often. They're unique, and special, so it was pretty wacky. All good players, obviously. I love Kim Mitchell's playing, he's still playing wonderful stuff. I remember Mitchell just capturing those vocals in such a way that he just knew exactly how to deliver those vocals. He didn't need a whole lot of coaching. But he is like that. He has that edge and he spent enough time with those lyrics, and knew where Pye was coming from, and of course he crafted all the music to go with those lyrics, so when it came time to do it, he just nailed it. They all knew what they were doing. Terry (Watkinson) was a real stickler for detail, a perfectionist, always well-rehearsed and organised. No, they were all on top of the game, no doubt about that."

"As I say, Paul Kersey had a drum kit with a very, very large bass drum which drove me absolutely crackers trying to record it properly. Because it was very big and quite boomy. So that was tough. I believe he still has that kit in fact. 'Toronto Tontos' was pretty wacky, putting it together, and trying to keep a handle on the tune as a whole. Because it was such an unusual song. But we didn't do anything obscure in the production, other than try to capture the mood of a song which was already pretty abstract. It's not your average pop song, that's for sure."

As for how Pye and Kim collaborated lyrically, Terry says indicates that, "Pye's lyrics were always ready to go. And Kim would go through and sort those out, prior to going in the studio. I was never privy to that. It wasn't one of those workshop things in the studio. It was always done. The songs were always ready to go when we got down to recording them. The guys were pretty straight-ahead to be honest with you. Wacky personalities, and still are, but no, there was nothing crazy going on. They were crazy enough just in what they were trying to put across in their music. I think that was quite enough to deal with. But no, it wasn't a drugged-infested session or drunk session. They were all very on the ball. Very focused. Kim Mitchell was always very focused."

"This was a magical time," adds Pye, on the creative flow within the band in the early days. "For the life of me, I can remember, something went down with a song called 'X + Y,' and the line in the song was 'My Libra lies in Malta.' I can remember having a discussion. I overheard this with Terry Brown and somebody else, that they were fighting over this song. I remember thinking that was the first time I ever heard some controversy where I thought they were going to pressure Kim or somebody or me into not using it or rewriting it. Up until that point, nobody ever said anything! Not one word was ever said to me, like, write this, don't write that, rewrite that, don't do this. It was just a wonderful playground of toys, these words and guitars and sounds—it was great."

"I think it has character and it has a sound of its own," says Terry Brown, asked if he is happy with the production of the album. "Whether it's better, worse or indifferent, it is what it is. It captured the mood of the record and I think it worked for that particular record."

"'Coming Off the Moon' was pretty much straight up," says Paul. "We'd been playing that for a long time; that was a very early song." As for bearing witness to the generation of the lyrics for the track, or any others that magically appeared out of Pye, Paul says, "You know his real name's Paul Woods, right? He was a good friend of Kim's, and he just was always writing down little things. He had all kinds of inspirations from here and there, and just wrote them down on a napkin or a piece of paper, anything he could find, stick them in his pocket, hang onto them. Later on he would get together with Kim, and just say, 'I got some words,' and sometimes Kim would have some music first, and Paul would say these words would go with it, or Kim would say these words would go with it or vice versa. There was no standard way of doing it."

Why the alias? "No idea, other than I don't think he really wanted his name known at first or something."

"I always remember Pye pointing to his nose all the time," recalls Kim on the album's next flashy rocker, "Only Your Nose Knows." "It's like, 'Fuck, I don't know; I don't know what's going on with this,' and then he would point to his nose. Only his nose knows. It's like, we have to write something around that. I just started to slam on the riff (sings it), and he wrote down, 'Only your nose knows I've been fooling around.' I sang that, and that's how it happened. But when I think of that tune, I think of Pye pointing to his nose all the time. He wouldn't say anything; he would just point to his nose."

"That was pretty fresh, that one," explains Kersey. "I remember, we went back to the original way of recording it, in so much as we were facing each other not set up as on stage anymore, which we did for 'Lily.' We went through it two or three times with the click track, and we said okay, take the click track out now, we're gonna do it without the click track. It was that take or the next one after that and it was done. Nothing took long. It was all really a couple of takes at most."

Indeed "Only Your Nose Knows" was recorded on September 18th, 1975, along with "Lady Let Me In," which wasn't to make the album, again, marbled between constant live bookings. This puts it at the tail end of the sessions, which were conducted mostly in June and July.

"It's not hopeless, but it's not so great, really," is Watkinson's nonplussed assessment of the track. "I guess it was the first one to be not played live (laughs). I don't know. It's like, there is some stuff that you just don't even want to look at again. But most of the stuff, my role was to just kind of not necessarily double what Kim did, but play in parallel with him, and then add flourishes here or there. I think that worked to make the band sound very cohesive and a little different than the way most bands with keyboards approached it. Every album I would write one or two or three songs. I sang a few songs, but basically my role was to make Kim's songs work."

Lots of guitar in this one, including some manipulation through a Leslie speaker at the end of the track. Kim hasn't entirely found his style—it would take the rest of the Max catalogue and a few Kim Mitchell records to reveal the singular genius of Kim on guitar. But a bunch of things nifty and even novel for 1976 are going on here, and he's well on his way.

Kim's often said that jazz players influenced his soloing style... "Yes, a little bit of Ornette Coleman, who was a sax player, and I really liked guys like John McLaughlin. But some of those guys really pissed me off, too. There are a lot of guitar players out there who go, 'Look what 6000 bucks at G.I.T. can get you,' or the Humber program. They basically use music as a vehicle to blow their shit on, you know? I find there's a lot of guitar players like that. Some of those guys were really good. I thought John McLaughlin just had a deeper thing going on. Allan Holdsworth had an amazing thing going on, whereas Joe Satriani is just a pile of fucking technical shit, as far as I'm concerned. I hate to say that, because I may offend some readers who really like him. I've seen Joe Satriani, and it's like, Joe, your music is nothing more than a vehicle for you to go, look what I can fucking do on the guitar. You're not making music to me. Like, the first and foremost thing should be, I'm making music. That's why I loved Eddie Van Halen so much. Because he was a songwriter and into the band and into the performance, and he just happened to have all these chops, that when it came time for him to blow, he just seemed to be floating through the tune. Not, 'Wow, watch this.' Anyway, so... sorry to get all crazy like that."

Concerning his own style, Kim says, "My guitar playing is, at this point, I think I do have a very different unique style of soloing, and I think it could just be called kind of a fuckin' guy with a bit of a screw loose, you know? I do bump out into areas where I have no idea where I'm going, but for some reason, I like that. And half the time, when people say, 'Oh you're using a Phrygian mode,' I wouldn't know a fucking middle C if it poked my eyes out. Yeah, there definitely are couple of spark plugs missing in my playing. I'll be playing a solo, and then all of a sudden, I'll be like, 'Whoops, whoa, where's he going? Okay, he's back.' It is dissonant, and it is outside, and I do like that. I couldn't play on a fucking Bryan Adams track, ever. Because they don't know how to... Keith Scott is a great guitar player, and he's a great jazz player too, by the way, and I know Keith, but he can come up with those solos that just... the kinds of solos you hear on hit records that you go, 'If I were to cover this tune, I would have to play that solo exactly like that.' I've never been able to come up with those. I'm more of an improvisation, blowing, kind of guy, more like an Angus Young, where you just kind of float around. So that's more what I like to do."

As for Kim's oblique Robert Fripp influence... "I listen to him a little bit. He's a very cerebral, spiritual player to me, really different, unique, and seemed to think a lot about what he did. It was planned out a lot, it seemed to me. All that stuff has an influence on you as you're growing up, in respect to, what do I want to do? What *don't* I want to do? What don't I want to be? What do I want to be?"

Back to 1976 though, and Max Webster closes with two tracks somewhat lost in the canon. "Summer's Up" is a jazzy, lilting pop ballad perfectly in tune with all the other intelligent soft rock on the album. It's got ample and erudite key changes, and some complexity from Terry, but none of that distracts from its flow.

"I think 'Summer's Up' got switched up too," notes Kersey. "I think we used to do it differently before the album, and then I think all of a sudden we changed the groove for some reason and put that bounce to it." Curiously, Kim opined in 1977 that the only Zappa-esque flourish on the first album is the opening "lick" to "Summer's Up," eschewing any thought that "Toronto Tontos" goes to those places.

Closing the record, "Lily" rides much the same vibe as "Summer's Up," although it's actually quite epic of scope, with Watkinson playing a fair bit of artful piano around the percolating, insistent prog arrangement. Uncommonly, the lyrics comes from Kim, who also wrote "Anna Lea" and that's about it.

Similarly asked about influences, Terry says, "A lot of jazz players, all the way from Duke Ellington, Thelonius Monk... rock players, I liked Manzarek from The Doors, Jimmy Smith, of course, who was preeminent on organ. All the great keyboard players from the '70s, including Keith Emerson and Rick Wakeman. We all loved Frank Zappa and Captain Beefheart, and we listened to a lot of jazz. We weren't into the big bands at the time, more the musical oddities. I don't think anybody called us a heavy metal band. But I think we were called progressive rock. We were into alternative ways of making music."

"We saw Captain Beefheart twice," adds Pye. "Yeah, Captain Beefheart at the Colonial. I never really thought Kim emoted much watching a band. I knew when he was having a great time, but Captain Beefheart did this one song, and Kim actually stood up, just like, my God, that's good (laughs). Might have been 'Bat Chain

Puller,' I don't know, but Kim and I were just having a wonderful time. It was so good at the Colonial, so I think that would have had some effect on Kim. Plus, we went to see Mahavishnu Orchestra, with John McLaughlin and Ravi Shankar. We saw that live—and you can guess what that was like (laughs)."

Adds Paul on the first album's strident prog-inflected closer, "What we did for 'Lily,' I know, we set up as if we were on stage. We were all facing one way. I remember we did that one really quickly. Well, actually all the songs we did really quickly, because we played them so often in the bars—we had them down, no question about that. 'Lily,' I remember, I think we did only two or three takes and that was it. I remember saying to Kim, 'Kim, you're doing this really fast.' He says, 'No man, this is right.' He was hyper that night. We played it through, I looked at him said, 'Kim, that's really fast.' Kim says, 'No man, that's right, this is right.' I said, 'Okay, I'm telling you it's fast.' We did it again, Terry goes, 'That's it, that's good, we got it, we got it.' We went in and listened to it, Kim goes, 'Oh god, that's fast.' But we kept it, and Terry tuned it down. He dropped it a semitone. So, if you have an old record player with an adjustable speed, click it up a bit, that's the speed it was actually recorded at."

But to clarify, Kim's vocal was added after the fact; in other words, this isn't Kim sounding throaty because he has a cold. "That's right, no, he would've sang to the lower speed. But he could sing to either one. It didn't matter. The band was dialled down and he sang it naturally. But he could've sang it at the faster speed; he could've sang it at either one. It's just that it was too fast. I could feel it. I'm thinking, oh man, we're just burning through this thing."

"Oh my God, no," says Terry Brown, discounting the story, although, granted his memory on much of this stuff is none too clear after the years. "I don't remember that! I find that hard to believe, to be honest, being in analogue mode. It's not the easiest thing to do. But he could be right, could be right. I was listening to it just a little while ago; it's possible." In truth, there was tape manipulation, with the final result ending up in a key somewhere between E minor and E-flat minor.

"I loved 'Lily' because it was proggy," adds Mike Tilka. "It was influenced by Kim spending the summer in Greece. So, he played weird open tunings, because he had been listening to bouzouki players all summer. A lot of that sustained open tuning stuff, he used to play on a 12-string Hagstrom guitar, and he took some of the strings off and had open tuning, so he could only use that guitar for that song. It was proggy, it was interesting, and there really was a person named Lily, and it had that Greek thing, that chimey stuff. But that was an oddity on that record."

But as Kersey explains, "Lily" was even proggier in the months leading up to the crafting of the album.

"Oh yeah, 'Lily' used to be a twenty-minute song. It used to be, really, a little much; all kinds of parts. Then I remember Ron Scribner from Music Shoppe saying, 'Not a bad song; it's just a little too much—there are too many directions.' Then all of a sudden it got chopped way down and ended up to be what it is. But originally, it just went through a lot of different changes. It was as if you were writing songs and putting them together. It was overdone and needed to be reduced."

I asked Paul if "Lily" bore any influence from the band's consistently proggier and more successful Canuck brothers in Rush.

"No, they didn't influence us one little bit, not even slightly," begins his curious response. "I think the only real influence, in my opinion, would be Zappa. That's pretty much the only influence I can think of. Because of the timing. I know Aynsley Dunbar was playing with Zappa and he's one of my faves, and I wanted to try and play like him, but never succeeded (laughs), unfortunately. Zappa would be the biggest, if not the only influence. But everybody had their own influences within themselves and the type of music they'd been playing and we just came together the way we came together."

"It's odd, but Kim used to complain about everybody," continues Kersey. "I don't know if I should tell you this, but it's true. He used to complain about Mike Tilka's bass playing, and I'm sure he complained about my playing, and he complained about everybody. His frustration... he wanted to be more successful, I guess, and just didn't know how to do it and he didn't know why he wasn't. He would just point fingers, and then it would cool down, and again, why don't we try a lead singer? Why don't we try adding a violin? Why don't we try adding a rhythm guitar? Try this... and then you'd go, holy cow. He was just looking for something. Well, if you check out his career, obviously you've seen all the players he's gone through. Because I saw them once in Sudbury in the '80s, and I think they had seven guys on stage, if I'm not mistaken. They had two guitar players from Wireless in the band. This is Max Webster. McCracken was playing. I don't know if Terry was there; it might've been after Terry left. Mike Tilka wasn't there and Myles wasn't there. I think Mike Gingrich was playing bass. But I'm going, 'What the hell are you doing, Mitchell?'"

That's quite the concept, that Max Webster would consider adding a violinist. "I didn't—Kim did. As I say, Kim was searching for something. I think he was just insecure. He used to get frustrated the way he dressed on stage. I remember him saying to me, 'How am I supposed to pick up a chick looking like this?' I'd go well, you get them, so what's your problem? I don't know. You know what you're getting, I guess. Yeah, I would say he was insecure at first, because he just wanted to be, I don't want to say rock star, but he just wanted some success and he wanted it now. If it's not there, what are we going to do to get it? He was willing to try anything."

Except bend musically. In other words, there wouldn't be much compromise out of Kim, to have hits. The integrity of the challenging music remained, as did, for that matter, the quirky wardrobe, the surreal, multi-coloured lyrics, everything...

"Well, he didn't have a problem with playing Terry's songs," counters Paul, the implication being that Terry's writing was poppy and accessible. "He had no problem with that. I remember, I think the first song Terry brought in was 'Let Your Man Fly.' And that was well received in the band, and with people. And I'm not sure the second song. I know there were a few we used to do, of Terry's. Yeah, Kim was open to Terry's contribution. I guess if Mike or I would've brought a song, I'm sure it would've got done, but our way. The band was this way, or whatever would happen would happen."

Because it's something we can see and touch, the first Max Webster album is often viewed as drummer Paul Kersey's most indelible link to the story of Max Webster. In other words, we tend to forget his role in the formative years leading up to the first record, but also the rich experience touring it. Paul says, as far as he recalls, he never played the States with the band, but he did most of Canada, including a western swing that took him to Victoria and Vancouver. He was also in the band when they backed up Rush as they were recording their *All the World's a Stage* double live album at Massey Hall in Toronto. More intriguing, as alluded to earlier, is the fact that the band during his tenure had as part of their set list, all manner of future Max Webster classic.

"There's not many songs I didn't play," reflects Kersey. "'Paradise Skies,' I didn't play that one. There's not much I didn't play though. 'High Class' and for sure 'Oh War!.' Yeah, it was ready to go. We were ready to do it. Every song, for sure. I played all of them live. 'A Million Vacations,' not sure the lineup on that album. 'Blue River Liquor Shine;' I played that; I think we learned that in Quebec City way back in '75. Also, the other moon songs, like 'Beyond the Moon.' Probably those last two albums I didn't play a lot of things, but up until that, I would say most of them. You know, you're writing all this stuff..."

Indeed, there are early tapings of Max shows from 1975 and 1976, for example one at Larry's Hideaway in Toronto, where Paul is drumming up a set that featured no songs from the debut, but most of *High Class in Borrowed Shoes* in preview form. As well, confirming what he says about "Lily," that track is captured live in 1976 from Winnipeg, and is a progressive rock firestorm with extra features, driven by propulsive drumming from Paul and sprinkled like pixie dust with Terry swirled in B3 tones. Kim's solo at the end is a maelstrom of clean notes, inventively organised. The playing is so tight that one can understand how Max, and many other bands from the '70s, were able to record even the most daunting material live in the studio for permanent public consumption.

Confirms Tilka, "By the time the first album was done, we were doing at least a third of the second album, or half of the second album. Because we were a working band. We didn't take two months off to do an album. We recorded at night, and we played all the time. And we rehearsed all the time. If we had two days off, we rehearsed. We had a big old house, and we would rehearse. So, we were constantly working."

When they were out working, the band was, in the main, more experimental and Zappa-esque than what we got to hear on wax. We've talked about the lunacy of "Toronto Tontos" and "Lily" live, but beyond that, there was an epic prog rocker called "Don't Be a Moon, Be a Star," which might be described as serious Zappa mixed with silly Mothers of Invention, crossed with "Lily" and heavy metal Max. It's an ambitious track, and one thinks that perhaps it was just a bit too out there to unleash on the Anthem office. Additionally, the band's on-stage banter often stretched toward meandered comedy bits, just like Frank, and most of that came from Tilka.

As alluded to, just before Paul left the band, Max supported Rush while they slammed out the performances that were to be their supercharged post-*2112* live album, *All The World's A Stage*.

"Well, it was three days and it was phenomenal," recalls Mike. "I do remember, when we finished, you get to play Massey Hall, you think you're gonna be invited to a party, reception, something cool, something neat, something whatever. Yeah, we got in the van and drove to Winnipeg. You know what? That was cool. In fact, that was very cool. We were a working band. We had an opportunity to go... I can't remember if that's when we met up with Styx or where we were just doing our own dates, but we went home and took a shower, packed the amps, the roadies went straight from the gig, and we were gone. Although I do remember, I think Rush had a party after the first night, and then it was set up for the second and third night. It was phenomenal."

Further conversation with Mike hashed out that this story of driving to Winnipeg was after one of Max's own headline shows at Massey (1977, with the first stop being Brandon, Manitoba, not Winnipeg, and indeed to join up with Styx).

"Well, we definitely drove to Winnipeg right after a Massey Hall show. Maybe it was that we headlined Massey Hall and we couldn't have a party and then we drove to Winnipeg. Unless I'm looking at my own calendar and I can see stuff, I get it mixed up. But in any event, the guys in Rush, even then, they were a pretty slick band. It wasn't like everybody was nervous, how is this going to work?, etc. They had three nights, which is wonderful. They had a really good sounding venue, not the Gardens or something that's big and boomy and echoey. But they had three nights of material to pick from. I certainly don't know which nights the majority of it is from, but I do know having read a lot of rock magazines, when bands do multiple nights there it tends to be one magic night over the other two."

The band played Friday, June 11th through to Sunday, June 13th. On the Friday, the guys played "Oh War!" for the first time, and Kim did the gig dressed as a sheik, complete with head garb. On the Saturday, they conducted an autograph session at a store called Record Rocket.

Reviewing one of the nights, from a Max perspective, back in August of 1976, *Nightout*'s Stan Lepka wrote, "As the opening set progressed from zany comedy numbers like 'Toronto Tontos' to polished rockers like 'Coming Off the Moon' and 'Hangover,' it was obvious that the same mania was there. The boisterous response— culminating in an encore—told the whole story. The locals were getting off on Max Webster, just as they had when Rush opened for Nazareth two years earlier. Max Webster's stage show doesn't have the flair of Rush's, but what the band lacks in gimmickry, it makes up for with a well-paced repertoire of original material that leaves you one step behind, leading you on with bizarre discords and lyrics in tunes like 'Toronto Tontos' and then dazzling you with the *Tommy* feel of 'Lily.' Indeed, the group is a progressive rock band without the predictable guitar riffs and runs. Just as their stage performances are outstanding, the *Max Webster* album is refreshing. Void of the tunes that begin to sound the same after a while, the set pushes the limits of progressive music. The group conjures a collage of insane incongruities, largely contributed by lyricist and unseen member Pye Dubois. Then the band gets down to some dynamic tunes that are both melodic and harmonic—highly unusual intellectual rock that you can dance to, if you can stand the pace of syncopated rhythm cadences."

"Most of the really important concerts are engineered by either management or a record company," said Mike Tilka at the time, in conversation with Lepka. "The only question is whether the band has the talent to capitalise on the opportunity. We hoped to get a lot of mileage out of the Rush concerts, but we didn't expect the phenomenal reaction we got. The crowds were really great."

"And it's been like that everywhere," added Terry Watkinson. "We did The Electric Circle in Quebec a couple of months ago and some of the reps from London Records (distributors of Taurus) flew up to catch the act. From then on, they were behind us 100%. We're not knocking the majors, it's just that they distribute about 20 labels and they have their priorities. Taurus has fewer priorities and more at stake, so they can devote the time to promoting upcoming concerts and ensure that there's product in the stores."

"We've played every bar in Toronto," adds Kim, "not to mention the ones from Thunder Bay to Quebec. We've all gone the usual route from playing Elvis Presley numbers in small town hotels to starving while we got it together."

Indeed, as Terry says, from March 15th to the 18th of '76, Max was set up at "Le Cercle Electrique" in Quebec City, to be seen by label reps. Fortunately they'd had time to mend from the crushing hangovers experienced a few nights earlier back in Toronto, when Kim introduced the guys to a ghoulish liqueur from Greece called Ouzo.

Reviewing a Rush date in Lethbridge, Alberta—light on a Sunday night, at 1340 tickets sold—in the fall of '76, the local newspaper's Mike Rogers wrote, "The first band up was Max Webster, a Toronto bar group trying a bigger stage. The Zappa-styled quartet leaped and jerked about the stage in stark contrast to the almost immobile Rush. Their music was different too. When the band's sound man was awake, the music was very good. Webster's lighting was good, what there was of it. Guitarist Kim Mitchell proved he has what it takes to get to the top of the rock pile, but the powerhouse of the group was keyboard player Terry Watkinson, whose abilities gave the music its beef and gravy."

As for fond memories of hitting the tour trail, Kersey has many. "Boy, I remember opening for Rare Earth, in Max. We opened for Rush a bunch of times, lots and lots of times. We opened up for April Wine, Bachman-Turner Overdrive. BTO... back then, you came down to the dressing room, and our dressing room was smoke-filled, different kinds of smoke-filled, booze flowing, chicks screaming and yelling in different states of dressed or not dressed, more chicks than guys, and just an absolute insane party in a small room. As you walk by BTO's room, there's dead silence, and the four of them are sitting in there. Not a sound. Nothing. They drove in on their station wagon with their guitars and sat there and went on stage, and went back to their station wagon and drove away. And they made the money and we didn't (laughs). One of those deals."

"Rush were great guys. Really, they are. They deserve what they're getting for sure. They worked very, very hard. Their touring schedule was very tough. I remember I was amazed at their touring schedule. Because we played Cochran with them one night. I remember we left right after a gig to go to Cochran, the next night, and there was a little bit of grumbling going on, saying holy cow, this is... we're a little tired, we're a little worn-out getting there, and we're thinking, yeah, this is a little rough. We got there, we're trying to sleep in the van, bouncing around, laying in the back, and Rush gets there, and they came in from Winnipeg! I'm going, my God, and they're headlining. All we had to do was play half an hour, forty minutes, and okay, guys. We just walk up and do our thing, we're done, we leave. They've got to shine—we didn't have to shine. We just had to be there. I thought wow, now that's tough. They were like that a lot. They had a gruelling schedule at first. Ray really put them through it. I appreciate that. They worked hard."

Going against the consensus that the Max guys were never resentful at the resources spent on Rush, Paul adds that, "Kim was never happy. Just because it was always Rush, Rush, Rush, never Max, Max, Max. That's about all I can say about that, because no matter what, Rush was always number one, in Ray's mind. Just because, they were friends, and they were whatever they were, and Max was second, simple as that. Kim didn't like that. That wasn't sitting well. But we also knew that Ray was the guy. So, what are you going to do?"

"We were quite fond of them and they were fond of us," reiterates Pye, concerning relations with Rush. Still, there was a rocky start to the rock 'n' roll marriage. It turns out that the irritation Pye was experiencing trying to interview with the author at a noisy pub... it was because it brought back bad memories of how communication can fail.

"Yeah, why I was a little bit upset at that restaurant, with the whole restaurant talking loud, Max's first tour with Rush was almost sabotaged by people in the restaurant unknowingly speaking about Rush. Someone from Rush was in the restaurant, and it got overheard and it got back to Rush, or someone, and Max is off the tour. I don't know how it was resolved. But something was said, and it was considered pejorative, and Max is off the tour. But then it was resolved. I don't know who said it—I don't think it was me (laughs). I'm sure it wasn't me. But someone said something."

Paul has an additional "get in the van" routing tale to the one he relates above, regarding the time the band backed up a fledgling Rainbow in Montreal, at the St. Denis Theatre on July 20, 1976 (Rainbow's second ever Canadian show). "When we left Toronto, it took us 24 hours to get back, by the time we were done—and we played for twenty-five minutes! Yeah, we had a forty-minute set that got cut and it got cut and it got cut, and we ended up playing five songs. But the reviews said we blew them off the stage."

That's pretty much the case, with *The Montreal Gazette*'s Juan Rodriguez reporting that, "The atmosphere was just what Max Webster, the opening act, needed, and the Toronto band didn't miss a trick in winning over the ripened fans in their first local appearance. Webster, a singer and guitarist backed by three strategic sidemen, has obviously researched the rock market before designing his act. He has adopted numerous popular styles—from the jigsaw structures of Queen to the pop-boogie of the Doobie Bros., to the Bowie-Jagger syndrome of stage presence, and even a little Frank Zappa kitchen sink measures thrown in for effect. Unlike many Toronto bands that play Montreal, Max Webster performed with the kind of confidence that strikes straight at the hearts of the local buzzed-out rock cognoscenti. He was careful to include several 'merci''s in his patter, and the bass player added a few bon mots himself. Lo and behold, Max Webster won over the Montreal crowd—perhaps the day is not far off when he joins Shawn Phillips and Genesis in the affections of the local audience."

Paul recalls also that after the band had done their sound check,

Ritchie Blackmore went and limited the band to five songs. They were also banned from the dressing room when Rainbow was on, with the guys watching the show from the audience. Two nights later they were back playing the Toronto bars, but by the following weekend, they'd found themselves on a festival bill with Roy Buchanan, Ian Tyson and Ronnie Hawkins.

To backtrack, sure, the *Montreal Gazette* writer assumes Kim was Max, but it's quite surprising how little that mistake was made, almost as if entering the Max world and analysing them demanded a tacit pact that you were a smart and dedicated enough music fan to get your powder dry. After all, this was a band that was already post-prog in the mid-'70s, and savvy enough to create an alloy that was as songful as it was left-field—like Blue Öyster Cult, Max Webster was conceived and put in motion for musos but specifically significantly hip musos.

Biggest gig? "For most people," qualifies Paul, "we did a concert in Windsor, I believe. It was with The Guess Who. I believe that was outside, 25,000, but I'm not sure. That's what I was told. It was a very hot day. I remember that. Not a festival, just the two of us. When we played with Rush, it was usually eight, 10,000. There were arenas and they were pretty full. Although I played arenas since, with my next band, The Hunt; we played arenas but there were other acts on the show."

As for intriguing wrinkles in the set list—future Max anthems notwithstanding—there were many, including non-album originals. "Max gradually got off the cover songs. We started flipping originals, and I remember 'Anna Lea,' 'Battle Scar' and 'Marmalade Mama.' I'm pretty sure 'Coming Off the Moon' was there early. We started switching them in. We started putting in one original per set, and then gradually two per set, and then three and then we just kept adding songs. 'Anna Lea' was actually really long, as was 'Battle Scar,' and Jim Bruton played on both of those, so those are definitely old."

"There were no drugs whatsoever in the band, zero, as far as know" continues Paul, as preamble to the aforementioned experience with Ouzo. "And on my part, not much drinking. The only time I'd drink was usually to get inebriated, and I got what I paid for. I remember, Kim came back from Greece and was talking about a liqueur called Ouzo, and we had a night off, and I think it might've been Good Friday or something, and we all went to a party and did a lot of Ouzo. And the next day, oh my God, it was rough. We had to play a matinee at the Knob Hill, and Kim, in the first set,

'Okay, this song,' and it was the drum solo song, and I was pretty much hurting. I slept behind my drums on the stage in the breaks (laughs). I was hurting. But he wasn't doing much better; everybody was hurting that day."

On the rise, the band was now in the position to get some press for more than just the odd live show backing up Rush. *The Windsor Star*'s John Laycock, in a May 27, 1976 review of the newly minted *Max Webster* album, called it, "Genuinely freaky. A slap in John Denver's face. *Max Webster*, their first album (on Taurus-London), is freaky music to astonish the neighbours. I don't mean outrageous, exactly, though it is challenging. Their tongues are stuck too firmly in their cheeks to really annoy. But the dissonance, the noise, the oddity and obscurity, certainly can perplex. We need Frank Zappa as translator. It's a strange feeling to hear the yowls of 'Hangover' and know you've joined your buddies in the band in that particular rite of atonement (and in the rituals leading thereto). Toronto, their hometown, and a city with some self-conception of itself as freaky, gives them plenty of support. 'In Canadian terms,' says Tilka's press release, 'We have proved that a commercial band need not be limited to a repertoire of boogie tunes.' That's for sure. Nothing on the album will be played in discos. 'Blowing the Blues Away' is a light enough little song that some radio stations can play; 'Here Among the Cats' is their popular thudder. Some of the other stuff on the album is more brash than substantial, but it's a carefully established debut, including the three-eyed heads in the cover painting by Terry Watkinson, who didn't learn to draw like that when he played the bars with the Yeomen years ago. Crazy? Like a fox, maybe."

"Max Webster—a four-piece Toronto group which sounds anything but Canadian—reveals a diverse array of influences on its premiere recording," writes Andy Mellen in the *Winnipeg Free Press*. "The band's hard-driving, guitar-keyboard-dominated sound utilises a lot of stock riffs, but still comes across as one of the more engaging hard rock sets from any recent Canadian band. The group's penchant for off-beat titles ('Toronto Tontos,' 'Here Among the Cats,' 'Only Your Nose Knows') and equally strange lyrics is complemented by guitarist Kim Mitchell's emphatic vocalizing, reminiscent of an array of singers including Iggy Pop (on the album's lead-off cut, 'Hangover') and a number of British vocalists. Max Webster's blend of clever lyrics and no-holds-barred rock and rolling establishes it as an act to be reckoned with in the months ahead."

Less complimentary but not altogether damning is *Cheap*

Thrills' Michael Raceway, who writes, "Appearing on a brand-new label (Taurus), Max Webster has finally come out with a record. Well-received wherever they appear, this LP might be disappointing. What often happens to a band that communicates frenzy on stage, is that in the studio this rapport is squelched. The polish makes the musicianship sound unsophisticated and unfeeling. To a degree this happened to Max Webster. The numbers that are probably slated for market are a little unoriginal. There are a couple of cuts that are what you may have heard at one of their shows; these pieces have an old Mothers quality which they do justice. As a package, the record is a good first try. It has highs (and lows) but sells the band's enthusiasm a little short. Even so, the band has a magic quality that turns up live and on record. You can't put your finger on exactly what it is, but it accounts for the band's popularity beyond fans of hardcore rock."

Pretty much in agreement is rock journo Jim Millican, who writes in his *Rock On* column, "The music is full of high impact with the songs varying in their precedents from the bizarre arranging styles and ordinary, everyday craziness of Frank Zappa to the infusion of the odd production hook more associated with BTO. Seldom does this inevitable borrowing process in rock music interfere with the delivery of an interesting thought; sometimes lyrical, often musical. There is seldom any playing on the Max Webster album that the group couldn't reproduce on stage. It's mostly guitar, bass and drums, with an overlay of gruff grabbing vocals... mostly good, tough rock with a distinctly eccentric if not progressive edge. This isn't to imply a lack of precise playing, much intriguing invention, mood-matching tempo changes and a degree of technical prowess that is a mark of maturity beyond the timespace of the group's apparent recording experience. Max Webster claims to be set on expanding the boundaries of what is considered commercial. To succeed, they need a lucky break, which includes your ears, to stand even a left-field chance, but that's a good part of what rock 'n' roll is all about."

Interesting that two of the three above reviews make note of Kim's vocals, and to be sure, what to make of them? Suffice to say, Kim's singing is very good, but his voice itself is neither particularly operatic or at the other end, rumbling or powerful. In a sense, he captures what it means to be Canadian, content at the middle of the pack, unobtrusive. He's also not particularly bluesy or particularly thespian. In other words, yeah, fair game to critics who don't sound particularly impressed. Fair game to Kim as well, who backed into the job and never felt comfortable doing it.

As for Kim's final assessment of the record, well, it's decidedly less complimentary than all the above. "It's really funny. Just this weekend I played the Barrie Sound of Music, and a young kid, he'd be 16 or so, had four Max Webster albums, and he holds up the first one, and he goes, 'That's my fave' (laughs). I couldn't believe it. I thought, man, it's hard for me to even listen to that album. But anyway, it's so many generations later. But yeah, I have trouble listening to the first record. Because it just sounded a little too rough to me. It's the same thing as... this is a bad comparison, but Jimi Hendrix's first record. Such an iconic album, but it just sounds like ass to me. Well, it does."

Flash forward a few months and Paul gets kicked out of the band. "I left in, I think, November '76. But at least I got to do the album. We were on Taurus first—that was Ray's label—and then all of a sudden it was on Anthem. I did get a gold one for that, thanks (laughs). But I was just told that it's no longer gonna happen (laughs). That's all because of Gary and... well, coming back to Kim pointing fingers why he wasn't successful, I knew Gary and Myles, they were always coming around, hanging out, jamming and doing things with the band. I knew in my mind, I knew eventually they would be in the band, because they were old friends of Kim's from Sarnia, and it was inevitable. But I thought once we put the album out, maybe, maybe this is the band. But Kim in his infinite wisdom..."

To rub it in, Paul's final days with the band would be on a string of dates supporting Rush across Canada, October 10th through the 27th, winding up in Victoria, BC, with a handful of small local shows to end his run. In fact, on the 15th, in Thunder Bay, that's when Gary asked to join the band. On the tour, the band got to see The Who live in Winnipeg. They also played tourist, visiting Lake Louise.

Kersey's final show would be at the Piccadilly Tube in Toronto, November 13, 1976, with Paul blowing it all up by extending his drum solo to half an hour. Kersey then moved on to Canadian GRT recording artist The Hunt. "When we first came out, it was very vocally strong and musically strong. It was a pretty straight-ahead rock band, really. Not the same as Max, no quirkiness, but a strong band, very strong, with all the players also being singers."

The Hunt saw limited success. "Yes, some. We had a chance at a few things that just the way the cards fell, it didn't happen. We had people in Texas behind us 100%, produced a guarantee, come down, we'll do it, we'll do it, we'll do it again, and therefore next time you'll be headlining here. They said it was a done deal. They were the people that did Rush there, Triumph there, they broke bands there. He said any tour you want on, here's a list, you just pick, you'll be on it, you can do this, you can do this, we'll put you on a third bill first and a second bill next, and then you'll be headlining. Guaranteed. Our management company wasn't what it should've been, and things just weren't falling into place. Frustration set in, and again, you start switching guys losing guys and so on. Financially, we were five, so we started cutting it down to four. We thought, well, we'll cut it to three, we're not getting anywhere, we can really still keep playing and making some kind of money to stay alive. We put out three albums. They were released in different places, in Australia and Britain. We got a review in *Billboard* at one point, 'Look out Def Leppard.' But things… we just didn't have good management."

"I just remember, one time when we were in Quebec City, and I'd heard Mike Tilka got the axe," continues Paul. "I thought, well, this wasn't a surprise (laughs). Because I think I mentioned to the guys, Mike'll be next. I knew it wouldn't be long. Like I say, Gary and Dave Myles were hanging in the wings. Once Gary was in, well, that's definitely a done deal. I didn't know which would be first. Well, we found out, but I didn't know if it would be a double whammy at the same time or one by one. Oh well, what are you going to do? Too bad. I wish Kim would've stayed… I wish we could've done at least another album or two. We could've still been quirky, because I still feel that, personally, the band really changed, started mellowing. People were really into them and all that, but it lost that that edge. That's just me."

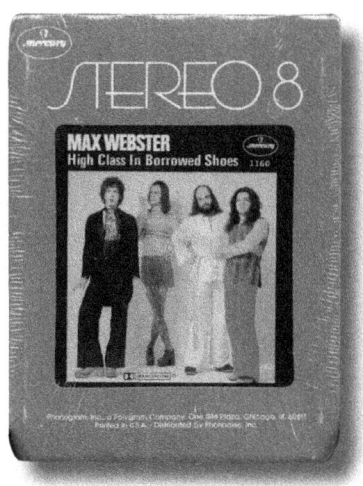

HIGH CLASS IN BOROWED SHOES –
"What, do you mean the clown suits?"

Taking it to the people constantly, winning them over one sophisticated yet stoned fan at a time, Max managed to find time in their schedule to craft—and I do mean craft—a second record to add to their arse-backwards arsenal. *High Class in Borrowed Shoes*, released May 16, 1977, would mark for the band a perceptible uptick in their talents, arriving from a number of whirled worlds. It was a nice foot to put forward too, given a new deal in January of '77 with Mercury Records for the US and the other territories outside of Canada, which saw the debut record get re-launched in the States, with, as discussed, a different cover and with the title *Hangover*.

Things were moving around back at the Toronto office as well. As Rush began breaking big with *2112*, the decision was taken to create Anthem Records. In conjunction, Ray Danniels and Vic Wilson brought in Tom Berry, later to become Kim Mitchell's manager over the ensuing decades.

Explains Tom, "My involvement starts... the first week I was hired, I went to see the band perform in the basement of the old famous Black Hawk Inn in Richmond Hill, which was the rock room in the north end of the city. It would've been right after the first record was released. I was the local Ontario promotion guy with RCA, and I was brought in to be the guy who looks after the records, very shortly thereafter to form a record company, because they were having trouble with, I guess at the time it would be PolyGram. Rush was signed to Mercury in the US, and I don't think they were getting the love they felt they should be getting from PolyGram. You know, Ray was always trying to build empires, and I say that in a positive way. He decided it would be better to do it with their own label, distributed by a major. They brought me in to open Anthem. I remember literally working on the logos and shit for Anthem Records. So, I was brought in to open and run Anthem Records in Canada, and be the conduit for Rush, and I guess Max, with the American record labels."

"I thought that Max was one of the few bands that was really doing something unique and different," continues Tom. "It wasn't just another hard rock band. It had songs that were relatively complicated. It went really simple to, you know, 'The Party,' lots of changes. The whole thing between the band and having a lyricist that was outside watching the band but inside writing lyrics for the band—kind of an interesting thing. Sometimes the lyrics didn't make any sense to me, but it was always interesting. Kim is—is and was—just an extraordinary front man. The rest of the guys were solid, relative to the positions they played, but Kim was extraordinary. He owned the stage and was an amazing player and was surrounded by this interesting group of guys."

"Marketing it and whatnot, you could see it grow. Every time they played they won fans. If you put them on as a special guest, with Genesis at the CNE for example, it would blow up really quick. Certainly, the audience would fall in love with them. Two-thirds of them wouldn't have a fucking clue what was going on, but there were always people that just absolutely adored it and fell in love with them. So, it was a great live act. It was saying something interesting, different, odd, weird. 'Oh War!'... these are songs, when Pye captured it, he really fucking captured it. When he missed, it just seemed like an artistic whatever (laughs), an indulgence that only he could get but was rather interesting as a concept."

"But yeah, it was pretty cool. The first couple of weeks I joined SRO, certainly within the first five or ten business days, the first band I went to see was Max in the basement of the Black Hawk, and I thought holy shit, what the fuck's this all about?! This is really weird. I just hadn't seen anything like them at that point, even though I did see bands in every room everywhere as a promo guy for RCA. But anyway, in the first two weeks, I was blown away by Max in the basement of the Black Hawk, and within five days, I was driving one of three Mercedes 450 SL's with the top down, with one of the Rush guys, on the way down Sunset Strip to special guest in front of Ted Nugent at the LA Forum—wow (laughs)."

A few things one notices digging into the wondrous box of tricks that is *High Class in Borrowed Shoes*, the new record is more textured and meticulously appointed, and much of this must fall to ever-exploratory keyboardist Terry Watkinson.

Second, the album is no less than one of the most high-fidelity records of the '70s, and much credit for this must go to Terry Brown, who was now four studio records deep into his knob-jobbing for Rush and thus vaulted into the realm of preeminent producers. English, Canadian, whatever... he's ours, a national treasure.

Third, as discussed, Max Webster had a new drummer in long-time orbital from the Max outreach program called Sarnia.

"Well, way better band. Way better drummer," muses Mike Tilka. "You know, not taking anything away from Kersey, but Gary's a way better drummer. When he joined the band, there was an immediate noticeable difference. Terry got better at being a white guy, rock, keyboard player. His influences were felt more. I became a better bass player and I sang better. We were just plain a way better band. It happens. You take three-and-a-half years of playing six nights a week, and unfortunately bands don't get that experience anymore. I don't know how you become a good band now. Kim was a taskmaster, and he was a great bandleader. We used to sit in the truck and listen to tapes and criticise each other after gigs. We used to warm up before gigs. I remember bands even joked about it. 'I can't believe how much you guys practice! I can't believe you sit in the dressing room practicing your vocals. You're going to play in twenty minutes.' But we did that stuff. I loved it."

"I don't think Paul leaving was acrimonious, the way it went down," ventures Pye, intriguingly blending two firings a record and a half apart. "I think there might've been a little bit of... geez, I don't even want to... I think there might've been a little bit of positive colluding to see what would happen if Myles and Gary got together. I'm not sure about that. I know, me, and I've told you this before, honestly, that I chirped in Mitchell's ear for a good year to get Tilka out of the band. I saw Gary as just a tremendous drummer, and I think he... I always thought he needed to be challenged, and a very good bass player would challenge him to make him better. And I always thought, well, that would be Dave Myles. I thought it would be Dave. Certainly, Mike Tilka wasn't that type of bass player."

"Gary was an old friend of Kim's and Gary was a really good drummer," continues Tilka. "Paul, I guess couldn't bring to the band what Gary brought. Paul has a great story where he says that they were gonna fire him, and he jokes, 'Hey Tilka, I thought it was you that was getting fired.' But I was the next one to get fired. But you know, whatever. All those reasons. Not to take anything away from Paul, because his drum solo was the highlight of the show, and people liked him, yadda yadda yadda. But you can hear the difference, I think. Whatever stiffness or lack of groove or whatever those words were that the first album has... it sounds like a first album. The second album sounds like a fourth album."

"Gary was an important addition," notes Terry Brown. "Yet also the material brought in for *High Class* was different; I thought it was a lot more commercial, more rock-oriented. The first album was more esoteric, shall we say. This time there was single-oriented material, given where radio was at that time, in Toronto and in Canada—we had a shot at radio. That's really the biggest thing. But certainly, the band was a little more streamlined, with Sticksy on drums. Gary was just a different style drummer and he played a larger kit, with a lot more forward energy, I think, than Paul. Paul had more jazz leanings—that was my impression at the time, especially with that big bass drum. Whereas Gary was flat-out rock. He had a big kit and he played the crap out of it. He was very good."

As for his signature tuned tom-tom sound, "Well, funnily enough, at that point in time, we were talking single heads. So, it wasn't the current trend of double heads and that sound. It was single heads, so microphones could be put inside the shells of the drums."

"The drums that I was using for most of that time period were Slingerland drums," says Gary "Sticksy" McCracken, by way of introduction. "I had three rack toms and two floor toms. Recording that album, I remember going through a whole lot of drumheads because I used all bottom heads, which are thin and not meant to be played on. But they have a really unique sound. But you'd only get one or two tracks out of a set of heads, and then they're totalled, right? So, I think I went through three or four sets of heads. So yes, they were on the top and they sounded great, but because they were thin, they didn't last very long. It was an experiment that Terry Brown was willing to take, even though it was going to cost a little bit of money—let's go for the nice clean tom-toms on the album, and we got it. Otherwise, what else? There's no double bass on that. I was playing double bass live a lot, but when we recorded, I used a single."

"We were sitting there waiting to go on," recalled Gary back at the time of his hiring, about his first significant gig with the band, after a debut show at Larry's Hideaway, November 25, 1976. For this next occasion, Max was on a bill supporting Strawbs at Maple Leaf Gardens no less, albeit in concert bowl configuration. The date was December 10th, and two weeks earlier, the band had done the first sessions toward the first record with Gary. "Kim asked me if I was nervous. I told him, 'Sure, a little.' Then Kim told me I was white. I looked down and my leg was shaking uncontrollably. Just a little tense."

But then it was back to the bars literally the next night, with Geddy Lee joining the band onstage at their last show ever at famed Toronto venue Gasworks, on December 23rd. Into the new year, late January, Max would conduct their first US campaign, supporting Rush.

"I grew up listening to Weather Report and Miles Davis; I was a jazz guy," continues McCracken, expanding upon what he brought to an already sophisticated cabal of players. "So, my inclination, if I sit down in front of the tape recorder, I want to play weird instrumental experimental music. Just to hear what it sounds like as opposed to, oh, I gotta put a B-verse together, and who's going to sing the chorus? Just to have a hit song that everybody is going to download for free nowadays (laughs). But collectively, at the time, I think everybody knows Frank Zappa had some influence on us. Certainly, Jimi Hendrix and Zeppelin and stuff we grew up with. But at the time it was progressive bands. And Rush, of course, who had a lot to do with breaking the band."

"At that time it was Billy Cobham who was my big influence. I always wanted to have a great big set of drums and go crazy on them, and I still do (laughs). Back then, having a big set of drums was show biz before anybody was doing it. '75, '76 were the first years you could buy these big sets so everybody started buying them. But Keith Moon, Ginger Baker, all those double bass drum guys, they were all just nutso, crazy. That led to the kind of drumming in Weather Report. But I didn't do any double bass on the records, except for maybe 'World of Giants.' It was reserved more for my solos and in other places live."

It's an attitude toward challenging music that served McCracken well as he propelled Max from the engine room right through to their demise, being the last drummer Max would ever have (or need). Of note, as far as Kim Mitchell was concerned, there wasn't much wrong with what Paul Kersey had been doing with the band, other than perhaps that he was "distant."

It was more the case of always having wanted to play with Gary. So, telling Paul he was out... the guys had to drink a couple bottles of wine to prepare themselves for the firing at hand, a firing that went against the band's atmosphere of appeasement when it came to conflict.

"As far as a drummer goes, I'm just trying to nail it, right?" continues Gary, nonetheless the team player, and, as alluded to above, not concerned with writing either. "I'm just trying to be as precise and as in-the-pocket as I can be. I have no control over the keyboard solo, I have no control over the guitar solos. I only have control over what I'm doing, so I'm just going to try to do the best I can; as it turned out, not bad. As soon as I joined the band, everybody made comments, but one of them was, the band started to smooth out. It straightened out. It was pretty polished and clean sounding, compared to the original band that was all kind of choppy, not smooth or whatever."

Upon hearing that that's pretty much what Tilka said, Gary laughs, appreciating the compliment. "Well, he nailed it, right? That's the thing; when you're talking to Mike, he does have a pretty good grip on this stuff as far as how it went. The results of it all. But anyway, so that's one of my things, just as a drummer. To be able to join up a band and actually make it sound better because of what you're doing. Well, that's the ultimate. So, I got that out of the deal."

Triumph drummer Gil Moore sums up Gary this way, albeit including him in a prodigious pairing with Kim Mitchell solo skinsman Paul DeLong. "Drumming-wise, whether it was Paul DeLong with Kim or Gary McCracken with Max, both of those guys are smoking drummers (laughs). Both really good. I always thought, if you don't have a good drummer, you don't have a good band. Not that the drums are the most important, but the drums are the thing that glues a band together and keeps it tight. If the drummer is all over the place, no one else has a chance to take. If the drummer's got his act together and he's got a good oily rhythm, the rest of the musicians are more likely to fall into the pocket. The drummers that I tried to emulate were in the pocket, so to speak. Like most of the guys that I was looking up to are guys that looked up to Al Jackson Jr. from Booker T & the MGs. They were disciples of that very, very, in-the-pocket 'rhythm is everything' type of playing. As opposed to what I see today a lot, where drummers are thinking of fills first and rhythm second. They don't get the foundation under the house, and they're starting to put fancy accoutrements on a shaky foundation. So, Gary is from that school where you build a solid foundation of smooth, oily, greasy rhythm pocket. Then the flourishes and stuff are very good. But he's not without that really solid foundation, which I think is part of what Max's trademark sound was. Now Mike Tilka was a very solid bass player as well. But when you get a combination of a drummer who kind of locks in with his bass player, now you've got a rhythm section that's in good shape. I have no idea if Gary ever saw, or paid attention to Triumph, but I paid attention to him, that's for sure."

Oddly, despite the perception of Gary and his tom-tom fills and his big drum set, Gil Moore is right in that McCracken's more about a solid foundation. Indeed, a studied analysis of Gary in general versus Paul on the debut essentially turns up a quicker tendency of Paul to break into jazzy note-densities. Yet we never really cotton to that, distracted by the boxier recording, the less sophisticated texturing and the harder rock sound of *Max Webster.*

Gary's one of the few Max guys ever to bring up Rush as an influence per se, but Geddy, Alex and Neil in fact inspired the band in so many ways, says Mike Tilka. "The guys in Rush were amazing. And they were diligent. They were wonderful to be on the road with. But we didn't hang with them and that. I know that Neil practices more than any drummer in the world. The guy has a work ethic that nobody has. But no, it didn't have anything to do with Rush. It had to do with the fact that we wanted to be better. We wanted our grooves to make sense, as much as they could. We wanted to excel at what we did. We didn't talk about it a lot. We just did it. It wasn't like, oh, God, we have to rehearse again. It wasn't like that. It was like okay, we're off Tuesday and Wednesday, let's rehearse. Or we're sitting in the dressing room for four hours, have the crew bring in a snare drum and set up some little amps and we'll practice."

"Basically, Paul Kersey made it known he was leaving the band," furthers Gary, offering some specifics of his hiring. "I was playing in Windsor at the time with a band called Meadows, who were a real good vocal band. We were playing a tavern thing, and we were between sets, the phone rang in the kitchen and it was Kim calling to say hi or something. He said they were in Thunder Bay and were starting a tour with Rush and I said, oh that's great. This is when they were just coming out with their first record. He said, 'Well, would you like to join the band in a couple of weeks?' I went yeah okay. So, the next thing I know, Kim and the boys are at my house picking me up with my drums and I'm on my way to Toronto. We had, I think, eight or nine days of rehearsal, and then we went out playing, and within two or three months we were in the studio doing *High Class in Borrowed Shoes*."

So, the arrival of Gary, as well as a blossoming of skill-set out of producer Terry Brown... things got pretty high class for *High Class*.

"Well, we spent enough time," says Gary. "Actually all of those records were $100,000 budgets. They weren't cheap. And a hundred grand back then, well, a hundred grand now, you can make a nice record, right? A really nice one. Back then, you're buying rolls and rolls of tape. Away you go with your master. Back then it was rolls and rolls of tape, and then the tapes all had to be preserved and put in vaults and stuff."

"You've got to remember, we co-produced the records with Terry," continues Mike. "That's not to take anything away from Terry. But Terry had just done two Klaatu albums, which sound amazing. By then he'd done what, two or three Rush albums that sound amazing. So, he got better, I got better, and when I say I got better, I sat next to Terry through both of those records. That's why I got to produce the third album. So, I understood the studio, I understood the sonics, I made Terry change the monitors we listened to. In fact, back then, a whole bunch of studios bought small monitors like we used. Because back then, the Yamaha and its ten-inch monitors didn't exist. But I used to listen on these very hi-fi-sounding Electropoint (ed. Electro-Voice?) monitors. Terry bought a pair, they had a pair there, I had a pair. Tons of people bought them."

Mike also had a reel-to-reel deck at home, so he was able to take the tapes away and study them. He recalls that at the end of the process, in the mixing stage, he brought in a Kansas album for reference, notably praising the album's drum sound.

"If I'm not mistaken, it was evening sessions, which went pretty late," recalls Brown, "much like the first album. I don't think we recorded during the day. By the time we actually got into the studio, the tunes had been chosen, and it was just a question of producing the best album we could with the tunes we had at that point. I had the reputation of recording only what we needed—I never recorded more than what was needed. It just seemed to work out that way. Like the Rush albums, we've only got so much time to do these albums. Back then, it was done in a short space of time, so to record extra tunes and have them sitting in the can was not really an option."

"Well, other than the fact that we achieved our objectives," laughs Brown, responding to the assertion that no record from the entire decade could be said to sound better than *High Class in Borrowed Shoes*—at this level, there's only different choices made for different frequencies. "Sure, I think it's a good sounding record. I love it. Still to this day, I enjoy it. We had put in a Neve console, and so that certainly gave us good sounds. But other than that, it was just really what I did at that time. I was just using my skills and the way I worked, transferred to Max Webster."

All business as well, except, "The only thing we did was play table tennis. We would do that in our time off, just to relax. I remember one thing, which is trivial, but one night we were working away, and we ordered Chinese food during a break. And it was the last time I allowed Chinese food on my session, because everybody has their Chinese food, and of course with the MSG and all that, we got nothing done for the rest of the evening (laughs)."

For some reason, just like most of the Rush albums, *High Class* feels like a winter album. Maybe it's the cold steel efficiency of the performances and the sound, and maybe it's the gunmetal blue bordering the front cover. "I think it was recorded in the winter," says Mike (indeed, the final mix was conducted April 7, 1977). "Because if we did the first one in the spring and played it all summer and everything, then the second album was done very similar to the first, although I think we actually had a couple of weeks where we could keep the drum kit set up."

As for the front cover, which, let's face it, reflects a substantial degree of career suicide, Mike figures, "You know, by then you had to get promo pictures and stuff taken. So, we had gone to various photographers, some of which took good pictures of the band, some of which didn't. A lot of them we, as a band, didn't care for, because there was something about that pose that you see on the 8" by 10" glossies the bar bands had to have, that was hokey. We knew we had to have them, but ours were like that first sticker we had with the high-contrast photo. When Terry joined the band, he just took Jim out and painted his face in there. That's not even a photo. Again, no money, we couldn't reshoot it. So, it was really easy to just get it right, because Terry was an artist. Now that we had a photo shoot, everybody decided that the mistake we made in the first record was band identity. So, we were going to have a picture of the band. And then we liked the picture enough, and the record company liked them enough, that it was the front and the back cover."

Asked about that absurdist cover image, Gary says with a chuckle, "What, do you mean the clown suits? I think we were just trying to make an impression, just shock value. And the music certainly had just as much shock value as anything. But I think the strange clothes and stage antics, it was the same thing—we were just being weird (laughs). Rather than just everybody going out in jeans and T-shirts going, 'Hey, "Here Among the Cats"' (laughs)."

Adds man of few words Watkinson, "Really, we just dressed up and stood in front of the camera and the photographer posed us around a little bit and took a couple dozen pictures."

"We all went shopping and grabbed stuff," recalls Pye, who is nonetheless not in the shot. "Yeah, it was funny, absolutely. It wasn't a matter of needing agreement. It was just go for it. No permission was asked or needed."

It was merely an ethic carried over from the live show, continues Dubois. "It was always a goal to find something quirky for Kim to wear, or sometimes Terry all of a sudden had makeup on and glitter. Of course, Gary was completely different. Just in his wonderful own world playing the drums. He loved what was going on, but he was pretty straightforward, where Terry was a little bit spacey. But Kim and Terry always had something going for them visually on stage, whether it be their dress or makeup or hats. It wasn't that it was feminine. I think the idea was to get it as colourful as possible. He had the orange and purple... these big, what do you call it, Egyptian balloon pants or something. You just couldn't miss them. On the *High Class in Borrowed Shoes* album, that thing he wears is really great under lights. The idea was everyone having fun, and when you do it a couple of times live, initially, and people react, it becomes part of the show—it's part of entertaining. Fun to do and fun to watch too. People always anticipated something was going to happen. That was Max—Max really had the reputation that something was gonna happen."

"Not much," laughs McCracken asked about what he now thinks of that photo session all these years later, which, incidentally, might not have happened—the original plan was to use the Hugh Syme design we see on the cover of the *Lookin' For Trouble* album by Toronto. "I remember we had driven overnight from Montreal or something, had to be at the photographer's at 11 o'clock in the morning. I remember that. We were trying to figure out what to wear. Kim at the time was getting into funky outfits. I was always a blue jeans and T-shirt guy, right? Because when you play drums, you don't necessarily have to get dressed up too much. You're just going to ruin whatever you're wearing anyway. But Kim's the front man, and a lot of it was handmade for him and stuff. I finally ran into someone who actually made a few outfits for me, basically glorified sweatpants and a wedding vest, type situation. But on *High Class*, I've been accused of wearing a red dress in that. I hate to ruin it for you, but that's not a dress."

Once past the cover, which betrayed not a trace of what kind of music was to be enclosed, *High Class in Borrowed Shoes* opens with its high-octane boogie woogie title track. What's it all mean? Don't ask Terry Watkinson, who says with a shrug, "I don't know. Pye wasn't really into explaining his lyrics that much. He said, 'Well, what do you think it means?'"

"It's a little bit like 'Distressed,'" says Pye, offering a crumb of a crumpet, "in that this couple, this male and female, are having an argument. Yeah, no more, no less. There's tension and anxiety, a little bit; that's what I wanted. It's everyday, how you work things out."

Kim kicks the attractive track off with an abrasive riff, Terry announces his presence with arch-'70s synths and then it's off to the races. Boogie, to be sure, which is an odd idiom for Max, but they make the rootsy blueprint their own with ascending and descending prog flourishes that are Zappa-esque of chord sequence and melody and rhythm.

"It's a little more sophisticated," agrees Terry Watkinson, so much now a magic part of the Max brew. "We knew more about the studio and I think the songs are stronger too. That was really, I would say, the most fun, because we were getting known and doing really well in clubs and having a lot of fun on stage. Doing some abstract, outrageous stuff as well as some really great songs. So, it was good. The big improvement was in the drumming, because Gary was way ahead of Paul Kersey as a drummer, as a timekeeper and creatively.

So that was big, and then the band just felt a lot more powerful and together. So that was exciting, to have a new band going into the studio. The music was a pretty logical progression from the first album, I would say. There were always some new things we tried. You can look at the tunes on the first album, and you can see that stuff like 'Coming Off the Moon' and 'Hangover' and 'Toronto Tontos'—that's the Max Webster signature there, already, pretty much."

"I also had several unsatisfactory electric pianos," adds Terry, in an email to the author. "Keyboard players in those days would have killed for one of the many great stage pianos available now, such as the Yamaha P155 that I currently use. But the real thrill was when I got an ARP Odyssey synthesizer. The pitch was unstable, it could only play two notes at once, and you couldn't store any of your sounds; you had to recreate them from scratch every time. But it was great to enter the world of synthesizers, with note-bending, portamento and timbre control. Starting with the *High Class* album, it was along for the whole Max ride. Other instruments that appear on the albums: a magnificent Petrof concert grand on 'Astonish Me' and other tracks, a Polymoog that happened to be in the studio for 'Diamonds Diamonds' and various polyphonic Yamaha instruments. At the end of the Max Webster years, many great keyboard instruments began to appear using sampling systems, built-in effects and sound storage abilities made possible by computer capabilities that were not even dreamed of in the '70s. Nevertheless the '70s was an era of great keyboard players and innovations, and it was wonderful to be in a progressive band with great players like Gary, Mike and later Dave Myles. Especially it was great to work with Kim, who was a master of the guitar and an awesome musical mind."

"One moment I remember vividly as when we were cutting the title track," says Terry Brown. "Mitchell was playing a Travis Bean at the time, and it had an aluminium neck. Great sounding guitar, but because of that, the tuning aspect of it was driving us absolutely crackers. The aluminium heated up and cooled down at a different rate from the body of the guitar and the strings, so he was having a really hard time keeping it in tune. He's a stickler for tuning, as you know. So, I remember he was yelling at me. We were just about to take it, and 'This expletive deleted guitar is driving me expletive deleted crazy.' We had a couple of bricks in the studio, which we had used to put in the bass drum to hold down the blanket we used for dampening. We had taken them out of the bass drum and they were sitting in the studio. So, he laid the guitar across these two bricks, from the neck to the body about a foot and a half apart and jumped as high as he could in the air, on the neck and then he picked it up, 'Okay, let's take this.' That was the song, that was the take—we kept it. So that's the one story I can remember vividly. Didn't do any damage, but I remember it being extremely dramatic, going oh my God, are we going to be sending out for a new guitar? It played just as well after he jumped on it, although it didn't fix the tuning problem."

As for other gear Kim used to get his sound on the record, Terry says, "We used a Fender Twin if I'm not mistaken. He just cranked it up to 11, and that was his sound. He was a great player. He gets so much sound out of his fingers and the way he frets and everything— he can change the sound of the guitar with his hands. It's that Jeff Beck thing going on with his hands; great player."

"I think the meter in that song is wonderful," notes Pye, back to "High Class." "It's a very unusual meter. It's really, in my opinion, a wonderful mix of songs. No wonder the record company was going, now what do we do? Diversity is not the home of art. For them, although it was for me. But the sound of that record, that's Terry Brown. Hats off to Terry Brown. I remember in the studio, he was just amazing. Terry was great to work with; he was funny too. You know, there'd be a really serious moment in the recording, and he'd be like this on the board (head down, two arms thrust forward on the faders), and you'd get closer, and he would be asleep! It'd be like, 'Terry, this is a serious solo!' (laughs)."

Adds Mike, "I always loved 'High Class in Borrowed Shoes' because it's fun to play. It's rocky and the thing just flies. That whole album we'd been playing. In fact, right after we finished that album, we were already playing 'The Party.' That's how fast these songs were coming." Indeed, as *High Class* was being issued, Kim was on radio reciting lyrics from "The Party," including the redacted, "We're musicians catching the colour of your skin."

Kim also said that these more high-energy numbers were necessary if the band was going to tour heavily in the US, where pulling out a plastic guitar and playing a ballad to a Rush crowd meant certain death.

"'High Class,' it's not fancy drumming, but it's nice and rockin'," opines Gary, who cites this as one of his favourite Max drumming tracks of all time, along with "America's Veins" and "Diamonds Diamonds." "You're going full-on on that one. But it's not particularly hard to play. The only challenge was I was trying to play everything as good as I could. We had played for a couple of months, learning the material, getting it worked out, and then we went in to record. Being the new guy, I was just thrilled to be there and do the job. We did a couple of songs a day, bed tracks, and as far as recording, you want to get the good drum track, back in those days. Then you would build off of that. So, I was always the most worried one (laughs)."

Asked if they used a click track, Gary answers, "We rehearsed to a click, but we didn't record with one, oddly enough, for *High Class*. We would rehearse, we'd run through the song a couple of times, click, click, click, and then when everybody got the idea, okay, that's it, we're going for it, 1,2,3, go, bingo. What's really neat is these albums are not Pro Tool'ed at all. There was no fancy manipulation. But 'High Class' is one of my favourite songs; that was one take— after rehearsing it. We would rehearse the stuff till like 11 o'clock at night, and then we'd all go home and go to bed and get up and go back to the studio at 11 o'clock in the morning and nail it, whatever we had been working on. That's what happened with 'High Class in Borrowed Shoes'—it was a one-taker. It was always the whole band, including guitar and keyboards; it was always everybody involved. If somebody had to repair something, well then you go back and you repair it. But everybody wants the drums to be as good as they can be. Once the drums are done, then you can go ahead and fix other areas, right?"

Next up was "Diamond Diamonds," a quaint, magical, child-like ballad with Oriental melodies. Not really a hit, it's managed to ingratiate its way onto Canadian classic rock radio, not to mention its use as the title for the band's greatest hits album, annoyingly, with comma added, although inconsistently. "'Diamonds Diamonds' I thought was very commercial," notes Brown. "I think it proved to be—it got tons of airplay, even to this day."

Kim decried at the time of recording how nervous he was singing the ballads for the record, intimating that he was losing sleep in the days leading up to his takes, rehearsing the songs in his head over and over again. Indeed, Terry rode him hard on this one, imploring Kim to sing it like he believed it.

Kim also said that the song was stuck on the record due to the strong response it got when they played it live. He particularly loves Terry's keyboard solo and Mike's bass part on the track, which, according to Tilka, was the only time he ever overdubbed a bass performance, although, even still, he nailed it in a single take.

"I was never privy to those conversations, but I think they went down," says Pye, asked about discussion over the picking of singles. "I'm not even sure if Kim was involved in that. I think the record company was rather arbitrary about that. But I don't think Max Webster was really single-oriented. I think 'Diamonds Diamonds' was a single, but 'Beyond the Moon' was never gonna be a single (laughs). To the record company's chagrin, what do you do with a band that is that diverse? But 'Diamonds Diamonds'... yeah, she's beautiful. I love her (laughs). Do you want me to say anything more?"

"Gravity" (working title: "Traces of Gravity and Clouds") brings the prog, with the band presenting a structure that feels like a working paper for the majestic masterwerk that is "Paradise Skies." Is that a key we hear drop? The story persists that it's Kim, in the vocal booth, flipping one of his own keys, and then dropping it while doing a take. Kim, at the time, said it was a bottle opener, that he had dropped, but Duncan, the engineer, said that he saw it vibrate its way off the amp, a victim of gravity.

As with many of Max's most enigmatic tunes, the song is a chimera, offering glam, pop, pomp, unexpected twists and turns, visceral guitar out of nowhere, and an oddly thespian vocal from Kim that has him sounding like a bemused adolescent. "I couldn't see 'Gravity' being a single," says Brown. "I thought it was a really commercial tune, but not in a radio sense; more like it was a good selling point to that album."

"I think it's a very typical theme that people have to get over their angst to expect some things to change in their life for the good," suggest Pye, asked about the lyric. "But I think I'm gonna make a comment that, 'Forget that fear of gravity...' many Max songs came from one-liners, and that's a one-liner song. 'Forget that fear of gravity.' I always had that in my mind. I didn't necessarily write it down. But 'Forget that fear of gravity' was always... I guess, people are going to call it a hook. I didn't call it a hook. I just called it an idea. So that floated in my brain or stayed on that piece of paper with all the other one-liners and eventually I found a spot. Or I found another line to go with it. That's one of the writing processes that I have, the one-liners. There are many one-liner songs, including 'Go for Soda,' 'Gravity' and 'Toronto Tontos.'"

"'Gravity' is my absolute favourite song of all of them," says Mike. "just love that tune, I love the way we recorded it, I love the accidents that happened."

But it wasn't so accidental in all departments—Kim confesses that the way he sings the song was inspired by The Sensational Alex

Harvey Band, which he was listening to a lot during the making of *High Class*. Kim has also said that there's an Alex Harvey influence to both "America's Veins" and the rock 'n' rolling title track as well.

As with most songs on the record, "Gravity" gets a Mitchell/Dubois credit. "You know, there's a whole school of thought on arranging, playing, formulating a song," reflects Tilka, asked about this contentious part of being in a band. "We did that as a band. Should I have gotten a songwriting credit? No. That's my personal feeling. Did I help make those songs happen? Absolutely. Did I help arrange them? Sure. On 'Gravity,' that's my voice in the lead on the chorus, but it hardly means anything. All three of us are singing, but you'd never know that. You know what I mean? It's not like the spotlight turned to me, you know what I'm saying?"

Concerning Mike's view of Pye at this point, "Again, when I was in the band, I didn't… His relationship with the band is that he hung out with us. He was in the house all the time. I don't think he ever lived there. He didn't go on long road trips with us. That was all later. Him and Kim were friends. I don't know, he wrote the lyrics. Kim wrote better songs, and edited his lyrics better. I'm not sure."

"Everybody recognised that it was Kim and Pye who were the driving force of the band," adds Watkinson. "And I was happy to get a song or two on each album. Pye has a real gift for saying things in an unusual way, that lights people up. Like people who are into that kind of thing. His lyrics are like a puzzle, and he generates new ways of saying things. I just consider him a great lyricist, really."

Proposed the idea that there's a particular challenge Pye rises to in terms of being obscure, artistic and poetic, without being dark or pessimistic, Terry says, "Well, yeah, but nothing the matter with dark or pessimistic lyrics. Look at Roger Waters. I'm playing keyboards for a Pink Floyd cover band on Canada Day. I'm just learning the songs, and every song is about here comes death or I'm going crazy. So that can work too; everybody loves those songs. But Pye had a way of expressing the ideas of young, rebellious guys, I suppose, more than women. I suppose some of those ideas are of partying and stuff. Everybody writes songs about partying, but he had a way of making it different."

Is there a sense of childlike wonder there? "That is not an expression I would think of using with Pye. No, he saw things in a unique way."

Also key to "Gravity" is Gary's groove and pocket as he commandeers the band through artful time signature changes.

There's a crazy instrumental break halfway through this five-minute mini-epic at which time McCracken gets to work out those arch-'70s tuned toms.

"Words to Words" touched many a couple's hearts to the point where this delicate acoustic ballad was used regularly as a wedding song. Notes Pye, "That's another song saying I love her. It's just about the beauty of being in a relationship, including the angst." Befitting Max's skills at the sophisticated, the track builds to new melodic possibilities, all the while with Terry Watkinson proposing new keyboard sounds. Kim augments the eventful track with clean electric soloing and deft acoustic licks as texture set against the central acoustic premise.

"Words to Words" was issued as a single, backed with "In Context of the Moon." A second single paired "Diamonds Diamonds" with "Rain Child." Both were non-picture sleeve.

Closing side one of the original vinyl is one of Max's angriest, most heavy metal tracks, "America's Veins." Its riff is legion, its detailing and appointments amusing and impressive. Lyrically, just like there's a "moon" suite, "America's Veins" is one of a handful of tracks on which Pye addresses the conundrum of America. It's a subject that popped into view given his upbringing close to the border as well as from his touring with the band all over the land of the free.

"Yes, there are a few digs about America there. 'Oh War!,' 'Battle Scar,' 'America's Veins'... During the time I grew up in with the Vietnam War, there was a high incidence of draft dodgers," reflects Dubois. "I couldn't believe it, that the person standing beside me was in Canada because their parents had to sneak them across the border, or if they didn't get across the border, they'd have to go to Vietnam and either be killed or kill somebody. It still makes my skin crawl thinking about it. These kids are my age, and they're killing people or being killed. It didn't make any sense to me. They were just fodder."

But, as it turns out, it was a good thing that the guys had a compartmentalised and specialised wordsmith to consider these vagaries of the times. Richard Nixon was ousted for Gerald Ford, with Ford replaced by that Allman Brothers-loving President from the south, Jimmy Carter. Asked whether everybody in the band was feeling political in the mid-'60s, Pye says, "No, and I'm glad you asked that. I never resented it, but I was acutely aware that I seemed to be the really sensitive one. No one ever talked or thought. Nobody ever talked about some of the issues I talked about, Vietnam or some of the political views or religious things, some the things that I thought were egregious. It certainly came up lyrically, but I never remember anyone caring. Maybe they secretly wanted to talk about this stuff, but certainly not to me. So, it was good, because it left me alone in my profundity. I just got to sort that out."

"Something I wanted to say," continues Pye, warming to this disconcerting topic. "You need to know, in all the years, this is really the only time I've ever really talked about lyrics. I still have a little bit of misgivings interpreting lyrics. I would never do that years ago. But it's okay now. Like I say, no one in Max ever talked to me about lyrics or asked me about lyrics. No one. So, I was really, really, just the guy on the side that wrote down stuff on paper. Even the record company never really said, well, what's this about, what's that? No one. Even sometimes Kim never asked. Still, I think Kim enjoyed and knew intuitively that what I was handing him, or I was reading him was very different. I think he thoroughly enjoyed that."

The "America's Veins" lyric, says Pye, is more directly, "about graffiti. I don't think you can find anyone that writes better anti-American graffiti than me (laughs). I just happened to put it in songs. For a good blow job, call… (laughs). The stuff that you would see in a washroom. But I wanted it female, because I snuck in the girl's washroom, and they write graffiti as well. But that's really a touchy subject for me as far as America goes, because I had this proclivity to chastise America. 'America's Veins,' 'Battle Scar,' 'Oh War!'—they're anti-American. I had to find a way to be anti-American without being too… without getting myself in trouble. I thought back then, the connotation with the graffiti was this was something that you would read, rather than something I would say about America."

But in the end, Pye's blood is made of laughter. "Well, yeah, that's me. That's me. But I would suppose that I'm not the only one with the feelings I have. The feelings I'm writing about. I think there are people my age in America that feel the same way. Even though I might have these feelings, I have a great sense of humour about it all."

"That, we worked on more than usual," says Mike, of "America's Veins." "It didn't just come together. I loved the fact that I got another tune with keyboard bass, which I got to play. Because I'm a keyboard player too. So, the whole notion of playing keyboard bass, like at the beginning of 'Diamonds Diamonds' and on that tune, etc., I loved it."

"Oh War!" opens side two with fighter planes humming and

rapid machine gun fire before the band collapses into what amounts to a prog band churning through a propulsive slow blues. After one verse, Terry tears into an essentially visionary burst of post-punk licks, followed by Kim with a tasteful axe solo. More machine gun fire and we're back into another verse. Of note, Kim was aware when making the record that he was soloing less than on the debut, quipping that he sometimes felt guilty about wanting to stick in solos. Indeed, it is Terry that picks up the slack, who really comes to the fore as a soloist here more so than on the workmanlike first record.

"'Oh War!' I loved, and it was the set-opener," says Tilka. "When we did the reunion, it was the perfect set-opener, with the bomber noises. The day Kim brought it to the rehearsal, he says, 'Tilka, you're gonna love this tune; this is one of your songs.' Because of the shuffling blues bass thing. The day we learned it, I loved it. I loved the lyrics, I love the song, I loved everything about it. It worked immediately."

The typical somewhat laborious process of turning Pye's words into songs worked a bit smoother this time, first because Pye indeed had a long poem ready and second, because Kim was able to lift, as a fairly large chunk, a portion from the end of the piece, for the lyrics of the song.

"'On the Road" is just a precious little song," muses Pye, on the record's campfire respite, an acoustic folk song fulsome of joy, analogous to the vibe of Kim Mitchell solo track "Cheer Us On." It's a pert song with forward motion, but yet again Terry gets to add a beautiful yet innovative part, despite this being a stripped-down version compared to how the band played it live.

"I hope someone plays that at my funeral," laughs Pye. "Because I think it's just a good lyric. I don't know, what do you really call that? A coming home lyric? It's just a pretty lyric. But I don't think the lyric is important. For that album, once we got into the studio, everything went fairly well but the only one Kim had trouble with and couldn't resolve was 'On the Road.' And Kim had trouble with it because he didn't like what Mike Tilka was playing and he didn't know how to deal with that. Didn't really tell Terry Brown about that. So, it took a while for some kind of momentum to get it corrected. I don't remember how it started, but eventually Kim played the bass guitar on that song. That's the important thing about that song more than the lyric: the way Kim recorded that song—Kim played the bass, the guitar and Terry Brown produced it—it was just a gem on all levels."

"Oddly enough, I got more pedantic as I got older, as it went on," continues Pye. "Back then I was pretty loose. I seemed to be able to peel these little things off quickly and easily. Maybe it was just the immediate access to Kim. Kim more or less knew I was writing every day. I didn't have a problem with him being an editor and me more or less giving him something right away, what I did that day or the night before that I thought was good."

Proffering a little more detail about methodology—or the small variety of methodologies—Pye says, "I think the process is twofold. I would be writing all the time. Probably not the best example for you because you're dealing with Max, but in my journal, I would say, 'Hey, Kim what do you think about this?' I would read him 'Patio Lanterns.' Which is right straight from my journal. And Kim would go, 'Oh, that's great,' so I would just copy it off for him and he would take it and it was done. So, I would either have one line to give him, or, I would have one line, and I would just put it in my mind or put it on paper and write to that one line. But generally speaking, if you see my journals, all of a sudden my mind seems to go outside the box, and gets away from the prose and the daily activities of living and into this bizarre-dom. So, I have thousands of these little passages, but I would underline one line. Sometimes I would read that to Kim, 'What about this?' And 99% of the time, I would read it aloud to him, because I had this intuitive sense of cadence and meter and what I thought it could sound like. It was important to me not to influence him musically, but this is what my mind hears when I write this, and that would come out when I read it."

Pye says "five out of ten songs" would be fairly complete and ready to go, but as far as repeating passages, banging things into verses and choruses, "Generally speaking, that's a decision Kim would make. He would be filling in the gaps and arranging the song. Sometimes I would repeat, if I heard it in my mind, this is a strong enough line to repeat that part. Or even if it's just something in the background, this is nice, yeah. But that's really part of the writing process. That's the kind of stuff that just goes hand-in-hand."

As alluded to, "On the Road" began loud and got quiet, as Gary explains. "We spent six months or so, or better, every night playing 'On the Road' as a band. When we got in the studio, Kim decided he didn't want to do it that way. It ended up, if you listen to it, with just him playing everything, with just a little drums from me, a little train beat in the background with brushes. So that was all fabbed up in the studio—that wasn't pre-planned. Basically, it didn't sound the way we thought it should with a full band, especially in Kim's mind. So, he decided that we'd be better to try salvage the tune in some manner. Because it is a good song—'On the Road' is an awesome song. It just went that way. It's like okay, we're gonna scrap the band idea. Kim played the bass, Kim played the guitar parts and then it was decided, okay, get in there, Gary, and put on the train thing. It turned out to be a good choice, and bingo, we saved it by reworking the song."

Second to last track on the album is "Rain Child," one of those elegiac deep album prog tracks that quietly adds class to a Max spread. This Terry Watkinson piece features the man himself on vocals, the Ty Tabor to Kim's Doug Pinnick. Chuckles Watkinson, "I don't know, it's another one of those where at that time I was trying to write songs and some of them worked and some of them didn't. I would say that is one that didn't really work so well."

Terry added a dimension to the band over and above his bag of key tricks and his singing, namely this bonus situation where he didn't feel he had to write with Mr. Dubois.

"I just felt like I could be a lyric writer too," explains Terry. "So, I just tried to do that. I did work a little bit with Pye, but nothing really came of it. He had a method of working with Kim that we weren't really privy to. He was more of a poet than a songwriter, and he would just give reams and reams of stuff to Kim, and Kim and Pye would dig through it to see what could be a song. I have a lot of admiration for Pye, but he was kind of an eccentric guy."

As for Pye's view on Terry's wordsmithing, "I thought he was okay. Yeah, and almost the diametric opposite of me, right?" And having this second lyricist in the band? "I think it was a good idea, and Kim agreed. Really, like I said, diversity is really the home for Max. So, I think that was good." Surely there could be, therefore, a few ego battles? "I think there was, but for me, I never noticed. I knew that there were a couple of songs I didn't want, that I didn't like. I don't remember if they got on the albums or not, but I remember I didn't like this, didn't like that. But I never had any problems with Terry."

"I wasn't very prolific then," points out Terry. "Took me months to write a song. So, I was lucky if I could come up with a couple for the next album. It's different now. I've got a lot of great songs I've written over the last fifteen years that would've been just terrific for Max Webster, but there you go."

When we call "Rain Child" proggy, it's more in the erudite melodies than anything. Fact is, it's essentially commercial and accessible, if a level of compromise between crafter and listener can be negotiated, hand extended.

"Well, there was grappling going on," notes Terry, on the eternal dance Max had to do with the business interests of the band interested in making it resemble, at least by cursory glance, a business.

But prog was still a big part of the band's sphere of influence. "Sure, yeah. Rick Wakeman, Keith Emerson, for sure. That was a period when you actually had keyboard heroes. And now keyboards can do anything basically, but who knows the name of the keyboard player anymore? Kim was a big Frank Zappa fan, first of all, and he also liked people like Captain Beefheart, all the usual suspects, The Who, Led Zeppelin and so on. But Kim, I kind of bent towards his vision when I joined the band. Because it was really interesting and exciting to me, and it freaked me out a lot, rather than playing in the normal rock band mode. The songs were a little more experimental and sometimes goofy, and sometimes very intense."

"What happened was," continues Terry, addressing the shift of studio to stage, "we got to play a lot, opening for Rush, in the States and in Canada too, at first. In that situation, when you're playing in front of, say an American crowd that doesn't know you at all, you can't be too self-indulgent. You've got half an hour maybe to make a statement, and so I think that was when we started to become more conventional in our stage approach. Probably a good thing too. But we were listening to everything, and developing our own sense of what works. The band scene was a very different scene than it is now. Because most bands that got to where they were—like, moderately successful—played five or six nights a week in clubs. So, playing every night is something that bands don't do too much of now, and it's too bad, because it's really a good way to solidify everything and work everything out."

Asked to toot his own tweeter horn a bit—which is hard to do with Terry I might add—Watkinson acknowledges his import, which includes serving as some of the inspiration for Geddy Lee to bring keyboards into Rush.

"Well, I would say I was one of the pioneers on synthesizers. At that time there were just a few different kinds. I got an Arp Odyssey and had a lot of fun with it and worked it into the music and that was good. I developed ways of playing kind of solo guitar or interacting with a guitar. Yeah, strangely, not that many rock bands are guitar, bass, keyboards and drums. Kim liked the way I played, I guess. I played with him longer than anybody did."

Charting the evolution of his gear, Watkinson explains that "The basis was a Yamaha transistor organ, through a Leslie speaker. It had some bells and whistles you didn't have on a normal Hammond organ, plus it was cheaper and more portable. So that was the basis, and I used various things. In those days, it was hard to get real piano sounds. So various different kinds of pianos came and went. And synthesizers, I used that Arp Odyssey for a couple of years, and they started making polyphonic synthesizers, which were exciting. That got really expensive, but great, so..."

Specifically on the Leslie tip, that's something we all associate with the great Jon Lord. "Well, that's just a given with organs. There's not too many organists that don't use a Leslie sometimes. I really liked guys like Ray Manzarek and the guy in The Animals, who used a transistor organ; they really got that bite, that you don't get in a Hammond organ. Because a Hammond organ doesn't generate any sound higher than, 5K or something like that."

"I love 'In Context of the Moon' because it's proggy," remarks Mike on the album's slightly Zappa-esque closing track. "But it's a proggy song that was listenable." To which Pye chuckles, "Yeah, I got my moon song on the album. That's a sort of moon song love song—that's all that is. It's not a moon traveller, but this person in the moon series is a person there, this spirit. You know, it's neat to talk about those kinds of feelings like devotion or acceptance."

Indeed, this one's got signature Max twists and turns but its central verse structure is based on heavy power chords. Essentially, tracks like this support the premise that Max, despite greater diversity, were in there toiling with the likes of Rush, King Crimson, Styx and Kansas in the invention of what we might call "progressive metal," although the lion's share of that mantle has got to go to Rush.

Album concluded, it was now time for any press the band could conjure. Canada's fledgling *Music Express* abided with an 8/10 review, stating, "Max Webster has been called many things— brilliant, eccentric, whimsical—but above all, this band has the musical ability to override their esoteric presentation. Kim Mitchell's excellent lyricism and the group's tight instrumentation has been well exhibited by almost faultless production. The album's cuts are in the four- to five-minute range, allowing the band to indulge in some rather exotic arrangements. But Max Webster are equally capable of straight hard-driving rock numbers like the title cut and more plaintive acoustic numbers like 'On the Road.' Max Webster's debut album was critically acclaimed but did not fare too well commercially. *High Class in Borrowed Shoes* deserves a better fate. The ingredients are all there for a hit record."

For his part, Kim was calling their music at the time, "High class curiosity rock. It's the best thing we could come up with. It's not punk and it isn't heavy metal. My weirdness is consciously cultivated. It's part of being an entertainer. It's a growing thing like the songs. It's all part of the process, including each person's personality. We're not a bunch of high school kids farting around anymore. We've turned pro, so to speak."

It's interesting hearing Kim talk about genres, for indeed, in context, 1977 marked the height of punk, the best year for ridiculing prog, and a continued celebration of all-American heaviness through the success right then of Ted Nugent, Kiss, Aerosmith, Boston, Cheap Trick and Blue Öyster Cult. Where did Max fit? Well, one would have to say they were defiantly anti-punk, although presciently post-punk. Plus, out of step, they were quite proggy. And yet somewhat aligned with the times, they were accessibly heavy and humorous like Cheap Trick and BÖC.

Now two long-players deep, Max Webster found themselves out supporting Rush yet again, but also sharing stages with Starcastle, Derringer, Cheap Trick, Angel and most extensively, UFO—Kim has fond memories of the Max and the Rush guys stopping mid-bite at dinner, jaws agape, listening to Michael Schenker play his guitar during sound check. As well, Kim participated in his own cool sound check event, woodshedding 'Xanadu' and then playing it with Rush once, when Alex knew three days ahead of the gig that he was going to be late, due to flight logistics. Another head-shaking recollection for Kim is of all those shows where he had in effect been playing with two drummers, Gary and Neil Peart, given that a scrim-shrouded Peart had drummed often times Max's whole set as his warm-up, with his microphones turned off, in preparation of the Rush set to come once Max said their goodbyes.

Other career highs... there was a debut headline stand on March 26th at Toronto's New Yorker Theatre, with the band selling a thousand tickets and playing two sets at the 500-capacity venue. That was an important milestone to be sure, but it was the band's even bigger hometown headline show at Massey Hall on June 9th, supported by A Foot in Coldwater, that earned the Websters three encores from a crowd 2000 strong.

Two nights later, Max found themselves on a Western Canadian swing in support of Styx, ending on June 26th in Nanaimo, BC. Into August of '77 and it was a short Ontario headlining leg, with Goddo and A Foot in Coldwater as support. August 23rd found the band playing outdoors in Toronto at Exhibition Stadium, with Rush, to a crowd 23,000 strong. This was followed by more dates supporting Rush in Western Canada, on a campaign sponsored by the Thrifty's clothing chain. Then it was off to the States with Rush and UFO.

Asked about those ragged days on the road, Mike responds with, "Remember the big fuel crisis in the '70s? There was a huge fuel crisis in the States, and I remember playing in Tennessee, and it was an extremely cold winter, and it was really hard to get gasoline. We're driving in the van and we'd put a piece of cardboard in front of the radiator, so the water gets hotter, because we were driving with blankets on our knees. Because the front of the van is just tin. It was freezing! The guys in Rush would sometimes... Kim and Gary would sometimes ride in their bus. We played an arena, and I remember the kids were all wearing jean jackets and stuff and it was freezing. UFO was nuts. Phil Mogg was crazy. I saw them later with Wireless; there's even more stories. What's his name, the guitar player, Michael Schenker? He practiced all the time. He never talked. He didn't socialise with us in the band. In rehearsal, you could hear him practice; if you're at a gig, you would see him practice; the guy was scary. Pete Way? Yeah, he was drunk all the time. He used to fall over—on stage."

The Max guys, however, were pretty even keel, something they shared with Rush, who, collectively, one would think subconsciously, shared that Canadian trait of feeling like they had to have their wits about them in big, bad America.

"We could drink and we could party, but we were pretty boring," says Mike. "When you get right down to it, in my whole life, I experimented, yes. Did I do it on a regular basis? Never. I don't remember Kim hardly ever doing drugs. I think when he was younger he might've. That's not to say we didn't take a toke or something. We were certainly drinking; we had parties. Terry and Gary were a bit more maniac, but you know what? They were maniacs off the clock. One time in my life, I played after having three beers. I remember Kersey was in the band. I swear it would never happen again. Three beers is not a lot of beers, but I just didn't play well. I knew it, the guys in the band knew it, nobody said anything to me, I never did it again. I remember Paul got drunk once too and he couldn't finish the night, and he never did it again either. But whether or not Terry was drunk or stoned, who knows (laughs). I couldn't tell; he was a pretty out-there guy. Kim was never a 'bottle of wine before the show' guy."

"Everybody took their turns at being steady and being crazy," laughs McCracken. "Sometimes I was the crazy one, and other times it would be everyone else that would be going nuts."

September into October of '77, in the midst of dates with Rush and UFO, the band found themselves at the Whisky a Go Go in LA for four nights supporting Blondie. "I remember it; it was amazing, so cool," says Tilka. "Blondie was cool, the gig was cool, being in LA was cool. And the building was kind of chilly, but back then..."

But why Blondie? "It didn't work like that. You took any gig you could get. If you were a touring band that had an audience... and we didn't ever play with Blondie again, but there was no other reason that Blondie wasn't available. Ray Danniels got us that gig. So, we needed the work in LA by then, yadda yadda yadda. A year earlier we played with Handsome Dick Manitoba and The Dictators in New York to three people. We drove all the way to My Father's Place in Roslyn, New York, because the agent wanted to see us. They were a heavy punky band. We made no sense with them, but as it turned out, it didn't matter. But we drove 700 miles for 300 bucks to play a gig. If that's what you get, you do it."

As for Gary's memories of Blondie, "Just the fact that we were standing there right beside her in the middle of the afternoon doing sound check. It's Blondie, man! Everybody became a lot more famous twenty years after. The Whisky had history, plus it was neat to say, yeah, we opened for Blondie. What's with Max Webster opening for Blondie? But it turned out to be one of those deals where we had a full house, and whether they knew us or not, we just blew the place apart and did really well. People went nuts—we were the good ol' Canadian boys."

"Agents didn't know what to do with us," continues Gary, on the subject of winding up on oddball bills like this. "So, okay, let's try these new wave gigs, right? Yet we were sort of heavy metal, just a bit left of centre, weird, but musically quite good. That's what always over-rode the imagery of it. But ultimately, we sold all our records in Canada, and we sold all those records because we showed up at these places and played. We show up again and we played. And everybody who came to buy a ticket bought the album, right? And we went gold just on Ontario sales."

Rocking with Rainbow is another fond road memory for McCracken. "Ritchie Blackmore used to come and sit in our dressing room because he didn't like hanging out with his band. So, he'd come in with that white Stratocaster of his and he'd sit down and say, 'Would you mind if I just hang out with you guys and warm up?' He put out the impression that he was a mean-spirited kind of weird guy, right? He's actually a very nice guy, and mellow. I never thought in my life I'd be sitting there talking to the guy from Deep Purple. Then Cozy Powell, we ended up being quite close. When we went over to play in England, he showed up at our gig over there to say hi. That was a real trip for me because I grew up listening to Cozy Powell myself. That's the thing with being out there on bigger gigs— you get to meet a few people that are your heroes. You're sitting right beside them on the same tour, doing the same thing."

"I remember Richie Blackmore punched out a guy," adds Pye, offering his own Rainbow tale. "There was Max, Ritchie Blackmore and REO Speedwagon, and this is in Texas. And REO Speedwagon used to carry... the road manager used to carry this clock, put it at the side of the stage, and this is your forty-five minutes. If you were a guitarist, there's no way you couldn't see this clock. Ritchie Blackmore just came forward towards the end of the forty-five minutes or whatever it was, he was kicking over amps and he looked at the clock. He was doing the solo like this, standing at the side of the stage, turns and bam! Punches the guy, goes back to his guitar solo. It was hilarious. Ritchie Blackmore's keyboardist was Dave Stone, and they hated each other, so Dave Stone would have all the wires and be playing in down the hall, right around the dressing room, in the cafeteria while the concert is going on, because Ritchie Blackmore didn't want him on stage. This was all the gigs. Because he probably signed a contract, said you're going to be on tour, you get this much, but that didn't mean he was going to play on stage."

Flash forward a couple years and Dave Stone would be punching the keys for Max Webster. "Well, I guess they met there. I guess that's probably it. But it was so odd to see a keyboard player set up nowhere near the stage, and playing the songs while Ritchie Blackmore was playing on stage."

"I didn't like the guy," continues Pye, back on the Man in Black. "Arrogant twit. I remember after one show, we were up at the bar and he had these magic cards and coin tricks, and it was just the dumbest, pathetically dumb, trite, and he just thought you had to be an idiot if you didn't like what he was doing. I remember some Texas town, and how he used to just pile up the amps, and he was overdoing his guitar solo, and he had his foot on the amp. And he just kicked the amp over and there were hundreds of people below him. He was a dangerous man. This was a dangerous man (laughs). But because of Ronnie, I always made sure I saw them. Because I love that kind of singing. He had a pretty unusual stage presence. Stiff but not stiff, small in stature but unbelievably powerful—and demon-like and angel-like. It was a real contradiction."

"We toured twice with Rainbow," continues Pye sifting through his memory banks. "So, for the first time it was Ronnie James Dio; the second time, not sure. What was nice was a calm in the middle of the tour where there was a week off, and everybody went home except a guy on the road crew and me. That was all through the southern states, Tennessee, Louisiana, Mississippi, Arizona, Texas, lots, all around the Gulf there."

"Somehow, we found out there was this concert in Phoenix. It was Bill Bruford, the violinist Jean-Luc Ponty and this kid who came out of nowhere, Allan Holdsworth. These guys just got together, Billy Bruford, Ponty and Allan Holdsworth. I don't know how they got to Phoenix, but when we got to it, there were eighteen people there. We just got the concert of our life! These guys were just rocking. It was great. I think Kim came back, because I don't think he'd ever heard of Allan Holdsworth, and he was like, oh God, this guy's incredible. This guy was the nerd of all nerds. He had a shirt from Kmart and kept going (laughs) like this, and playing the guitar, and he didn't have a clue what he was doing as far as being on stage. That wasn't UK, because I remember, we later went to Europe and saw UK with Bruford, but I think they had the same bass player, really tall guy, Jeff Berlin? I might be confused."

Other than Rainbow, Max shared stages with—and most often—UFO, as well as Rick Derringer, T. Rex (once) and Cheap Trick. "Oh, they were terrible," says Pye, confirming industry chatter that Chicago's finest were never the most amiable tour mates. "It's very true. Yeah, Kim went to the mic in Chicago and the monitors didn't work, the lights didn't work. I think that all came back to haunt Cheap Trick. The dirty tricks caught up with them, and when they started opening for other bands, the rumour was that they weren't very nice, and bands did the same thing to them that Cheap Trick did to us. Yeah, Cheap Trick were the rudest people I ever met. And

Blackmore, really moody people. But Cheap Trick wore it; they got their just desserts by treating people like that."

On press duties back in the day, amidst all these tour dates, Mike Tilka had told Boyd Tattrie of *Music Express*, "The places that didn't like the first album, we're pretty sure they're gonna give airplay on the second, because programmers and record people have told us that it's a lot more programmable. You know, 'Toronto Tontos' is great for Toronto and we love it—it's a great song—but it's a little weird for a guy in Davenport, Iowa to relate to what a Toronto Tonto is and even how to work that into his program schedule."

Added Kim, with regard to US radio, "They're so tight. Mercury Records has taken the album to some stations that have fairly straight programming and given it to them, and they've said, 'Oh, man, that first album, I dunno...' Like they don't even want to listen to the second album because they still remember the first one. You have to twist their arm a bit." However live, says Mitchell, "We've been getting very good response. We've been getting encores, and that's hard for an opening act. In this deal, there's an opening act, then a special guest, then the headliner. If you're an opening act, you're playing while people are still coming in. But we still pulled off encores."

As for the new album being less nutty than the debut, Kim was buying it... sort of. "We had so many tunes, and those were the songs that we wanted to put on. We have a lot of crazy stuff. But we have a lot of straight stuff too. People relate to us as a crazy oriented band, but we're not really. I think we're really normal. Like after being in a band three or four years even 'Toronto Tontos' seems normal."

"We've had a lot of trouble with covers," continued Kim, on the *High Class in Borrowed Shoes* cover art, which was bound to upset some people. "Initially they hated the cover of the first album, so we made an American version. 'Just have one head, and make it look like it's got a hangover.' So that's what Terry did. They still hated it, and they came back and blamed us. 'That cover's terrible.' We'll never live it down. For the second album, Hugh Syme did a really nice charcoal sketch of a little 12-year-old chick in your basic jeans, smoking a cigarette, and she's got her mother's shoes on, beautiful shoes. You know, *High Class in Borrowed Shoes*. The cover was gonna be grey and white. The record company says, 'Child pornography, we can't do that.'"

"We play with different bands," explained Mike, back to the touring experience, in the same chat. "But it's the same sea of kids.

It can be divided up differently; like Rush's audience and maybe Starcastle's are a bit different, but there's so much crossover. I think maybe they just take different drugs depending on which band is playing. I think there are places along the east and west coast where we could play to a different type of audience. But basic Midwest Great Lakes audiences are pretty similar, whether it's Rush, Starcastle or us. You should see the American audiences. Bars are tame compared to how drunk kids are there. A lot of the concerts are not, 'Let's sit down and act nice for the band;' they're much rowdier than bars. A lot of these places—the arenas—serve booze too, so they're like a huge bar. Plus, every kid in the place has a bottle in his pocket."

Mike set the record straight on how the money flows were working for the band back in 1977. "The lean years are now," explained Tilka. "The lean years weren't playing the clubs here— those were the fat years. Going on tour gets so expensive. Hotels for eight people every night whether you play or not; gasoline expense is just enormous... We've been making some decent cake in some places; in others we're unknowns and we're paid like unknowns. It's as simple as that. But fortunately enough we can come back to Ontario and we have a good market, a good following here. So, we subsidise our own tours. We have record support, too, of course. You can't do it, I don't think, without a millionaire or some record support. But fortunately, we can finance it ourselves 'cause we can come back to Ontario. Like right now we're here for two-and-a-half weeks, we've got a lot of dates to do, and we'll bank the money—to lose on the next tour. It's the name of the game; everybody does it."

Also sharing stages with Max Webster in the States was Angel, a band that was in a sense at another point on the progressive metal trajectory, very much textured like Max but without the humour. Also, like Legs Diamond, Angel were considered America's Deep Purple. And weirdly, with Terry in the band, when Max Webster played heavy, they could sound a bit like Deep Purple as well.

"Oh yeah, interesting band," continues Mike, back to the present day. "Keyboard player was a really nice guy. We talked to him a lot. Punky Meadows was the guitar player. He was gorgeous. As Frank Zappa's drummer used to say, 'I'd love to sleep with Punky Meadows, and I'm not gay!' They spent more time doing their hair and they never did sound check. They were like the white Kiss. I was not a fan, meaning, I wasn't a fan, but they had a thing, and the drummer was the only one with dark hair; the rest of them all had long blond hair. Good band. Again, not my taste. But lots of layers, textures, keyboards, but more of that than we had, more Yes-like. Kim was a better guitar player, but Punky was good. The drummer was similar to Gary, really good pocket drummer. So yeah, they were similar. Blondie was a way more interesting band. I wasn't into Blondie, but they'd just fired their bass player; they had one guitar player who played bass, and they were really rough, really crude. She looked entirely different every day we played with them, but they were mesmerising."

Adds Gary, "The only thing I remember about Angel is watching them run offstage in-between tunes to check their makeup. Yeah, they had actually put six-foot mirrors on the side of the stage, so they could run off and check if they looked right, between songs. I'll never forget it. I don't know whether that's because they were getting pictures taken or that was just the way it was. But we thought that was pretty strange."

With Starcastle, what Max had there was another appropriate band with which to share a bill, although comparatively they were more so straight progressive rock, Yes clones, as it were. "Their singer," recalls Mike, "I ran into him years later in LA. We shared a cab. He was working for a record company and I was working for SRO, and we both transitioned into the music business. They were a good band. I was from near Chicago, so we had a lot in common. Styx was really cool. We all wished we could sing like that. Starcastle was a good band, although I don't think they were good songwriters. Nice guys, and the white Kiss, Angel, they had the shtick. But we already knew what we were. We worked really hard at being what we were. You learned about music, and you learned about the industry, and you learned about playing live, and you learned about playing simpler in arenas, but none of it terribly consciously."

You look at that smear of bands—heck, UFO and Derringer included—and one can envision, within the great leveller that is a rude and crude live show in a concrete hockey barn, that Max made some semblance of sense on bills with all of them. But there's one act I've always compared Max to with my American friends, that Max never played with, and that would be the legendary Blue Öyster Cult. The laundry list of similarities is long, including lyrics of the utmost and upper echelon (many by people—poets and near-poets who were not in the band), hard rock mixed with pop, a dedicated keyboardist (although much less keyboards in BÖC), an element of prog, regular power chords, and a vocalist in Eric Bloom that could sound like Kim at times, most notably in terms of nasal twang.

"No, never listened to Blue Öyster Cult," says Mike. "I knew who they were, they had a couple hits, they were rocky, but no. When we used to sit around the house, we listened to Jethro Tull, The Who, Frank Zappa, Captain Beefheart, and for poppier tunes we listened to The Doobie Brothers, because they were good, and this is pre-Michael McDonald, when they were rockier. We loved early—or I did, and then I turn the guys onto them—early Queen, the guitar-heavy Queen and all that stuff. That was what we listened to. For textures and stuff, like when Gary Wright came out, I remember Kim listening to that album over and over and over again, just to hear the textures. Of course we loved Steely Dan, because they were a muso band."

Again, just like the mix of Max live partners, there's another "smear" right there in Mike's recollection of influences, that adds up to the complex stew that was Max Webster at the time of *High Class in Borrowed Shoes*. Fortunately for aficionados of fine music across this great frozen nation (and in pockets the world over), when it came time to construct a third record of maximum Max Webster genius, our heroes with zeroes in their bank account would stay the remarkable course and deliver the goods yet again.

MUTINY UP MY SLEEVE –

"Fix it?! I got fired from that band!"

Come 1978, Max Webster would bravely issue a third record that certainly did not bow to continued pressure to temper and tamp down the band's fearless sound. *Mutiny Up My Sleeve* was every bit as sensually and sumptuously confounding as its predecessor, and maybe even more so, if one allows a surrender to the few tracks that are most pointedly weirder, in conjunction with the record's album cover and general vibe toward obscuration.

But like a last kick at the cats (despite a hopeful move outside of Canada from Mercury to Capitol), there was personal drama to spice the tale of senses already overloaded. Bassist Mike Tilka would be ousted from the band, replaced by old pal from the outback of Ontario, Dave Myles. Tilka, however, would not land far afield, winding up as the (limited) producer of the new album as well as busy bee back at the offices of SRO, where he would look after Max's tour finances as well as other duties.

"Mercury didn't give a fuck about us," Pye told *Sounds*, about the switch in label representation. "They didn't care one bit. The band would play in Milwaukee or wherever and it'd be great and you'd walk around town, go into a record store, and would they have a Max Webster album on their shelves? Nope."

"You get embarrassed," added Kim. "When you're a support band in the States—these days we're headlining in Canada—I don't expect to see an enormous Max Webster display in the window, but I do expect to be able to find our records."

"They weren't feeling the love at Mercury," reiterates SRO's Tom Berry. "Max was not easily understood by record company people. I loved it. It was my favourite thing. I just loved it to death. It was such a crazy, wonderful combination of everything that I felt was good about rock—and they were just staggering live. But Americans just thought it was some weird Frank Zappa-esque, Captain Beefheart, 'What the fuck is it?' kind of thing. I'm pretty sure that the Mercury deal was done just because they had Rush and did a favour to Ray. Because Rush loved Max and were determined that they were going to open a lot of their shows in the States and whatnot. So, Mercury knew they had that going for them. I think that the lack of them really going for it at Mercury ended up in Deane Cameron, who loved the band, and was the president of Capitol, or maybe only the head of A&R at that point, at Capitol in Canada. He just loved the band and made an offer."

Subsequently the deal worked out well in Canada, not so well in the US, but also nicely in the UK. "Yes, certainly in the UK; David Munns was a friend of Deane's and actually did something in the UK for the band. Capitol in America, well, they never 'got' Deane Cameron, let alone most of the acts he released, and I'm pretty sure they never got Max. But David was around a long time. He went from Capitol to... Jesus, he was a major player at PolyGram (ed. Munns had eventually become Jon Bon Jovi's manager, before rejoining EMI). But he was head of marketing at Capitol in the UK. He was Deane's good friend, and they were the ones that did picture discs and had the band come over and perform."

"In my view, they were one of the first artists in Canada with a truly unique and innovative sound," begins Deane Cameron, positioning the band in territorial context—sadly, we lost Deane, age 65, in 2019. "I consider them among the first—along with Rush—that were different. But Canadian radio and the Canadian public, if they were going to eat and digest something different, it was probably going to have to be international. We've come a long way in three or four decades, but we always wanted something to be endorsed by somewhere else first. Rush was probably in amongst the very first, and they, for many reasons, became international stars. But I remember in the early days, working for EMI, which was a British-based company, I travelled a lot and certainly to the UK a lot, and the attitude was always, yes, Rush is incredible, but a surprise that they came out of Canada."

As for hauling the band over to Capitol, Deane explains that "One of the co-managers of Rush at the time had lived in the UK, Vic Wilson, and I had taken an interest, obviously, in Max as an A&R guy at Capitol. I knew they were with Anthem, so I made a play for getting both the Anthem label in Canada with the commitment that I'd love to have Rush, but they're already signed to Mercury. But I will get a US deal for Max Webster. So, when it came down to the deal part of it, it was really to have both the label and Max. But yeah, going back to your original question, Max were one of the markers, and then much later on, The Tragically Hip would really cement with Canadian audiences the idea that we can like our own music, even if it's different."

The deal between Capitol and Anthem would last, "for a period of just over fourteen years. We always expressed... Capitol Los Angeles always expressed an interest in Rush, if they were to be free and available, but I don't think Mercury was as stupid as I needed them to be."

So, jumping in with *Mutiny Up My Sleeve*, Deane remembers the timing as follows. "When it came in, it was done, delivered, and the first track was already in the market, I think. I liked it. I thought the production was a little thin. But it obviously had a couple of strong tracks. I liked the image and the cover art image. I wasn't sure it was going to be the record for the US. But all along here, I was a fan as well as trying to be an objective A&R guy helping the Americans and the Brits to try and pick this up and do something with it."

"I know exactly when it was," recalls Mike Tilka, reminiscing over his last gig as bassist perceived as not up to scratch. "New Year's Eve at Seneca College. Mike Reno was singing for the band that opened, Moxy, and then he went on to become famous in Loverboy. He wasn't the original singer; Buzz Shearman was. Reno was the singer in Moxy, and I think maybe Wireless opened the show. I think it was a three-band bill. We played not the theatre, but they had a triple gym, with the big folding doors, and they opened them all. It was 3000 people there—so a bittersweet gig."

The Seneca College Field House gig would also produce the crowd singalong famously used on *Mutiny Up My Sleeve* anthem "The Party." It was done three times, with the third take being used. So, we're hearing that from Mike's last gig, even though he's not the bassist on the record. Furthermore, Dave Myles had already been working with the band, with a *Globe and Mail* article at this juncture indicating that the bed tracks of the album had been recorded three weeks earlier.

"And it's funny," says Gary McCracken, "when he left the band, he just went from the band up to the office and he was still looking after Max Webster's receipts, just as if he was in it. So, nothing changed. Weird. He's just... he's just not in the band anymore, but he was very instrumental in starting it. Kim was like the crazy guitar guy, but Mike was the guy that made sure that the PA system was there, and the lights, oh, we need a truck, we need this, we need that. He would always rent all the stuff back to the band. I'm sure you've heard stories when the band actually pays for all the gear that the one guy owns? That's Mike (laughs)."

It's no secret that Mike and Pye weren't the best of buddies, and things came to a head with Mike's removal from the ranks. "When Tilka left the band, the band members were very passive about the deal that was struck with Tilka leaving," says Pye. "When Mike Tilka was leaving, he was going to work for SRO. The separation agreement was that he would get a piece of the publishing. I said wait a second. Ray Danniels was quite upset at me, although I think he isn't now. I think he might respect what I did. I was the only guy who said, no, this is not happening. I'm not going to give a part of me to someone who doesn't practice and is not a very good bass player."

"Nothing to do with money," continues Pye. "It was the principle of the thing. Absolutely the principal. That he was, that Ray was negotiating for Mike Tilka, who is going to work for him after he left the band. Absolutely, the idea that Mike would get a piece of the publishing was ridiculous. He never wrote a song, and he was essentially on paper a side man."

Pressed for more detail and a clearer run-down of these events, Pye goes, "Again, Mike Tilka, I gotta tell you, I was the only one who stood up. Because I was not happy. But my vision of Max... it really probably started with me. Because I was determined to get Mike out of the band. I had a vision of Max, and maybe it was shared, but they never spoke about it. But I had wanted Tilka out of the band. My reason was that he wasn't good enough. Never practiced, never wrote songs. I didn't like his stage presence; I didn't like the idea of someone looking at their watch when Kim was having a solo. So anyway, that came to fruition. Mike was kicked out of the band. We were going to get a new bass player. But coincidentally, as Mike was leaving the band, Ray Danniels hired him to work at SRO, to work at Anthem. I'm repeating myself, but the severance package was that Mike took what he was going to take with him, as he left the band, the points in the publishing, like points on this, and I went no way, uh-uh, stop. Well, all the other guys in the band were picking their nose and eating their toenails, 'Yeah, sure.' But not me. It's not gonna happen."

But is there not debt attached to any and all members of the band at this point? How did that enter into it? "I don't think so. No. But it wasn't going to happen. I'm not involved in that. That was with them, certainly not with me. I was in a very awkward, and perhaps envious, situation."

I asked Pye if this was because he personally never incurred any repayable or recoupable debts.

"No, except that I, when I wrote a song, they owned it. So, I had an interest in giving up the publishing, or parts of the points, the publishing points, to Mike Tilka, for someone I desperately wanted out of the band, and someone who never practiced and never wrote a song. I'm not going to give him money. I never put that in the contracts for my money." But publishing points... "were miniscule back then. They were the typical contract you would have and were really in favour of the record company. Certainly not equal."

An excerpt from one of Pye's letters to the author applies here... "Re: Tilka's 'severance' meetings and his request for writer's royalties, Ray Danniels, leading. This was my introduction to the business of the music business. It was as good and as bad as losing my virginity and... and, yup! I'm gonna say it: losing my religion. The band's passivity was dumbfounding and I was the only fool to ask questions! My innocence was lost and stolen from that point on. I was vigilant of the band's business and its impact on me. From that point on, I developed probably the 'noli me tangere' (stance, façade, personae), and I think I lost—and they lost—the spirit of friendship. I don't know. I know they don't comment on that meeting. Loyalty, as I was to discover much later, is the loneliest number."

We'll leave it at that, namely murky, and for a couple of reasons.

One, as with too much numbers talk with McCracken, one senses there are pieces of the puzzle missing, or gaps in the explanation; and two, for the sake of the relationships between these guys, I didn't want too many detailed financial debates tainting a story that is ultimately about creativity in full bloom.

"I'll never forget, when we did *Mutiny Up My Sleeve*, we were recording at Sounds Interchange," relates Gary, on what happened next. "I'm walking with Kim, and he says on the way in, we were just walking in the front door, he says, 'Oh by the way, Terry Brown quit last night.' We're like halfway through the record and Terry Brown quit. He had a big argument with Ray. That's the story I got. Apparently Kim was trying to do certain ideas and this and that, and then Ray was trying to squeeze a hit song out of us. Like, if you ever listen to *Mutiny Up My Sleeve*, you're not getting close to a hit on there out of anything. But anyway, as it turned out, the session turned into too much of a headache for Terry Brown and he goes. He doesn't show up anymore and it was over. Guess who finished producing the record for us? Mike Tilka. He was the babysitter."

"I may get this backwards," adds Pye on the subject, "But I think Kim and Mike Tilka disliked what had gone down, and Mike and Kim had tried to fix it. I think it was just Mike and Kim. Mike probably had an ear for the sounds, and it's more of his forte to do that. I remember them doing it, but I don't remember paying a lot of attention to it. Because it was left up to them. It was very odd to me. But there's a sequence there."

Asked to compare the new crucible of an experience to the previous record, Kim opines that, "*High Class* I see as Captain Beefheart's *Clear Spot*. I think *High Class* is great; it was a great album for me. And more like a luxury car. *Mutiny Up My Sleeve* was more like a muscle car. You know, like a pimped-up something, totally altered and fucked with. But *Mutiny* was a pretty creative album. That's when we met Black Sabbath, was when we were doing overdubs for that. Sadly, that album was just a nightmare to get finished. Yeah, it was just horrible. Terry Brown started out on it and then went... we were doing 'Beyond the Moon,' and I kept saying, 'No, this is a good enough take, this is a good enough take.' He goes, 'No, it's not. I know you guys can do better than this. You guys aren't rising up to the bar.' He saw the bar at a certain point and he didn't think we were coming up to it, and I was disagreeing with him. He left, and then the bass player, who we fired, Mike Tilka, Ray put him in charge of producing the album, which was... we got through it, but holy fuck, it was just a nightmare. Now with hindsight, many decades later, Terry Brown was right. We could have done better. *Mutiny* had a few things that could've been way better, felt better. As it was, it felt a little mechanical and stiff."

As Kim had alluded to, Black Sabbath were struggling with their own record for 1978, *Never Say Die*, struggling in fact way beyond the intensity that anybody from Canada could conjure, much less the ultimately sensible Sarnia folks in Max. Writing in a freezing cold theatre in Toronto now completed, the band then stumbled over to where Max was at, with Ozzy booze-addled and about to get booted.

Relates Kim, "Max Webster was finishing up our third album at a studio in Toronto called Sounds Interchange. I remember while we were doing overdubs, they were in the main room starting up some stuff. They were great guys. They invited us in for a playback after about the second night or something. I think Ozzy's dad was sick, and he was spending a lot of time just in the TV room watching TV. So, you'd walk in to get a coffee or something and Ozzy would be sitting there. It was just small talk, but it was kind of cool, sitting there listening to a Black Sabbath track, where they just cut a bed track. 'Hey guys, come in; you wanna hear it?' 'Yeah' (laughs)."

"Well, Mike sat in there," explains Gary, back to the baking of *Mutiny*. "He sat there while we recorded, and he said that's a good take and that's not a good take, and yeah, he sat there and he finished off producing the record. Where the big difference is made is when you listen to the quality and the pristine-ness of *High Class*; you don't hear that on *Mutiny Up My Sleeve*. It's a much drier... I think it's the worst sounding record we ever made, with the best songs on it. You know, 'The Party' and some of those tunes are fantastic."

Offering Gary a bit of pushback, I propose to him that *Mutiny* is nonetheless an above average sounding record for the late '70s, and more dynamic sonically than the debut (which of course, Gary wasn't on).

"No, not bad sounding, but at the time that's how that ended up. That's where I'm starting... the light bulb over my head is going, what the fuck is going on? All of a sudden Terry Brown just quit. Again, I'm thinking, man, I really liked having him. He made my drums sound great, unique and polished, blah blah blah. The guy you just kicked out of the band is now your producer?! What's going on?"

These rumours about there being some rejected first version of the *Mutiny Up My Sleeve* album... Gary says, "No, there was just the album. The only thing that might've been rejected is that maybe the first time we mixed it, Ray or Kim didn't like the sound of it and they remixed it. Because that's the only time you reject anything. You know, you don't record all the songs and then reject it. You're not going to get that far if the songs aren't any good. Then, like I never heard anything other than, we got the record done, right? I was disappointed that Terry Brown just wasn't there. That set me off a bit. We made a nice record nevertheless, but in my mind, it would've sounded twice as good if Terry had mixed it and produced it to the end. Whereas Mike did it."

Yet the tapes from the initial sessions at Sounds Interchange (the back half would be done at Phase One), dated February 22, 1978, tell a slightly different story with respect to the record beginning significantly different to the final outcome. On there are "Silvery," written by Terry and beloved by Kim, even though Terry, typical of his disposition, wasn't so hot on it. There's also old Max live standard "X + Y," along with "Mash Moon," or "Mash Moon in Hawaii," which got edited down to become "Hawaii." Lastly, there's "Charmonium," which gets extricated from "Astonish Me" to become a stand-alone highlight on the next album.

"Mike did an okay job and everything else, but it's one of these things where the turmoil between management and all that was starting to happen," continues Gary. "Terry Brown has a fight with Ray Danniels, because Ray Danniels wants more commercial music. Kim doesn't (laughs). Kim just wants to do whatever he's doing. There was no... we used to go to have meetings, 'You guys need to come up with something a little more user-friendly,' type stuff. The more we got pressured to do it, the less we wanted to do it."

"Oddly enough, it seems when the solo career came along, it was no problem coming up with commercial tunes then. You know, 'Go For Soda,' 'Patio Lanterns'—there's tons of them. So, it's not like Kim didn't know how to put together, again, radio-friendly songs. At the time, he just didn't want to be that guy. He wanted to be like the Frank Zappa weird guy; that was his thing. That was my thing—I wanted to be the drummer for that guy. It worked, plus we were friends on top of it all. It's not like I didn't know him. I'd known the guy forever. So, it was just one of those deals. All the stories you hear about, some of them I've never heard ever. Then other ones, like I know a lot, again, 90% of what happened. Any private stuff wouldn't matter to me anyways."

"Mike was the business head for a while," recalls Tom on Tilka's transition to the office. "That was not necessarily... Mike was always appreciated as the least musical guy but also the guy who could do a budget and keep everything running. He's very important for that element. So, he joins the management company and then starts to have a say on some of the creative things. So, it's like, oh my God, and there's rebellion. Instant rebellion. That didn't work out well."

So, they weren't buying Mike's ideas.

"Not a chance. I don't know how many ideas Mike had creatively at that point. But it was just... it's not a negative on Mike; it's just who Mike was. Mike left the band and became part of the management company, who was not at war with the band, but trying to figure out what the hell they were doing. It was very messy."

Buffalonian bass player Billy Sheehan, physically and perhaps somewhat mentally speaking, a Tonawanda Tonto, a US version of Kim, almost wound up as the replacement for Mike Tilka.

"A month earlier I had been fired," relates Mike. "I introduced them to Billy Sheehan, who was an amazing bass player. He was out of Buffalo and he had a trio, Talas, and they used to play the Gasworks. By then we were too big to play the Gasworks, so when we had nights off, we would go to the Gasworks, and I would just sit there with my jaw dropped, because the singer was so good and Billy and this band were so good. They were a great band. I think Kim wanted a better bass player; I don't know. Billy travelled with us for my last month in the band. He sat on the side of the stage and watched me. A month later, they fired me. He never did a gig, he didn't record, he didn't do anything. He rehearsed for a month and then they fired him. I knew it wasn't going to work. Billy was a nice guy, Kim was a nice guy, they were both nice guys, and in some ways they were similar personalities. Physically they were similar, tall guys, and they were both lead players (laughs)! You knew it wasn't going to work."

Recounts Sheehan, "When we started playing there in Talas, it was about '74, '75, and we started at Larry's Hideaway and Piccadilly Tube and then we got to the Gasworks. It was definitely the mid-'70s, I remember, because Kim Mitchell came down. The first night we played at Larry's Hideaway, I saw this guy sitting up—there were like five people there—and he ran out, and he came back in, and all of a sudden all these people started showing up. Apparently, he made a phone call for people to come on down, and I've been friends with him ever since. That band, Max Webster, no cliché lyrics, taking chances. I just got all the rest of all the records. I found them online and have them all now, the whole collection. Kim gave me a live tape to learn some songs one of the times I was almost going to be in the band, and it was in my trunk and it got stolen. It was a live performance, and I tell you, it was one of the best shows I've ever heard. When I see him, I'll describe it to him and maybe he has it archived. Just incredible."

Adds Gary on the Billy Sheehan summit, "I remember auditioning with him. We're sitting in there, we're going through some tunes. We knew how good he was, right? He was insanely good. But it was almost like he was too good. We were looking more for someone who was going to be a bass player, rather than a lead bass player? No matter how good he was, we weren't looking for someone to play lead solos—that was Kim's job. Dave Myles was just a better choice, in terms of an overall band. Because he came in and played fantastic bass parts. He plays awesome, has a great sound, but he wasn't trying to be the lead guitar god. As opposed to Billy Sheehan. It's not even personal. I quite like the guy; he's a nice guy. We just thought we were going to run into trouble somewhere, trying to get him to play normal bass, right? So, we just figured we'd avoid the whole situation by getting Dave."

Once Dave Myles was in, he immediately began noticing the dissention between Terry and Kim, often around Kim's singing, and he also found himself embroiled in frustrations due to production issues.

"You only hear what you want to hear," reflects Dave, asked if he had heard grumblings externally about Kim's singing. "I felt, when I listened to Max's records, they had a very compressed sound. They did not sound really open. Part of that was that sound was coming off the stage too. It really was. It was full, but it wasn't expansive as when you listen to a lot of bands. I remember when I first joined Max, Kim said, we've got to go get some Taurus pedals. And that's where I met Billy Sheehan, because Kim and I drove to Buffalo and Bill had an extra set of pedals he wanted to sell. Kim and I went and bought them because we said we have to have these on stage. We need that huge imperial low end, and of course we'd seen it with Rush too."

"When I see Kim live now, he is so much heavier in terms of sound, generally, and his vocals are much better. But at the time, he was still getting his licks, I think, to a certain extent. Because that took me by surprise too. It was like, well, how good is this going to be? I remember Terry Brown turning around and going, 'You gotta sing better than this. This is not going to fly. You have to make me believe that you really believe this song.' For Kim, I think that was, we all do what we do. There are better vocalists out there for sure. Like, when we would do things in Max, some of the songs we would do, and the way they would be arranged, it was so oblique. It was like, this is different than everybody. I think where we lost our appeal to some degree was when we weren't able to continue to be the quirky, fun band that we were, or that Max was, on *High Class in Borrowed Shoes*. People wanted more of that; they really did. Still, Kim on guitar, I'll tell you, there were times I would go on stage and I would look over and he would just be zoning out and playing a solo with his head back, and just amazing, amazing guitar. He was really intimidating on stage. The guy is so good that you just go wow, what can I do? (laughs). What can I do to impress everybody?"

So, Dave is in and out goes Mike, who winds up in the offices of SRO Productions... "I managed Max Webster and Wireless and Gowan. You know, I worked there, on the management side. Not the record company side. I certainly knew how to do it. I've been an agent, I've been all over the world, produced records, produced the Wireless records, produced Frank Soda, and knew all those guys, I could talk, I was smart, I was a manager. I worked for Ray Danniels."

But not actually "managing" of Max Webster. "No, no, it officially was Ray Danniels, because it was his company. It didn't work like that. But I got to the point where I was, after eight years, I was vice president of SRO, on the management side. So, for Max, I put tours together, did their budgets, I did a whole bunch of the things I used to do, but no decision-making, because as I told you, Ray Danniels' management style wasn't like that. Although if there was a problem, it had to be fixed, so he said, walking by, 'Tilka you're fixing this.' It's working for the management company. What are you gonna say— no?"

One of this writer's favourite people, and for decades a huge player in Rush's business empire, is Pegi Cecconi, who has since passed away, in 2024, at the age of 70.

"She got there about a year-and-a-half after I started," says Mike. "But I knew Pegi then. She was a high school buyer. I knew her years earlier. I loved working there! It was great (laughs). It was great. You know, I wasn't surprised when Ray and Vic (Wilson) separated. I wasn't surprised at all. But I liked Vic, nice guy. You know, like Ray used to say, a manager can't make a band happen. A manager can just put a band in front of an audience, and then they make themselves happen in front of the audience. I agree with that. Ray would offer opinions on songs and opinions on things, but he was the business guy. He was the deal-cutter. Ray came from the agency side, not the record company side. I'd worked with Ray when he was an agent, so I knew that. Tom Berry was the label side, and Tom was good."

Contrary to some views, Mike says Kim was never resentful of the resources put behind the company's proven meal ticket, the band who wrote "I Think I'm Going Bald," which, although an allusion to Alex Lifeson and his concern for his coif, could have just as easily been written about Kim Mitchell or Mike Tilka.

"No, never. They were a hard-working band. They were wonderful guys. How could you not like Geddy and Alex?! I didn't really know the drummer very well, but I knew their first drummer really well, John Rutsey; he was a sweetheart, John. But you don't meet a nicer guy than Alex Lifeson. Geddy, he had a brain, that guy. He was a smart guy; they were great."

As to why things didn't eventually blow up even half as big for Max as they did for Rush, Tilka figures, "Well, one reason, they fired me. Because I started the band with Kim. I was a lot of the brains of that band. I don't care what anybody says. They floundered, although *A Million Vacations* was a great album; it had some great tunes. Although if you listen to the production, I think it sounded soft. *Mutiny Up My Sleeve*, it had the great tunes on it, like 'The Party' and 'Waterline' and stuff, and I was glad to be involved. But it was all over the map, because the band tried to... Terry Brown tried to deliver an album, and that wasn't going to work. And it was partially because I wasn't there."

"He started that album, and then he was fired," continues Mike. "Then they tried to deliver the record and it was awful. They turned to me and said, 'Okay, Tilka, you have to fix this.' I said, 'Fix it?! I got fired from that band! I don't even talk to those guys!' Because at that time I didn't talk to them. I felt bad, and I think they felt bad. Everybody felt bad, and all of a sudden we're in the studio and I'm the boss?! How much fun do you think that was?!"

It's in fact Mike that is one of the big promoters of this idea of a rejected album... "Yeah, yeah. They delivered nine, ten songs, whatever, so I walked in and said, 'Okay, these four songs don't exist, they're toast, here's all the new edits on "The Party." Here's edits on this, and we're going to do that tune "Waterline," because it's a great tune. You didn't even put that on the record. Maybe go write a couple more, and we're going to edit the shit out of these four songs. Here we go, let's go.'"

As for these rejected songs... "I'm sure they became parts of other songs. I really can't remember. They could have been recorded just by the band. I wasn't involved, so I don't know what they recorded before or with Terry. I didn't even know that Dave Myles played bass, because there's a fair amount of keyboard bass too, that Terry Watkinson did."

"It was agony, but it was neat, it was fun," says Mike, on being producer of necessity after the mutiny on *Mutiny*. "It was freaking amazing, because I got to do it, but I remember the palms of my hands had blisters all over them from being nervous. Anyway, there were a lot of neat things and a lot of tough things. 'The Party' was all a knife job and then a remix and as I said; I love 'Waterline,' just love it."

"Terry was great," says Watkinson, offering his version of the producer switch story. "He really liked the band and he was really helpful, and a good producer. Right up until he dropped out in the middle of the *Mutiny Up My Sleeve* album, and that was exhaustion. The first day we went in to work on *Mutiny Up My Sleeve*, he had been up all night frantically trying to finish mixing a Dominic Troiano album (ed. 1978's *The Joke's on Me*). So, he was burned out, right from the start, and I'm not exactly sure what the frustrations were. But after a few days he said, 'I can't do it.' Mike Tilka actually took over to help finish the production. So what happened was, we came in all just really gung-ho ready to record on the first day, and Terry Brown was sitting in front of the console and he said, 'Can you guys go and have breakfast or something? I've got to finish this mix.' He was exhausted. We could just tell that. So, it had got off on a bad foot there, because we had the time booked, we had this period set off to record, and Terry was just, he couldn't get into it. He was just too tired. Then we got pissed-off at him for not being ready. There were kind of bad feelings there. But we did record, I guess half, maybe more than half of that album, with Terry, or sometimes just with the engineer. Then SRO brought Mike Tilka in to take charge of finishing off the album."

Terry had confidence Tilka could handle the task. "No, we knew. Mike is a good organiser. He's got a good head on his shoulders and he was not the kind of producer that told us what to do musically. He just kept everything moving. So that worked out pretty well. But I think the best tunes on that album are the ones we recorded before

Terry left, like 'Astonish Me.'"

"Well, we'd lost our studio, Toronto Sound—we went bankrupt," explains Terry Brown. "The first Rush album was even recorded at Toronto Sound. It was recorded on an eight-track, originally. I recorded three tunes and mixed the whole album at Toronto Sound. Toronto Sound was in Leaside, on 14 Overlea Boulevard. After I lost the studio, we had to work at Sounds Interchange, which was on Adelaide at Parliament. Actually, right on Ontario, Adelaide and Ontario (ed. 49 Ontario St.). So, it was a little weird for me. Plus, there was some unrest going on in the Max Webster camp, and I just lost my patience and said, 'You know what? I can't deal with this. I've got enough of my own problems. Go finish it yourselves.' It was a weird thing to do, but at the time I just lost my patience, and they end up doing it themselves. I think Tilka did it, did he not? But they managed to get it finished."

"Yes, I was working with Dominic," confirms Terry, addressing that part of Watkinson's tale of the tape. "But I don't remember that being the reason. I remember there being some acrimony, and I just was tired of it, and just didn't want to be involved. There was a lot going on from the that point. So, who knows how I was reacting? I had lost my studio at that point, so we were working out of Sounds Interchange, and I just didn't want to be dealing with these arguments that were going on back and forth, so I kind of just stepped away. What happened after that, I didn't keep a handle on it because I didn't think there was much point. I had passed on the gig."

The source of the band's internal acrimony? "Just small, trivial stuff, but stuff that would get on your nerves after a while. Deciding who was doing what and what tempos and who's playing this and who's playing that—too many loose ends. All I remember is being uncomfortable. Mitchell and I were talking about it recently and he said to me, 'I don't blame you for walking out—it was a friggin' mess at that point.' (laughs)."

"It was a new studio for us," explained Kim back in 1978, speaking with John Lamont about the necessary switch of venues to Sounds Interchange. "We were working on the bed tracks, getting them to feel good, when this uptight vibe started happening; it was just nuts. Halfway through, we switched studios, co-producers. Terry Brown, our co-producer, picked up on the ugliness and quit; 48 hours later he was back, saying he'd put up with the weirdness. By that time, we felt strange. So, we shut down for two weeks."

Mentioning a dissatisfaction with the studio monitors, Kim goes on to explain that "It didn't sound like us for some reason. Black Sabbath went through the same thing when they came in. We had some beds down and were doing overdubs in another mixing room, and they would come in, freaking out, checking our monitors. But Phase One is really nice. The halls seethe. Max has really found their element in Phase One. Nice atmosphere, a really nice place to record. The monitors are great, the people are great, and there's enough room. The tapes from Sounds Interchange that didn't make it, we canned it and just went on to different stuff. We wrote for a week... and now it's done."

"Kim and I, we went way back," explains new man at the Max bass position Dave Myles. "We were practically playing together when we were going through puberty. Well, maybe not like that, but very early when we were in our teenage thing. So, I knew Kim pretty well and I knew Gary very well. He actually lived in our house for a while and we were buds together in high school and we played in the high school band, and he played drums and I played bass. We would jam on the weekends, just the two of us. Which would drive our parents crazy. We'd go in there for two days with a decent amount of amplification, and of course Gary played pretty aggressive drums and we would go nuts for two days, and then the parents would go, 'You guys gotta get outta here.' So, we would just go over to the other parents' house and set up and do it there for a while."

"He's working out great," said Kim, back at the time of Dave's hiring. "Although he's still a little scared. He came from Sarnia, moved himself and his girlfriend and all his furniture and everything, and plopped himself into this band. He left a solid career where he could have owned a dog and a lawnmower and stuff. Then everything started going weird. He's a new member of the band, recording an album and we're freaking out. You can imagine how he felt. But he's onto it now. He's just worried about the firecrackers and the bullets in the States."

"The only thing I really hate about it is the driving," continued Kim, on what lay ahead for the band. "The rest of it I can handle. It has its crazy moments, because you're constantly around crazy people who think you're weird all the time. At a point when maybe you're having a bad day and feeling a little weird, someone will come up and lay that shit on you. It gets difficult. But the rest of the time, it's neat. It's a great way to make a living, playing for crowds of 16,000 blitzed-out, bloodthirsty punters. You've got to deliver your goods."

"Gary and I knew each other in Sarnia, but Gary knew Dave better," explained Kim to his hometown Sarnia newspaper in March of '78, on the subject of bringing Myles to Max. "Dave's working out great. He's even started writing a little, though at first he was confused. It's not like high school anymore. There's a great deal of pressure and you have to be more professional. At first he was a little blown away by it, but now he digs it. It's expanded our range and now we can do more things. There are things the last bass player couldn't do that Dave can cut with ease. Dave was thinking of giving up music because all of his past experiences with it were bad ones. But we caught him just in time. Firstly, he said no way; then we convinced him to give it a try. So, he came down and rehearsed; then he left. A week later he was back for good."

Charting his own trip out of Sarnia year earlier, Kim recalled that, "It seems that all the friends I hung out with in Sarnia were really into drugs. There was no reality left in my world. They were all content to stay there, which is fine with me. I'm not knocking it, but I had to go. Pye left earlier. He was my only contact to reality in Toronto. At first everything was weird, but Sarnia has always been the weirdest place I've ever known as far as art. It always had amazing musicians and writers. There's something about that place. Everywhere I went there was art."

"Mike is a great guy," continues Dave, on the mad Max man he was replacing. "But his abilities as a bass player, I guess, weren't up to what Kim wanted to do. He wanted somebody that could play more, could add more to the situation than what it was, than maybe what Mike was doing. The only thing, really, that brought me to Max Webster was that Gary showed up at my door one day in Sarnia. I had been following Max, and *High Class in Borrowed Shoes* I really thought was tremendous. I was listening to it and going that's so cool. Then Gary showed up late one night and said, 'We're thinking of getting rid of Tilka; do you want to come and play?' But it was probably a mutual thing. Mike I think would have liked to have rode it further, but these things just happen. People get replaced in bands all the time. Actually, Rainbow even wanted me to play with them. But I knew enough about the business and going, you guys are just plugging people in because they're leaving you. But it perked my ego anyway."

"Mike loaned me his bass," continues Myles. "He had a really nice bass, and he said, 'Here, you can use that if you want.' But I don't remember him having that big of a part in that album at all.

Except probably a fresh set of ears when it was being mixed. He was not there for any of the bed tracks or anything. Because, Kim, the band had decided to not use him, and I was offered the gig and I got it, and I don't recall Mike really being in there. I was reading it as he made the transition from musician to working in management, and it was like, 'Don't worry about me, everything is fine, I'm not mad, I'll go on and do this.' I thought, well, that's very noble of him to do that. But I really don't recall him being a big force on *Mutiny Up My Sleeve*. Mike might have been involved in remixing, but he wasn't in the studio on any of the bed tracks. Nothing like that was ever done. I do remember Terry Brown saying to us, 'You guys have to get hot or go home.' Basically. Kim was singing something, and he says, 'You gotta put more into it here. You just can't be this safe. You've got to make me believe this is really something that you're doing.'"

But as alluded to, the gig almost went to Billy Sheehan. "Yes, it did. I don't know how Kim got to know Billy Sheehan, but Bill was in Buffalo, I believe, at this point. I don't know why Billy didn't cut it with Max. I would think that Kim probably offered him the position, but Bill, he's a force in his own right. He went on to do just fine."

Perhaps they didn't gel musically. Billy is such a radical bass player...

"No, I don't know if that would've been the problem," reflects Dave. "I know Kim really admired Billy's playing and his abilities and thought he was amazing. I don't know what kind of vision Kim had for the music going forward. He knows what he wants to do, but when you're young like that, relatively young, you don't know. You just ride the thing along to see where it goes. I think Bill had other things gelling, and he thought, why do I want to come and do this? I'm already cued in with what's going on in America. Canada has produced some incredible artists, but probably if you want to make money, you gotta be in the US market, or at least back then we did. Nowadays I don't know, because in terms of the internet, you don't really need to be where it is. You can do what you gotta do wherever you are."

To tidy up on what's just been said, Mike definitely had a lot to so with the second set of sessions, and yes, as Gary alludes to, Billy's frantic, burbly, lead style on the bass would have clashed with what the band was, or changed what the band was. It's an interesting point Dave makes though, about how by staying in the US, Billy would have been on a faster track to success. Although it took him a while, he did get to record music with Talas, and then he'd wind up in David Lee Roth's band and in Mr. Big.

So, in comes Dave, and... "I was just agog with what was going on around me," smiles Myles. "Kim would come with the riffs, and he would have had the lyric. Of course Pye Dubois was there too... Paul Woods, I knew Paul for a long time. In fact, he lived at my house too for a while. This was back in Sarnia, because things were not going well with him and his family, and my parents gave him a place to stay for probably eight months. But Kim would come with the tunes, or he would work with Terry on the tune. Some of the stuff was really spontaneous on the floor, and some of it we actually did some pre-production work. But again, I was agog at everything. You gotta remember, I was in Sarnia, and it was, 'You got the gig; be here.' I came to Toronto, and we started to record at Sounds Interchange. It was like walking onto the bridge of the Starship Enterprise—this was big-time recording. Not even knowing some of the people. I didn't know who Terry Brown was. So, I was pretty starstruck with everything that was going on. We did a couple of small gigs, and then we did the CNE (laughs), fronting Genesis. It was probably three, maybe four gigs and then into the record (laughs). I didn't even really learn the Max catalogue until after *Mutiny Up My Sleeve*. As a musician, to suddenly hear yourself back on tape, and you go home, my God, I gotta clean up my act here (laughs). You know, the tape doesn't lie."

"Boy, I'll tell you, when I first got with Max, I didn't have an outfit," continues Myles. "I didn't have anything to wear. I was coming from Sarnia. Kim would take us out, and we would go to these children's stores, and look for gear to wear. Kim was into wearing oversized kids' pyjamas. Of course on *Mutiny Up My Sleeve*, I'm wearing this outfit that looks like pantaloon pants—it was my wife's outfit. I had nothing else to wear, give me that thing, that will work. You look at it and go... but Kim would say, let's go down to some strip mall, into some family dollar clothing place, and we'd go through looking for different things that we could wear."

"Dave was a good guitar player and a good bass player, totally different style from what I played," opines Tilka. "He's a pick player, busy player, and he and Kim play like brothers, so that was nice. Was he a virtuoso bass player? I have no idea. That guy who played after Dave, Mike Gingrich, he had a reputation of being a really good bass player, and I used to see him play in other bands. He played more of a John Wetton style. Again, totally different from David and totally different from me."

"Dave was leaps and bounds beyond Mike Tilka," adds Watkinson. "Mike was okay. He worked hard and he was really good for the band, but Dave Myles was a really creative musician. He understood the songs on a level that maybe Mike didn't."

"Dave and I had a history," adds Mitchell. "Dave was... I can tell you exactly: Dave was like John Entwistle to me. He was really melodic, knew chord changes, knew a little bit of harmonic value, had great time, had a good sound. Mike to me was always... Mike did some great stuff on *High Class in Borrowed Shoes*—'Gravity,' 'Diamonds Diamonds,' really nice. But when it came to getting really rockin' and aggressive, I felt he was limited. He leaned always more towards Motown kind of bass—poppy, funky bass—whereas Dave would just grab a pick and go, 'danna danna danna,' really dig in like John Entwistle. I really like that energy underneath with Gary. Those two guys were best of friends and went to the same school together. So as soon as Dave was in the band, I felt there was this chemistry happening between those two guys that I was like wow, that's fuckin' different—and wonderful. So, it's nothing bad about Mike; it was just a different thing."

New bassist Dave Myles is featured prominently just as soon as *Mutiny Up My Sleeve* springs to life. Opening track is "Lip Service" and it's a funky proto-heavy metal rocker for the band, getting right to the point, with Pye getting political, Terry doing a light version of Jon Lord, and Dave and Gary creating a loping rhythm track on which Kim's vocal and guitar sit nicely, relaxed.

There's a darkness to "Lip Service" that comes from Kim's riff and a decidedly Sabbatherian turn of events. All told, an atmosphere is created that is a good match for the album cover. Figures Watkinson. "*Mutiny Up My Sleeve*, I guess the idea for that is somebody who has a secret mutinous streak or a secret grudge against society or something. So, it's a little darker. The album was dark too, in colour—it was all black. So that... smouldering flames and whatnot. Musically it was a continuation; we'd perhaps lost a little innocence."

Adds Dave, "When we did the cover for *Mutiny Up My Sleeve*, I went, 'Are you kidding?! You're gonna take Max Webster in glass and break it and light it? It'll look like turds.' But I went, I don't know, that's not my area of expertise. I play bass. But it was a tiny thing, eight inches (laughs). Yeah, it's all done with... it's all fixed in the mix later on, you know? In fact, there were a lot of times, I'll tell you, a lot of times with Max, I kind of went, 'This is *it*?!'"

The inner sleeve provided the lyrics in both English and French.

The idea to go bilingual wasn't so much because Max Webster were Canadian, i.e. mirroring bilingual packaging, which is actually mandated in Canada in many product categories. Rather, it was a peace overture to Quebec, a territory that Max Webster wanted to break badly. Which is an aspiration that made perfect sense. Quebec was known in the '70s for their progressive rock scene. In the '80s, they'd have a vibrant heavy metal scene to match, to the point where it was once said that 50% of all heavy metal sales in Canada came from Quebec.

Mutiny would represent the second cover graphic credited to Hugh Syme, but, as Tom Berry explains, "Hugh was like Rush's guy, and a lovely guy, and a quirky and wonderful character, and that's a whole other story. So, I think the band tried to draw a line on not overly depending on the Rush creative spirit, on their own. But this cover, I just remember it being done and most of us looking at it and going, 'What?!' (laughs). Album covers were always difficult, just because there were so many different ideas. There was the Pye corner and the Kim corner, and the Pye/Kim corner, and the Tilka and the Terry, who is actually a graphic artist and had done the first record and really created an image with that. Terry wanted, I think, to participate a bit more ultimately, than what he had. There was a lot of tension in Max Webster often. I think it worked for the band in a lot of ways, and ultimately, it didn't in the end."

"Another indictment of our society," sums up Pye, asked about the "Lip Service" lyric. "'So, you're the canker banker, hours 9-to-5 with fantasies of gold... hours 9-to-5 and fantasies of gold, vets, cheques cigars and Nassau, and the drugs work fast.' It's a collage of the banking system. When I look back, again, to these political themes of how the people in power, the people with money, are not to be trusted, it doesn't matter what they say or think. It's a nice lyric, but it might be just good as a lyric. It may not have any profound meaning. It may be just simple lines of lyric and poetry. A nice cadence and nice imagery and a nice thought. But does it have to be dissected? I'm not convinced of that. But it is political; it is a very well-tuned political theme. You like those lyrics, generally speaking, right? You don't get a sense of politics until I say it, right? You get a sense of entertainment. I hope you're entertained by them and not necessarily needing to find out from the author what they mean on a personal level."

"They talked to each other about small details within the lyrics and Pye would have musical input as well," figures Terry Brown, articulating how Kim and Pye worked amongst so much density of imagery. "But I didn't really see a lot of their relationship, because most of the time they would work together prior to going into the studio. So, when they came to see me, it was a done deal and things were in really good shape."

"Kim would write the part of the song," says Gary, "and he would go (sings it), right? Just sort of pretend sing, some phrasing and whatever, right? Pye would take that bit and then try to get words and licks out of the lyrics to go along with that. Then he'd give it back to Kim, and then Kim would in turn take Pye's lyrics, and there'd be choices, right? There'd be five lines that he'd have to go through at any given time to find the one line he's looking for. Then he and Kim would sit and organise lyrics, to where he was satisfied—that's basically how all those tunes went."

Often times, as with "Lip Service," Kim wound up with mouthful of words that would asphyxiate less adept and astute superhero front men.

"Yeah, yeah, I get what you're saying," figures Kim. "It was challenging working with him as a lyricist. Sometimes, because he understood... he was trying to say something in a poetic way and I'm trying to say something in a rhythmic way. He didn't get rhythm and cadence. He did, but it was hard. It wasn't an easy walk in the park. But fucking nothing is, you know? The end result was just amazing lyrics. Would I have done things a little differently if I could do it all over again? Probably. I don't think anybody sits around going I have no regrets. I would have changed a few things."

Is the extent of the collaboration that was necessary to wrestle Pye's voluminous musings downplayed too much? Not according to Kim. Pye gets about as much credit as Kim thinks he deserves. "I think I was a good editor. But it was hard to stand up to Pye. 'So come on, Pye, it seems like fuckin' one word here.' He goes, 'Yes, but you can't change it. It's going to change the whole...' Dude, it's rock 'n' roll, you know? But he's a good man (laughs). I probably remain his biggest fan."

The "Lip Service" guitar solo is drenched in fuzz, but through the sizzle, one can hear Kim's ability to do jazzy runs, as well as a degree of rock shredding before such a term was ever coined and conjoined.

"Kim took lessons from Tony Bradan, the jazz cat," offers Mike, by way of explanation. "Kim practiced a lot, and a lot of that very fluid, non-linear, jazz guitar solo thing from the '50s and '60s, that was the school that he taught him. You know, look at the chord and look at the alternative forms of the chord and where you can go with it. Kim sat and practiced that stuff for hours. A lot of rock guitar players, outside of playing blues riffs or copying rock riffs off of the records, they didn't have that facility that Kim had. Steve Shelski from Coney Hatch had a bit of that, because he'd been listening to it, and not just Kim, but Fripp and other people. Because remember, he's younger than Kim, and he went to Humber. So, he had the jazz-like approach, with more notes, as well. Kim would learn from horn lines, even bouzouki lines."

Then he'd have to pull off these riffs live, while singing as well. "Yes, he did, but he didn't obsess about it. He had enough other things to obsess about. But I think anybody that's a singer, writer, guitar player, absolutely has to think about that, number one, and number two, when you're actually rehearsing in the absence of learning a song and you have to play it that night at the Gasworks, some of its organic. In the beginning, we didn't stay a trio very long, and it was organic. We had the keyboards. Some of Terry's keyboard parts, if you listen to them, they're guitar parts! There are things that sound like a slide guitar—that's a synthesizer. There are crunchy things that are organ. So, we did that so as to rearrange the tunes, so they worked live."

Pye, like Tilka, places quite a bit of significance on Kim's period of jazz instruction as well. "For some reason, when we were living on St. Clair, he went and took some lessons from this guitar teacher that was well known. I think he was just enthralled with these new patterns he could play on his guitar. It was just a delight for him to get another perspective on this. So that's maybe where some of the jazz influence really started. He started to really think about it and apply it then. Kim was eclectic and very much ahead of his time."

"Initially, I moved to Toronto to study with Bradan," Kim told *Canadian Musician*. "Max Webster was supposed to be a side thing to pay for lessons and practice what he taught me. Life was wonderful then. Every week you knew you were getting ahead. I loved taking lessons. I lived for it. A lot of my style comes from that one year."

Muses Mitchell on his approach to soloing, "I just want to be disinhibited and relaxed. I don't want to be holding on tight. When I'm not hanging on tight, when I'm loose and not thinking about it, there is shit just flying out of me. That's when you're going to capture me as a guitar player the best. When I just play to the tune. Try to be as disinhibited as I could, without the aid of any other things, like drugs or alcohol. As for the jazzy thing, guitarist Kevin Breit, it's funny, he came out and saw me play, and he said, 'You know, you fuckin' remind me of Ornette Coleman' (laughs)."

"I just don't think Kim really plays like anybody else," figures Tom Berry. "I can't think of anybody that plays like him. It just seems like he'll take a solo to places other people wouldn't. Even if I don't like where he took it, it can be seen as pretty interesting. More often than not, on 'The Party' or any of these tunes that he's allowed to rip, I just think he's in the top ten guitar players in the world."

Next up, "Astonish Me" is a soft progressive rock masterpiece, a presage of pomp rock, a production tour de force, a delicate ballad punctuated by art rock flourishes. Its descending chorus riff is legion, fluttered by sympathetic drumming from Gary as well as church organ meanderings from Terry on top of all his other tones an' tricks throughout.

"'Astonish me' was something that I had read," explains Terry Watkinson on his gem of a piano ballad, slathered in synths. "There was a show business agent in New York who had a little sign on his desk that said, 'Astonish me.' So, when you went in to ask him for work or something, he pointed to the sign and said, 'Blow my mind or else I can't help you.' So, I thought that was pretty neat, and I transferred it to a kind of romantic song."

Terry says he took advantage of the Petrof concert grand piano they had at Phase One to come up with the introductory portion of the song, working during a break. The song runs 4:49, and he regrets that they didn't do an edited version of the track and put it out as a single.

"He's an extremely creative fellow," laughs Tilka on Terry. "A bit ornery. He wasn't very willing to budge on things. He had his own scene. But we always got along okay. But I love 'Astonish Me,' although, in hindsight—I still play 'Astonish Me' with Terry in our band right now—it was too long and needed more editing. But it was great, it was proggy, it was Terry, it was cool. A contrast to 'Lip Service,' which was a great rock tune."

"I could tell you the big mistake I made," continues Mike, wearing his producer hat. "There's not enough bottom end on the record, period. I let the engineer take too much of the helm, and he had engineered the last couple albums, so we all trusted him. But when we went to master that record, or when we were mixing it, it should've had more bottom. It had too much top. But it sounds thin, and that's all my fault. I didn't realise it at the time. I'll admit it now.

In fact, when I listen to it now, the copies that I listen to, I re-EQ the master tapes—because I am that big of a nerd."

There's an air of truth to what Mike says, but in perspective and context, we're talking about a beautifully produced record here, every bit as full-range and crisp as its predecessor, and also maybe just a shade less resplendent than the headphone heaven that is *A Million Vacations*. All three rival the very best recordings of the entire canon of '70s rock, and with these sterling, sylvan songs... well, I've said it before, Max becomes arguably one of the finest rock bands to ever craft sound.

After the genius of "Astonish Me," Max go modest with a boogie rocker with roots back to 1974 called "Let Your Man Fly," a bridge track vibing and vibrating between "High Class in Borrowed Shoes" to the frantic left and "A Million Vacations" to the relaxed right. The chemistry is there between the players, lifting it from the ordinary. Further elevating the song is its hope-bearing chorus. The guys sell the record short—like "Astonish Me," this might have succeeded at least modestly as a single.

"I actually don't like that song," laughs Terry. "I don't want to talk about that." Watkinson is indeed the culprit here, the song's sole writer, with the track representing the man's second and last credit on the album, with the balance going to Kim and Pye without complication. Adds Tilka, "'Let Your Man Fly,' I loved. In fact, that one, a couple months after I got fired, Kim and I were in the Gasworks, and Greg Godovitz wouldn't leave us alone. He wanted us to get up and jam, so we went up on stage and we played 'Let Your Man Fly,' which, as you say, is a Terry tune; I still love that tune."

"Water Me Down" is next, with Kim and Pye teaming up for a gorgeous ballad of almost child-like wonder, featuring sinewy guitar lines working in tandem with piano over big slow drums.

"A little love song," assesses Dubois. "I think I need to get a trophy for writing love songs and not using the word love too much (laughs). Don't you agree? I never liked... I couldn't write a love song. Not once have I ever thought that I was influenced by other lyricists. I liked love songs, but I couldn't write a song, 'I love you baby.' I just could never do that. I never wanted to do that. So, my influences... I don't think I have any influences. I was always the guy in the corner writing stuff on paper. Now, Kim and the other musicians may have been influenced musically. I was not influenced lyrically. I liked Captain Beefheart; I liked the way he used his voice as an instrument, and I liked some of his imagery. But I've always been doing that. That was nothing new for me—the proof is in the pudding. This is my writing style and I don't think there's another writing style out there like that. I'm not giving myself... I'm not complimenting me. I'm just trying to understand how I got to write what I write. Joni Mitchell, I enjoyed, 'And I dreamed I saw the bombers riding shotgun in the sky, turning into butterflies above our nation.' Brilliant, beautiful, but I'm not... that's not gonna influence me. I'm just going to be joyful that she wrote it."

Then we're into side one closer, "Distressed," another proggy ballad of wonderment like "Astonish Me," drenched in emotion, touched by deft female vocals from Carla Jensen and Judy Donnelly as well as Fripp-like licks from Kim. This one also hearkens back to 1974, but it's been rearranged, as well as slowed down.

Explains Carla, who wound up marrying Terry Watkinson, "I sang in a band called Mara Loves in the '70s with Judy Donnelly, Gary McCracken and Dave Myles, who played with us for about a year, I think. We went through thirty members over the years, did some demos but never had an album. There was an NBC special about us in '69 or '70. Anyway, that was our initial connection to Max. Judy and I were asked to sing backup for two gigs, at Mohawk College and Massey Hall. They were just bigger, special gigs for the band at the time and they just wanted to do something special and I think it was Gary's idea to ask us. We can remember rehearsing in the basement, probably at Heath Street, where Terry and Tilka used to live. Anyway, that was the only time we played live with them, just doing harmonies which we were known for. We just came on for two songs, three at the most. Then we recorded these songs for them and I think two on *A Million Vacations*—I believed we're credited in those two albums."

"That was the very first time I met Terry," continues Carla, "and there was a spark then, but it took him until, I guess, the Massey Hall gig to ask for my phone number. That's where it started." Separated since '91, Carla and Terry also have a daughter Chloe, who is quoted later in our tale. As for these recordings, "We were guided towards what they wanted on the songs, and whatever we did came from us. They told us where to come in, and we just did something and I really don't recall whether they said yes or no. But usually, Judy and I are so tight vocally that when we come up with something, it's usually spot-on and there's not much to do. They might say come in a little earlier or maybe raise the pitch a bit or throw your part on top of Judy's instead of below hers or something like that. But usually, we're pretty good at doing the parts."

Much is demanded of the listener who chooses to explore "Distressed," because despite the beauty of it, Pye is Pye, overactive in yet another one of his imaginings of unusual love. "I always liked the anxiety," reflects Pye. "I wanted to have a sense of anxiety, that this relationship was over. Or about to be over. Or maybe not be over (laughs). So, there's this nice anxiety in the lyric—I think there is."

All the while Yes is conjured, or maybe even Kansas, perhaps a touch of Genesis given all that melody, and yes, most definitely Robert Fripp at his most elegant, somewhere between Eno's *Another Green World*, Bowie from Berlin, and a record he hadn't even imagined yet, *Beat*.

Side two of the original vinyl opens with the band's most Zappa-esque song to date and probably ever. "The Party" is reminiscent of the faux-metal moments all over *Sheik Yerbouti*, and even lyrically, it represents a gentler Canadian twist on Frank's frankness about women and their self-abasement.

There's a reason, says Gary, that the song sounds chaotic. "The way those guys work together, quite often, we would rehearse a song without knowing what the lyrics were. For example, 'The Party,' we rehearsed parts. We learned the beginning of 'The Party' and Kim was like, 'Okay, that's good,' and then we'd do something else. Then the next rehearsal, we'll do, 'Okay, we've got another part to work on, and I don't have any lyrics yet, but here's where it goes.' So, it turns out that most of 'The Party,' the music part of that was written without anybody in the band, including Kim, knowing what the lyrics were going to be. We put the two together, and then when we went into the studio to record it. That's when we finally heard what the lyrics were gonna be. So, it was a big surprise, even for the band, right?"

"'The Party,' obviously, was one of our mainstays for the rest of the band's career," continues Terry. "That was a real pure Kim Mitchell music thing, along with some classic Pye lyrics, the kind that young drinking guys liked."

"It was just fun to write," recalls Pye. "I just remember it as being a great anthem. We just wanted to have a rock 'n' roll song. It was just a weird idea, the party, 'Lucy, who's choosy on the phone,' just fun lyrics. I tend to think… now I'm going to kind of pat myself on the shoulder here. Because you brought up the issue that a couple of the band members were a little bit annoyed with me always being with the band on tour. To be honest, the band doesn't get the song 'The

Party' if I'm not on the road. It's just not gonna happen. That song is never gonna exist. Because to the delight of the crowd, that was a song they could sing and party to. That's exactly what I wanted. It's an anthem, as far as I'm concerned. The band is secondary to their joy. 'Here to thin the thickness of your skin.' So, hard-headed man or whatever, whatever you want to call people, they have to look outside the box. They have to look beyond themselves. It's absolutely necessary. Especially if they want to be creative—and especially if they want to have a good time."

So yes, one famous dynamic in Max's career would continue to be the friction caused by having the band's lyricist on the road with them, even though he was not needed per se to perform. But, as Pye proposes, where would lyrics like that have come from?

"I never thought of it as I've got to work," says Pye, who, it seems never thought to lug road cases as a gesture of comradeship. "It was just something I would do. I would be so inspired by being on the road, being with these guys and seeing the concert and being with people. So, as I say, you get songs like 'The Party' from that. That's how you get those songs. That, 'The neighbours holler/This party's higher than the Eiffel Tower.' You get that from me being on the road."

"I think I heard it and dismissed it," says a defiant Pye. "If issues ever came up, like the people in the band are extremely passive. You heard it indirectly. They just weren't like me. I would speak up. But I would... maybe in hindsight I was being very selfish, but I just thought it was wonderful, that Ray Danniels and the record company was being so kind. But I never thought of it other than my opportunity to write."

And to socialise, and to see and experience and to be inspired by demonstrations of extreme character. "Yeah, in England, it was Alex Harvey," laughs Dubois. "You ever heard of Alex Harvey? We met his dad. His father was very proud. And we were very happy to meet Alex Harvey's dad, because Alex Harvey was quite the guy. Major drinker, but quite talented. Obviously, there was the booze, but everything we got to see of Alex Harvey was great. I don't know if that inspired me, but yeah, great rocker."

Plus, the English crowds, one half of the two clams of a rock show—them and us—they also entertained Pye, to the point where he would never tire of the opportunities to soak in the communication of the concert.

"It got better as the band went on," says Dubois of the band's lone English tour, the following year. "They had a tendency back then that if they saw you the first night, they would go to the next town and buy tickets to see you again. They would see you six or seven times. Then the crowds got bigger and bigger as the tour progressed. We met Thin Lizzy, plus The Tubes. They were great fun. Met them in England. They happened to be touring, and we saw them two or three times when Max wasn't working."

"But sure, someone in the record company had a good perception of me, because they had me go on tour with the band. I did go to England and I suppose I really didn't have to. I found out from you the other day, that there are rumours of resentment around inviting me there. But I think they were very smart because all I did was write. I did interviews. I got along very well with the A&R guy in England. David Munns, who I thought was the best A&R guy ever. Anyway, so I think, back then, Vic Wilson and Ray Danniels, they may not have liked me personally, but they were very good at seeing that I had a positive influence on the road."

So yes, one of Pye's main duties—and all rock stars consider this work—Pye would also be doing many of the interviews, alongside Kim. Doing just that, speaking with Geoff Barton on this trip, Dubois quipped about what else he was good for. "What do I do all the time? Well, I'm handing out the aspirins, sewing a cuff on a pair of pants... I do so many things. I'm very protective towards Max. I like to see the band treated in a certain way. I like to see that things are on time."

"That is my past," he continued, asked about his old day job back in Canada. "I am a psychotherapist. I used to practise in Canada, but there's no work for me there now; I cured them all. There are now no depressed people in the country. So, I felt I had to move further afield. Wherever I was in the world, I always kept in touch with Kim, made sure he had something. That's the way it works. We're always pretty close with our communication."

Back to Canuckland and the tracks comprising *Mutiny Up My Sleeve*, second selection on side two is "Waterline," a funky mid-rocker set to a lazy lope. Written as two separate words on the working tapes, the song would become a live staple moving forward. It's almost swampy, featuring some slide guitar at the end.

Pye turns in a dense, enigmatic lyric incongruously ambitious to the uptempo blues-tinged musical backing track. It's one of Pye's favourites in terms of live presentation, adding that, "'Waterline' reminds me that I was a little bit dark, but I didn't mean to be dark.

Again, another indictment of our culture and society. 'Rising slowly to meet the waterline.' It's not typical of me in the sense that I've internalised some things, and I may have tried to make it universal, in that I may be displeased or have some agony or pleasure in life and it's okay. It's okay, because if you're an optimist, you're going to get to the surface. Everything rises to the surface. You're gonna see the horizon of the waterline. You know, I don't know, am I dark? I don't think I'm dark. I think there's always a little element of hope in my lyrics. Some of the lyrics may be dark, but I seem to have this dénouement, where I say okay (laughs), enough darkness, let's go to the light."

"But remembering this sometimes is hard," cautions Dubois, "because I've never played a Max Webster album in my home. Once the album was done, I would hear it on the radio, but I never play the records. Plus, I would just hear the songs two or three times a week live, so I never needed to. But this one, yeah, some of this is almost far-fetched. Some of it is farcical. If I have to, I have my journals to refer to, with the coffee stains and cigarette burns and cheese stains..."

"Hawaii" ("That's the humour in me," says Pye) is essentially an instrumental, a soft, new age track emboldened by an elaborate arrangement featuring wind chimes, bells, triangles, acoustic guitars, various key sounds, plus occasional harmony vocals—from the guys themselves plus their two angels Carla and Judy. All told, it's a beautiful piece of musical craftsmanship prescient of the type of Zen-like mantra we might hear on a Steve Vai or Adrian Belew record.

If exercises like "Hawaii" sound somewhat like the work of perennial stoners, it would be a wrongful reading of the Max factor, says Pye. "I don't remember any drugs. I think there was one time it was suspected, but I never... I don't even remember pot. Well yeah, a couple of the band members smoked pot, but it didn't interest me or bother me. It never seemed to impede anything and never caused much trouble. Some of the bands we were out with all the time, you had a hard time to get them awake—that never happened with us."

Very interesting, but "Hawaii" just might have been some sort of prescient vision, some blue sky blueprint, of a strange place in the ether that Pye could see the band going. "I saw my role as completely redundant later on, as the band became a musical force. Because I saw them... well, Weather Report is what I saw. I envisioned this musical force, and I envisioned me being redundant, my role diminishing.

So, even at that time in '75 and '76, '77, I was writing these very simple lyrical, one-liners, hooks, that would just be a vocal, and not particularly important lyrically. But they would be something to sing. Because I always thought that they, this, Kim's vocal, or some harmonies or whatever, would be like another instrument."

So, in effect, the lyricist had the notion to write himself out of the band. "Yeah, and that's the only thing I can compare to, that resembles that vision, was Weather Report. When I saw Weather Report, Alex Acuña, Jaco Pastorius and the wonderful, wonderful man on the clarinet, on all the woodwinds. He's 80 now. Yeah, wonderful band, wonderful band."

Mutiny Up My Sleeve closes with another epic Max excursion. "Beyond the Moon" is a progressive rock behemoth that begins with a deliberate fingerprint upon Kim's odd pre-Max trip to be a sideman in Greece. The track then collapses, like a less traumatised version of something from King Crimson's *Red*, into malevolent heaviness. Then, brilliantly, that subsides and we're into a verse that sounds like "No Quarter" rendered new age. Much of the balance presages the instrumental majesty that would be "Battle Scar."

"Many of these were just a gas to write," chuckles Dubois. "'Beyond the Moon' was just wonderful to write. It was certainly a lyric that in part was inspired by my... I lived in Turkey for a while. Man, yogurt blood, lunacy shoes, zipper skies... the zipper skies was... I had stayed in Greece another year, and Kim went back to Canada. Eventually I went from Rhodes, Greece, on a rowboat to Turkey, and first stopped off at a little city called Marmaris, and just down the coast from that was this little town called Alanya. After World War II, the people moved off the mountain on the coast. The mountain was right on the coast, and moved into the beach, so they had a little place in the beach, and all the houses on the mountain were abandoned. But a couple of them had running water. There were seven or eight of us hippies, all with knapsacks, crashing on the mountain. Every morning the Turks would get the kids to bring us tea. The kids would climb up the mountain with little trays and give us our morning tea. Then they'd invite us down in the afternoon and take us out on boats and go out on the cove, and around the mouth. That mountain was just straight up and down. But there were caves in there, and you could row the boat into the caves. So, you get the image. We're in a boat in the water, going into the caves, in the mountain. I just happened to look up, and I could see the top of the castle. But all I could see was the parapets that look like zippers.

So right in my mind was zipper skies, because that's what it looked like. It looked like you could just draw a zipper across and open up the sky. So that's what I saw when I tilted my head back and looked straight up."

"But 'Beyond the Moon' was certainly of the moon songs, of a series. And 'Beyond the Moon' was supposed to be updated every year, or every five years. Conceptually, it didn't turn out possible to do that, but it was another mode of thinking. I can't remember exactly what I was going to do with it, but it was futuristic, and a criticism of Christianity: '2000 years we crossed up Jesus, thinking he'd make ends meet.' I posed the question: all these people were so delirious for their religion; how'd it work out for ya? (laughs). You crucified this man, and really, you crucified ourselves. However, I had to focus positioning "Beyond the Moon," because of its title. This is the moon song that's futuristic. It's gonna talk about, well, we have to let go of this religious crap because it never helped us before and it's certainly not going to help us again. So, we can't depend on religion. Forget that stuff; it's gonna be unnecessary. When we're going to be computerised, and our blood's gonna be yogurt and we're going to have little flying machine shoes and stuff like that."

The Greek letters in the sleeve, they remind of the origins of this song, but it's also in the spirit, says Pye, of, "Alpha and Omega, the beginning and the end."

"The moon songs stopped at 'Moon Voices,' where there was no lyrics," continues Dubois, referring to the fifth track on the next record. "That was exactly where I thought it should go. Where it was going to go—or eventually go. So 'Coming Off the Moon,' 'In Context of the Moon,' 'Beyond the Moon,' thematically, 'There's a time and place for me, futuristic, past, present...' and initially I wanted all the moon songs on one album. They didn't want that. I didn't have a problem with that. Ray Danniels was very, very kind to me, except that one day in his office about Mike Tilka. But he was very good to me. I didn't realise it until later, and they never made a fuss with me. They may have put pressure on Kim to write songs that our record company would like. But they never were that way with me—never."

Here's what Pye wrote to the author in a letter, musing upon the lyric for this strident, stretchy classic of a Maxer. "I know the aficionados of 'Beyond the Moon' will lose face and faith in themselves with this traduction/traducing. The initial drafts of 'Beyond the Moon' had the opening line as 'because books are obsolete.' For the right reasons, I changed it to 'because words are obsolete.' Anything said/sung after that opening line was redundant, circumspect and useless... words are obsolete. I wasn't kidding. I believe we had outlived our usefulness and I hung my 'voice paintings' of gnomic ideations in their faces!"

Continues Pye, as we try to stay faithful to his paragraph breaks, "There are Max Webster songs, then there is 'Beyond the Moon;' there are many a Max Webster lyric, then there is the 'Beyond the Moon' lyric. 'Beyond the Moon' is diametrically opposed to any other Max songs. It stands apart because it has to stand as my political statement of the destruction of my culture. I believed computers would do us in, just as any other addiction, including cocaine; I knew pollution would do us in, and in our infancy as a planet, 'acid' (rain or otherwise) was warping the foetus. I saw a culture vacuous and venal—a shoe culture! Yeah! Shoes! etc. etc. Cure: vitamin clouds—yeah! Sell us vitamins. Profit from placebos! The initial title was 'Test for Echo' until I gave myself a slap and then slotted in another 'moon' song. 'Test for Echo' was good. I like the 'canary in the mine' potential/ambiguity, but..."

"Pretty oblique, pretty mysterious," ventures Dave Myles, when I asked him about Pye on this track. "Delivery is everything with the lyrics. The stuff that he wrote, some of it was pretty oblique—it was just weird. But put it in the context of 'Lip Service' or one of those kinds of tunes, and it worked. But I wouldn't call him my favourite lyricist. That's just me. I was sad to see that he and Kim split eventually. Probably, from what I understand it was just over royalties. Paul wanted more money, and, hey, this is my deal, not yours. But 'Beyond the Moon,' the opening line, the first couple of lines on 'Beyond the Moon,' I couldn't cut it. It was just like a Greek bouzouki line. I couldn't cut that. I did after we played it for a while. But at first it was just too much for me to play on bass, and Terry Watkinson had to come in and over-do some of the bass licks."

Adds McCracken, "There were a few tracks we recorded where I overdubbed the drum kit, where the whole track was recorded to a click track, except the drums, and then I went in afterwards and put the drums on top of it. That was done on 'Beyond the Moon.' At the time, that was kind of a new way of doing things. Now they do it all the time. The drums are quite often the last things to go on a record now, not the first thing. But I'd have to say that my favourite songs, as a collection, are on *Mutiny*, even though it's the worst sounding to me. They all sound pretty good, they all had a character to them, a uniqueness. *High Class* sounds really good and so does *A*

Million Vacations and... you're right, they do all sound pretty good! (laughs)."

"We're definitely still defying classification," said Kim, to *Georgia Straight*'s Tom Harrison, summing up the band's third kick at the cat. "This album doesn't sound like *High Class* at all, and a lot of our feedback says this album doesn't sound like *Max Webster*. But that's positive for us because we want all our albums to be different. The minute you start following a format and direction, people are going to get tired of you. But if you half-ass surprise them all the time, it might take them a little longer to get into the album, but it's got a longer life. I think the new album is fuckin' great and I'm freakin' out over it. After we recorded *High Class*, I had to leave it for about a month, but this one we've been playing constantly, I enjoy it that much. Max Webster isn't going in any direction; it's moving in what could be described as a circle, but a circle that's expanding. That's hard sometimes because record companies beat their brains against the wall trying to market a band like that. We are what we are and we do defy classification."

"Lyrically, this album is going to blow minds," continues Kim. "There's absolutely no clichés on it and it's also up-front. Pye's writing his own book. Today's music reminds me a lot of being out of the same book. There's this book of rules you follow but Pye has his own. We end the album with a science fiction erotica called 'Beyond the Moon.' It's the last tune in our moon series. We've been dealing in moon songs; there's been 'Coming Off the Moon,' 'Don't Be A Moon, Be A Star,' which has never been recorded, '(Mash Moon Over) Hawaii,' and 'Beyond the Moon,' which is a look at the future. It's really a nice way to end off the album. It talks about some things like yogurt. Someday, we won't read books anymore; we'll just eat them. Someday we'll eat electric meat. We really don't know what we're in for, but maybe it will be called neo-beef. Cocaine-coloured computer cards and vitamins are a big thing. Vitamin clouds; clouds will be made of vitamins. There's a lot of futuristic images, but at the end is, 'Listen, you can't make the world to order like a hotel services food.' It's a great way to end the album. Because there's this whole album happening and then, 'Listen folks, it's another world we live in, because words are going to be obsolete.'"

Issued April 17, 1978, *Mutiny Up My Sleeve* had sold 30,000 copies within a month en route to certifying gold in Canada for sales of over 50,000 copies by September, with the platinum plateau never being reached. As alluded to, the consensus was that there was no potential hit on the album, so no single was issued, which would have contributed to the album stalling at No.53 on the Canadian charts, following a No.44 placement for *High Class in Borrowed Shoes* and a No.32 placement for the debut.

With the album now showing up in the racks, the band embarked on a cross-Canada tour supported by The Ian Thomas Band, beginning in Nanaimo on Vancouver Island and working their way back home, culminating in two sold-out shows in one night, at Massey Hall in Toronto. Playing in Ian's band is none other than Rush and Max Webster cover artist Hugh Syme, providing keyboards.

The piped-in music before Max Webster hit the stage is "Charmonium," recorded for inclusion on the current album and to be reworked for its follow-up, *A Million Vacations*. Next comes a grab-bag of shows in the States, in June and July, with a clutch of them supporting Rainbow along with Cheap Trick, who are second on the bill. Taking a break to support Genesis at Exhibition Stadium in Toronto, July 10th, they are soon back in America supporting REO Speedwagon and then, into August, The Dictators.

On October 25th, after a handful of Ontario shows plus a couple in Quebec supporting Peter Gabriel, the guys would find themselves holed up at the Sound Kitchen in Toronto, demoing ideas for their next album. After another productive session in late November, the band would close out the year, December 31st, supporting Rush at Maple Leaf Gardens. For New Year's 1979 as well as New Year's 1980, Max Webster would find themselves established enough to enjoy headline status at the coveted Canuck concert.

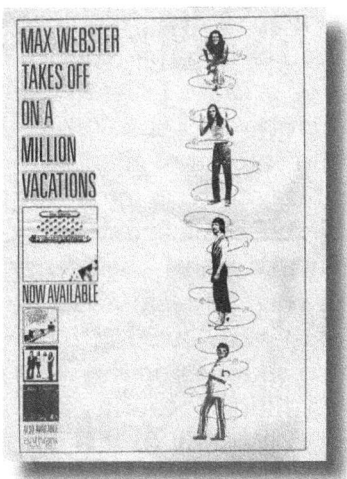

A MILLION VACATIONS –

"I mean, how many moon songs are there?"

If I may conjure up Rush again—a perennial but wry gold standard for Max, taking it or leaving some—album covers can affect greatly a fan's perception of a record. Witness the antique burnish of *Caress of Steel*, the wintery cold of *Fly by Night* and *Grace Under Pressure*, the pastels of *Signals* and that record's creamy swirl.

Well, Max, in 1979, boldly experienced now but still frustrated at not converting more minions, here they are emerging from the pessimistically titled *Mutiny Up My Sleeve*, with its dark and ultimately vandalised cover art, with a record that is all cartoon-appointed whiteness and hope, embodied in a title that is, for all practical purposes, infinite of fun.

"Well, *A Million Vacations*, right?" muses Pye. "Yeah, I was full-tilt boogie. My mind never stopped with those ideas. Postcards, get all our friends to write out the song lyrics in their own handwriting instead of one person doing it, making it look like you're on a vacation, and these are the postcards you're sending to your friends and family or your lawyer or your probation officer or whatever. Doesn't matter. So, it was just all geared to the pleasures of being on vacation."

"We hired a proper graphic design company," recalls Tom Berry, "and put our ideas together into that cover. I think it was me to a certain extent driving it, because I saw that whole thing as hugely marketable. But there's no way I could've gotten through that by myself without a certain amount of encouragement from the band. But it was a different situation. It was me sitting down with an agency rather than, the band would come in and have their meetings. But it would be me on the day to day with the agency, versus the previous one with Hugh Syme. Hugh is such a classic artist's artist, so it would've been more of them involved with him."

Berry says that everybody was on the same page with the album title. "Plus the song 'A Million Vacations' was so southern Ontario small-town—nailed it. If you talk to Pye you might find a totally different story, but again, this record was a step outside of the inner Max doing everything, to handing off certain of the creative reins to other people. Then we did all kinds of beach parties all over the place. We had so many fucking beach balls around *A Million Vacations*, which we had ordered up. That was really an odd Max Webster album as far as I was concerned. It was very light and airy, with the vibe of vacations and beaches and southern Ontario and summer and fun. I think we sent beach balls to everybody that worked the record, played the record or whatever. I just remember tons and tons of beach balls."

For no particular reason, the cover art was slightly adapted for issue in the US. The postcards are removed from the front, the rest of the graphics shifted downward, there are a couple graphic adjustments on the back, but the same photos of the band are used. Pointless, really.

"I'll give you the real answer," laughs Deane Cameron. "Everybody in the music business has an opinion. Certainly, in the early years, people felt that things coming from Canada, well, this is gonna need to be touched up. Unless it's a bottle of maple syrup—we can't really improve that. But I'm sure it's 'not invented here.' I went through that a lot. I went through that with Tom Cochrane on the *Life Is A Highway* album. The thing is, I really like the American cover more than the Canadian one now. It was the same in the UK. Throughout my time at EMI, all these people would like the American cover for the American artist. They'd want to change it. Every once in a while there was a cover that somebody put out from one country that was really going to benefit from being changed. But in most cases, it's a case of 'not invented here.'"

A Million Vacations - *"I mean, how many moon songs are there?"*

A Million Vacations, issued March 5, 1979, opens with a confident and even exhilarating whack from Gary McCracken—five of them, to be specific—before the band crashes into "Paradise Skies," their most famed song, their most beloved song, a track that embodies all the band stands for, lyrics of triumph, finely embroidered music of prog, pop and hard rock disposition living together in peace, resplendent production, texture, and McCracken whackin' those perfect toms of his.

"Because it had the two best songs Max ever did," begins Mike Tilka, on why *A Million Vacations* ultimately became the hit record that... well, let's just say it allowed the band to fight another battle and leave it at that. "Which was 'Let Go the Line' and 'A Million Vacations.' 'Paradise Skies'—I love 'Paradise Skies.' 'Paradise Skies' might've been an FM hit, but it was not an AM hit, whereas 'Let Go the Line' and 'A Million Vacations' charted. Maybe 'Paradise Skies' charted. I of course was less and less on the record company side at that time, because the management side was getting bigger and bigger and I was busy working, and I wasn't working that much with Max other than strictly numbers, budgets."

Indeed the producer-of-convenience role that Tilka had played last time out was subsumed by a new idea, a bold one at that, with Max and management bringing on a relative unknown, John de Nottbeck, to co-produce and, in the process, create for Max yet another record which is arguably one of the greatest sounding albums of the entire decade across all borders.

"Well, the managers, we weren't going to let Max produce the next record. The band wasn't going to ask me to produce it, that's for sure," says Tilka. "They had all these tunes, and they got... Kim got a buddy named John de Nottbeck. I knew John. John was an ad agency guy. Ad agency guys, the big record ads, which were huge back then, TV ads. So, John had a little background in audio, or in terms of putting together jingles. He was not a musician per se. Actually, he quit being an agency guy after that album and became a carpenter. He and Kim were friends. Kim trusted him, and against my better judgment, Anthem hired him to produce the record."

Adds Tom, "We went to a real corporate situation for that record; we went to a different producer in John de Nottbeck, who was a jingle writer and a friend of Kim's. It was his first real record. He'd convinced everybody that Max just needed to turn a little further to the centre/right to have a radio hit and improve upon... take more of a commercial stance generally. That ground its way through the sessions in that very yin/yang, yes/no, maybe I like it, maybe I don't like it, way. Then we finished the record and it was what it was. But I think everybody was quite supportive of John de Nottbeck around the office, because he was a producer that was used to deadlines and recognized hooks and those kinds of things, in songs. So, I think, the vibe between John and the office was quite tight—it was up and down between John and the band."

Capitol was happy with the arrangement as well, although Deane Cameron wasn't personally involved in the choice. "But I'd heard of him, and I think Ray and Kim knew of him. You know, I certainly interviewed him and talked to him. The concern was, again, okay, we're trying to make a record here that keeps the fan base going in Canada, but we're still trying to get something going in America. I liked *A Million Vacations* a lot, because I felt—and this may be a typical record company person answer—I loved them because they were different and new. I sat many times at the Gasworks and different places to see them, so I was a fan. But after a while I wanted it to happen. Globally, today people accept things from Canada as credible and we've really come into our own. I was one of those guys that was there in the pioneer years, and it was always, it can't be that good coming from Canada. Certainly, Rush, from day one, blew everyone away. They deserve it, and to me, they should all be Prime Minister. But, *A Million Vacations* was a little more traditionally produced and there were some great songs on it, although no better than previous albums, although it's got some of my favourite tracks. It was a bigger and fuller production. I felt pound for pound it was as good as anything from the band so far, but better production, or more relatable—I could hear this on American radio. I think as a stakeholder, as they say these days, it just made me feel that they're not selling out, but there's enough of a positive change that this is going to get us in the global game."

A Million Vacations as a whole possessed a buoyancy, due no doubt to the open architecture of the songs but also to the increased role of Terry Watkinson, at the expense of Kim and his gnarly, cantankerous guitar and the intrusive tone heard periodically—and even convulsively—on *Mutiny Up My Sleeve.*

"I think I was just playing better stuff and they let me play," quips Watkinson, who at this time had found himself offering tips and tricks to one Geddy Lee, who had been seeing what Max and other bands could achieve with keys. "We talked about it, yeah; I can't remember the substance of the talks that much. But he bought a big... I guess it was a Moog synthesizer with all the patch cords and everything like that. He was struggling with that, and I helped out a bit. But he used to pay a lot of attention to what I was doing and he picked some stuff up from me."

As for the band's new producer, "Okay, he was a guy whose main thing was producing commercials. So, he tried to make a very commercial album that still had the essence of Max on it. So, we butted heads with him sometimes. You know, about stuff being too commercial or too silly or whatever. But it turned out to be a really good album. By that time, we were kind of doing a lot of production ourselves, so it was more of a partnership than anything else."

"His forte at that point was he had an advertising company, or did music for commercials, jingles," confirms previous producer Terry Brown, concerning John. "It was usually a team, him and his partner, and they certainly knew what they were doing, and he did great work—very talented."

"John de Nottbeck was a friend of Kim's," adds Dave, "and I believe at one point when Kim first went to Toronto, he did some beer commercials for Labatt or something, and they needed some guitar work that sounded like Hendrix."

Muses Pye, "de Nottbeck was more or less Kim's friend, but I'm not sure why he was hired. Boy, that's a good question. I think Kim had grown in confidence in some respects and we went with his view of de Nottbeck's ability to do this. But I think Kim really had a project in mind, with those songs. I think Kim really is in the position of producer on that album. I don't know how he picked these songs, but it was a really good mix. I guess it's true that in general they are a little softer, except for 'Rascal Houdi' and 'Paradise Skies.'"

An interesting somewhat similar dynamic was expressed by Dave. "In order to really create like that, the people that Kim had around him... he had to feel comfortable with them. And of course, he frankly was going to have to be kept comfortable (laughs). I mean, everybody else could be replaced or overdubbed or whatever. Kim had to feel good, or it wasn't gonna happen."

And what a triumph for both Kim and John opening track "Paradise Skies" was—Pye says the lyric represented "a new beginning"—of production, of playing, with its ultimate joyful moment arising out of its Dave Myles bass line as much as anything else, especially come a lapse into the happiest of discos at 2:35 until heavenly close a minute later. Elsewhere, Myles is front and centre as well, such as during the driving verse section... if that can even be called a verse. Indeed, this atmospheric gem of a song confounds with two competing verses and not really a chorus and yet given its brevity and discipline—and much simplicity despite its strange frame—it's an easy pick for smash single. Of note, it's not one of Kim's favourites when it comes to his guitar solo, and he's proven as much by completely changing it over the years.

"That's just talking about how much fun it is when you let go," reflects Pye, on the wide-eyed wonder at the heart of the lyric. "It's like we're high, we're at a concert, so let's go. But I never promote drugs. It's more that feeling of, let's go, tonight's the night, let's get at and have some fun." There is Pye Dubois yet again, transfixed by the live rock show, an idea perennially at odds with his quiet and reclusive nature. Indeed, Pye is so much at the heart of what it means to be a rock audience, one imagines that there's not much difference in the tranced experience for him between a compelling live band that is not Max Webster and Max themselves, despite those being his lyrics rolling off the stage.

"I just think some of the nice elements that Max Webster had came together really nicely," adds Kim. "It was a good performance, and one of our better written tunes. I'm not patting myself on the back with that; I'm saying us as a band. Lyrically, Pye was pretty out there most of the time, and that one was just a little more relatable, I thought, to people. There are a few odd ways of saying things, but that was his style. But 'Happiness is beginning to ride, from the streets into paradise skies.' It was a nice image that I think people kind of dug."

The rise of "Paradise Skies"—charting at No.43 in the UK and No.21 in Canada—corresponded with the band's career highlight trip to England with Rush. A bonus related to that song ensued, once the band got there.

"That was so crazy! They went nuts; it was such a cool place," relates Dave Myles. "We did some shows, just Max by themselves, and then we hooked up with Rush. Rush is so huge in England, it's insane, it's crazy. We were doing the Hammersmith Odeon, the Marquee club, and the kids over there, they love their bands. They're extremely loyal to whoever they are. Just to play these places. Because we were with EMI Capitol at the time, they were letting us have a good time. They were letting us go to these parties and after-hours clubs that you had to know the magic knock to get into. It was pretty wild."

Pye was impressed with the English fans as well. "They seemed to grasp this 'No cigarettes, no matches,' because as the tour progressed, more cigarettes and more matches were thrown at Kim. But that was typical Europe—they loved the bands. They loved you more if you saw them the next concert, the same people out in the audience. They had a tendency to follow the bands around and stay with the bands the whole tour, especially in England. It was a lot of fun. Max Webster didn't have to back people up in Canada—they headlined. But the European tour was Max opening for Rush. I have the tour jacket at home, for *A Million Vacations*. These jackets were given to us at the airport, going to Europe, so it's *A Million Vacations* with a handmade crest. That was what? 29 concerts in 33 days? But that was just one big party. It really was a party because there's not a lot of distance between Birmingham and Manchester. There is quite a bit of distance between London and Newcastle or London and Glasgow. Those were the rough ones. But Coventry and all this, they were all pretty close together as far as traveling in a rock band. So, we were essentially always together."

Kim, in conversation with Roman Mitz just back from the trip, expressed a similarly favourable sentiment as Dave concerning Capitol. "You've got to picture the first night we were there. The record company loaded stacks of money into the band. They had picture discs, maxi discs and ads, and they just pumped us like they haven't pumped a band before. At the concerts, they gave away a sampler record which really went over well. The kids over there hold onto stuff like that; they like gifts. We played the Marquee, where people like The Who got their start, and there were four nights at the Hammersmith Odeon in London. That's a prestigious gig to play. There was an opera house in Hamburg that was so old that I'm sure all these dudes like Bach and Liszt had to have been there at one time."

"We had what is probably my ultimate in recording experience," continues Dave, citing another trip highlight. "We were set to do a show called *Top of the Pops*. At the time, apparently, there was some kind of rule that if you were going to be on *Top of the Pops*, it had to be a song that you'd recorded in England. I'm sure that's changed now, but anyway, so EMI said, okay, well if they're gonna be on *Top of the Pops*, we may as well take them into Abbey Road and they can record the song that they were going to do. But when they do it live, or when they actually do *Top of the Pops*, we're going to go back to the original tape, the original master that we recorded at Phase One (laughs). So here we are, and of course Rush came along with us too. They said 'hey, we'll go to Abbey Road.' So sure enough, they took us into Abbey Road, and we got to record... I think it was 'Paradise Skies,' I think, and maybe another tune, and we were in the same studio that The Beatles used. They had a very ancient board. We were down in that room, where you go down the side, down the stairs, and you go to the bottom. Our gear was there. We set up, and everything that came through the board sounded like 'Baby you can drive my car;' the guitars had that sound. It was bizarre."

"We went into Abbey Road Studios in the middle of the night," Kim told Mintz, who was interviewing him for *The New Music*. "It's pretty old and dumpy, actually, and ancient by today's technical standards. We used Studio Two, where The Beatles did all of their stuff. The old board in there looked like an airplane console, but when we started playing, the drum kit immediately sounded like The Beatles."

But the band's rock star tour of Europe was about to end—thanks Lerxt.

"Well," laughs Dave. "We tried to stay, when we went to England. We hooked up with Rush, and I think we went up to the north of England, into Scotland, and then we crossed over into Sweden. We got just to the edge of Germany, and we were to go into Germany with Rush. We heard that there were pretty good record sales for us there—people knew who we were. Alex Lifeson had his wife over. She had been flown over, and he had—I don't know if this is true—but he had hurt his finger in the bathroom, slipped on something or something happened, and he was... Rush was not going to continue with the tour. So, the whole tour collapsed and we went home (laughs). All because Alex hurt his finger in the bathroom. Yeah, sometimes you're the bug; sometimes you're the windshield."

But Kim was gracious of Rush's help throughout the course of Max's career.

"They've opened up Canada for us, they've opened up the States for us and now they've opened up Europe. They've been great guys to us. We've opened up for a lot of bands and it's never been as good as when we open up for Rush—only because we know what to expect. It's Rush's show, so there's a certain amount of lights, time and stage space. It was a case of take the encore if you want it and take the second encore if there's time. It was great over there. That's our element. We've got to follow it up because (the label) poured a lot of money into us and we didn't let them down. We blew them away. I don't know why, but it just kept growing and growing as the tour went on. Next time we'll break it; we've got our claws in it already."

Gary places the UK as probably the second-best territory for the band, outside of Ontario, and it was pretty much thanks to this particular visitation upon the nation.

"Absolutely, and it was because we played there once with Rush. We had gone and done the European tour there with Rush, which was really big for us. Canadian bands were huge in Europe generally, very popular; Europeans just loved it. And they also loved the music that we played, because it wasn't particularly commercial. We had all that tricky little stuff in there and the Europeans really go for that, which is why Rush is so huge over there. Europeans go for that instrumental, 20-minute guitar solo stuff (laughs). So 'Paradise Skies' was released over there as a single, in England. We did 180,000 singles. That's what I was told. Then it's like anything else, you go, well, I don't know if that's a lot or if it's not, but 180,000 seems like quite a lot for a single. That's the way I look at it. People wish they could sell 180 (laughs), let alone 180,000. So, we had a single that did well, and we ended up on *Top of the Pops*, which you can see on YouTube."

"They wanted to have us do 'Hangover,'" recalls Pye, concerning the TV showcase, "but we had no choice. 'Hangover' had Alka-Seltzer and Tang in the lyric, and because of copyright law, whatever law, you couldn't mention products, brand names. So, we went down to the studio and we recorded 'Paradise Skies,' and that was on *Top of the Pops*."

Asked about the routing of the trip, Pye says, "We went to England, but then Rush went to France, and we went up to Germany, and then Denmark, and then over to Sweden, and then over to Oslo. Yeah, here's an anecdote. So, I think we're in Oslo, and we're on the radio doing an interview, Kim and myself. We're talking, and one of the road crew snuck up behind me and whispered in my ear, 'Joe Clark is the Prime Minister of Canada.' And out loud I went, 'Joe fucking Clark?!' I couldn't believe it. So, Oslo got a little Canadiana on its tape."

"A few weird isolated moments comes to mind," contributes Kim, asked about the English swing. "We were all out for dinner at an Indian food restaurant, and Deane Cameron was sitting there, and all of a sudden Terry just starts throwing little pieces of rice at him, and the whole thing about Deane Cameron was, he wasn't reacting. He wasn't laughing or buying into it. He was just, okay, here's rock stars going weird and I'm supposed to maintain my... I was just losing it, because here's the record company guy just sitting there all proper and still. Meanwhile... and Terry wasn't throwing food at him. It would be a little piece of rice and he would just toss it and it would land in Deane's beer. It's just, I don't know, stupid shit like that. Just being hammered in England, walking down little cobblestone roads late at night."

"Where were we, Newcastle?" laughs Deane, adding a fuzzy memory. "We did a gig in Newcastle, and after we went out and got carried away, I remember we were trying to hang Pye from one of the old streetlights, on the back of his coat. He was in pretty bad shape. I missed my plane the next day and fell asleep in my clothes and had to take a later flight. But I was in my 20s back then. I also took the whole band to see Kate Bush. Most people think my career is about two things: Tom Cochrane, because I grew up with him and we played in bands together, or Kate Bush, because that was my crusade. So yeah, we all sat in a row, and I think Pye absolutely loved it. I wasn't too sure if Kim was enjoying himself or not, but I think so. I just went for that initial tour, because David and Vic Wilson had actually become personal friends. So, I always felt everything was in good hands, and that they were really trying to make it happen."

Recalls Pye, "Yeah, we saw Kate Bush's debut concert. It was really powerful. That was an inspiration for me. I was like, what?! Because no one had seen her. She was 13 or 14 (ed. actually 21). They basically sequestered her and taught her."

The moment Pye tells me this, during one of our many chats pub-bound in Toronto downtown, Kate Bush plays over the system. "Whoa, that's really bizarre. But they had her hid away, and she was obviously talented, but more piano lessons, more dance and more vocals, and she was just massive. She was a goddess over there. So, no one had seen her, and when she broke, and she came out... We were all there, but I don't know if anybody else was inspired. I'm getting chills, because it was wonderful. Chester Thompson and all these guys, musicians, who were on tour, went to that concert that night at the Palladium. It was wonderful. She was brilliant. I... I'm still in love with her. One of my favourite all-time songs is 'This Woman's Work,' this brief little song that just gives me the chills. It's the kind of song that, when I put it on at home, I don't do anything. I just stop."

"We all went out one night and saw the band U.K. on a night off," continues Mitchell, adding a favourite memory. "I had my mind blown by guitar player Allan Holdsworth for the first time.

I'm excluding the Rush stuff, because that was obvious, and playing the Hammersmith Odeon, which was incredible. I think we went back. I think we played there with Black Sabbath also; we played Hammersmith. I'm pretty sure Black Sabbath in London and in Leeds."

"What else? Yeah, I always remember the afternoon that we went over... we were gonna do *Top of the Pops* the next day. Leaning against the bar, I remember, just a typical English pub, leaning against the bar, and off goes the record company guys to make a few phone calls, to try and find a studio. When they came back, they went, 'Are you guys okay if the only place that's available is Abbey Road? Are you okay to record in that place?' I remember being halfway through a sip of beer and almost splitting it out like (laughs), just one of those things, like are you fucking kidding me? We have a chance to record at Abbey Road Studios?! That was probably one of the highlights of my recording career, even though I don't think the session went that well. But it was so vibey in there."

"'Mull of Kintyre,' two-inch reels," continues Mitchell. "We were sitting there and we were trying to bribe the engineer going, 'Come on man, give me an out-take. Like I would die just to hear an out-take. I'd like to hear Paul McCartney fucking up.' He said, 'You know what? I would,' but he says, 'Imagine if we did that, and that was the moment this machine fucked up and ate the tape.' So, and I saw his point. It's like, if I was guaranteed that this machine wasn't gonna mess up... but you don't know. These machines mess up once in a while. So, it was just so groovy. Yeah, walking across the street in the morning, and again, Abbey Road, people looking at you like, oh no, it's another drunk rock band. By then the sun was starting to come up and we had drunk a case of wine."

"But I do remember playing Hammersmith Odeon," continues Kim, shifting to the return trip on which indeed the band played with Black Sabbath, for but one show, not two. "There's a Whitesnake video out, of them doing 'Here I Go Again' from the Hammersmith Odeon, and it just takes me... I go watch that, not so much for their performance, but just to see the Hammersmith Odeon. That's a great memory. But the Black Sabbath gig, I remember being in Leeds, and that's, I would say, the scariest gig I've ever done. That's one of the three scariest gigs. The most afraid I've ever been going on stage. I'd say the first heaviest type of fear was Kingswood Music Theatre, for two nights, sold-out, and walking towards the stage and just remembering how terrified I was. The second one was in Buffalo.

There was about 25,000 people downtown, and it was a free concert. And I was just, oh, God I'm scared. But I remember the Black Sabbath gig going, holy shit. I remember looking out at the audience and I was going, 'We're gonna die.' Because it was just a sea of leather and studs. Like it was scary. I thought, oh, we're fucking gonners. As soon as we break into 'Toronto Tontos,' it's just gonna be all over. But we got through it. I'm here today, so..."

Moving forward, second track on *A Million Vacations* was one credited to Terry alone. "Charmonium" serves as microcosmic metaphor for the wider album. It's gorgeously prog-lite, angelic even, with musical sophistication for miles. As well, despite so many songs getting added at radio, it's one that made the grade too as Max wove its way into the pop culture fabric of its proud host nation. But it was belaboured of birth, with de Nottbeck having to rely on his rich past physically cutting tape to do many edits, including the excising of a whole middle section Terry had written, inspired by Duke Ellington's, "Diminuendo and Crescendo in Blue." As alluded to earlier, the song also arose from the sessions for the previous album, and was used instrumentally as the band's live intro tape. At the lyric end, some of the lines harken back to an earlier non-LP Max track called "Do You or Don't You Want to Know." As for the magical title of the song, it's a term used in particle physics.

"That was a Terry tune," says Dave, asked about "Charmonium." "He had a whole different point of view of what comprised a tune, which is probably a lot more commercially accessible than what Kim's was. Terry is a tremendous artist. Have you ever seen some of his paintings? Wow, this guy is not just a songwriter. So, it was a real pleasure playing with him. *Mutiny Up My Sleeve* was a very creative time for Max, but *A Million Vacations*, we were trying to live up to the expectations of the record company, and SRO. So, the songs became a little more commercially acceptable, basically. You know, it was like we were doing that, and we were part-time rock stars, at the time. So, there was lots of ego. There was tons of ego on that album. Tons, and of course by the time we got to *Universal Juveniles*, we weren't even really talking to one another a lot of the time. We would just show up and do it, you know?"

I wondered if Dave had ever wished he had been included more in the writing of the songs... "No, no. I was just there to play bass, to support. You always put stuff into records, into tunes, but it's just your creative contribution. I was just happy to play for them."

"Night Flights" is another progressive pomp rocker, lush and warm of texture, hopeful, buoyant, but contributing again to a record that was going to be in the main, much poppier than the three before.

"That was John de Nottbeck," figures Kim, asked why the album as a whole was so... pretty. "He got in there and worked our tunes and arranged stuff and picked stuff we were writing. And I think, in working with the label, the label's going, come on, we have to get some record sales here. Let's get something happening. He did and so, it was good."

"John de Nottbeck I met when I was about 16, 17," continues Kim. "I was in a band called Zooom. We were in Sarnia, and we moved to... What did we do? We moved to Toronto, we got a gig with Scott Richard Case, at the place which was the old City TV building; I think it was called Electric Circus. He saw us there, and he came back and went... his exact words were, 'Who the fuck are you guys and where are you from?!' Then he brought Jack Richardson to see us, and that's my connection. He recorded a couple of tunes with us with the band Zooom, at his studio that was right at Sumac and King; he had a studio there. We recorded a couple of tunes, as Zooom, and one was called 'Uniforms.' I think John de Nottbeck still has it."

"I'm not sure I co-produced," demurs Kim, answering to assertions that he really took quite a bit of control. "I'm the artist, it's my stuff, I'm always in there. I think every artist is always in there haggling away with what they're trying to say and what direction it's trying to go. John's strengths were getting a good performance out of us. And I think him having known Jack Richardson, I think John's strength was also arranging. Let's bring this part forward, let's bring this chorus, let's get this going. By then I was going, yeah, yeah, this is cool; I'm liking this. guess it was Max Webster's only platinum record."

"Night Flights" features the only Watkinson/Dubois writing credit in the Max canon, but the attempt to write with Pye went pear-shaped, with Watkinson retaining very little, if anything, of what Pye proposed for the track.

Next up is "Sun Voices," a pensive and ethereal prog ballad, arranged much like the song before it but not as uptempo. "I don't think anyone in the band would ever have believed that I was actually saying that I'm retiring the moon songs," laughs Pye. "I'm retired. I'm in the lounge chair by the pool, and those songs are history. Because that really was going to be the last moon song, except of course for 'Moon Voices,' which would have no lyrics. I mean, how many moon songs are there? There's got to be six or seven."

Including "Between Sun & Moon," which Pye contributed to Rush for their 1993 *Counterparts* album, plus lesser references to the moon hither and thither, there certainly must be. In any event, "Sun Voices" is indeed an eerie evocation of a retirement, perhaps the classic retirement, with all the imagery of letting go, slipping toward death.

And then we're into "Moon Voices" (working title "Avoid Moon"), a somewhat jumpy, dissonant instrumental that is still nonetheless light and delicate, like everything on the album so far, even the slightly heavy "Paradise Skies." "'Moon Voices' is the last moon song," reiterates Pye. "The plan was to have no lyrics, absolutely, and it's here because I think thematically, that's the only place in this series of moon songs it could go." There's an odd connection to the song "Hawaii" here—or a couple actually, first, in the Vai-esque progginess to both of them, but second, in this idea of Pye firing himself as lyricist because words are obsolete. In a live setting, moving forward, "Sun Voices" and "Moon Voices" were always played together, as a conceptual pairing.

Over to side two of the original vinyl, and the happy vibes continue with this successful and suntanned record's title track, a conventional, even shiftless boogie, different for the band in vibe, yet how could it not be, given that it's a rare writing contribution from the band's drummer Gary McCracken?

"I just did an interview with CBC in Halifax about 'A Million Vacations,'" begins Gary, on his moment in the songwriting sun. "They wanted to know how it was put together, and how we co-wrote it, rah rah rah, and we're going to include this with Gino Vanelli and all these people; they're going to do an hour on Canadian summer songs. 'A Million Vacations' is right in there for summer songs. So, I've got my own little piece of the action there from that one song. Even though a lot of people don't know I sing it. That's one of the things that over the years, I have to tell people I sing that. Because no one ever mentions it."

Gary certainly sings it well, his voice sitting closely with Terry's, both of them quite fragile and even naive, against Kim's singing, which periodically includes a slightly caustic Zappa-esque sneer—a wisecrack.

"Well, God, that just taps into everybody's head," muses Kim. "'Friday, Friday is a good time to shine.' It was just so Sarnia to me. 'You can only drive down main street so many times.' I can't speak for all the other people who liked that song, but to me, that was exactly what was going on in Sarnia, that song. We lived that song. So, I think he really did a great job in nailing that. I thought the rhyme scheme was pretty interesting too; it's all A, A, A. Good time to shine, unwind, losing all survival signs, time, mine—there's no A/B at all. It's all A, A, A; same rhyme. It's really funny in that way."

Adding additional back-story, Gary explains that, "At the time when we put *A Million Vacations* together, we ran out of songs. Kim ran dry, and we only had five songs. So, we had a meeting at one point, and he said, 'Listen, you guys got any songs? We need three or four more songs to finish this record. You guys got anything?' That was the first time he had ever asked anyone for material. I said I had one song that I know is a decent song, because it was—it was a song called 'Small Town Blues,' but it was 'A Million Vacations.' It was that song with my lyric, my 'You can only drive down main street' line, which is the big line, a lot of it. That's my line from the original song."

"So, when we went to record it for Max Webster, it was determined that Pye Dubois would have to do the lyrics to make it a proper Max Webster song. Versus just, here's a song from the drummer, kind of thing. So, I went along with that. I thought, well, if I don't go along with that, they won't record my song. So, there's your compromise. So, I ended up doing pretty good with, how when people split up songs, 50-50 and that—Pye gets lyrics and I get the music. So, I get the music +20% of the lyrics because of that one line. So, I get the lion's share of a hit song. Whether anybody knows I sing it or not (laughs)... So that kind of works out and is good for me. Kim even plays 'A Million Vacations' at his shows. He goes out and he sings it. People are listening to him, they don't know whether it's me or him singing or who, they just like that song. It would be neat if more people knew I sang it, but at the same time it's neat that they don't. Like how many bands do you listen to where you don't know who the singer is?"

"But Kim actually didn't want to sing it. He wanted me to sing it. He said, 'Oh, no, you sing it.' Now, when it was time to sing the vocal, and I said to everybody, 'Well, I'd like to take a run at the vocal tonight. Then if it doesn't happen, I'll be ready for tomorrow; we'll come in at noon and nail it.' So, John, the producer, goes, 'I think I'm just going to go home. Wait till tomorrow.' Kim goes, 'I'm... I want to go home.' So, neither one of them wanted to sit there while I wanted to sing. Terry says, 'Okay, I'll sit behind the glass.

Get out there and sing.' So, I went out and sang the tune. There's no producer and there's no Kim (laughs). They're gone. They're out of the building, gone. We ended up getting what we considered the final vocal, okay?"

"Then the very next day," continues Gary, "we went in, the producer listens to it, he goes, 'Holy shit. Run out there right now, and we're going to double it.' You know how they double vocals? So, I went out and I did that, and it took the length of the song, that's all it took, three-and-a-half minutes, and he goes, 'Okay, now come in and listen to this.' So, he doubled my vocal and that was it. The song was finished. Within that one time, the song is... and when it was all over, he said, 'There you go, now you got a good solid vocal.' Then that was it! Really cool."

"But it was funny how there was no involvement with actually the guy who was supposed to be looking after the record, the producer— he wasn't there when it happened. Sort of after the fact. Again Kim, well, the way it works when you're recording, is you don't have to be in the studio. So, if I have to sing a song, Kim doesn't necessarily want to be there to listen to you sing it. That's the producer's job. Terry helped, but I can't say Terry was that responsible for music in 'A Million Vacations.' That was, we just arranged my song and that's the way it went, just like when Kim brings in a certain song and we just add our stuff to it and it becomes Max Webster. So, I'm the one-hit-wonder guy. I had the one hit, and even though the lyrics got reworked, it happens to be a song I wrote way before I was in the band. So here I am, 61 years old (ed. 74 now!), and I'm getting royalty money from it; somehow that all happened."

Finally with respect to this loveable under-achiever of a song (highlight being, yes, Gary's perceptive quip, but also the car horns!), McCracken looks at the way Pye works with Kim, comparatively with having Pye put his stamp on his old song.

"They were songwriter-type partner guys for years, eh? The way it always worked, Kim had lots of musical ideas for any number of songs. Tons and tons and tons of music. But I think he was, like a lot of us, maybe self-conscious about his lyrics. I know that he used to not think he could write very well, the words. Dubois, Pye, his thing is, well, I can write all kinds of great words, and all kinds of imagery, and then it just seems like a good fit, not unlike Elton John with Bernie Taupin. You've got a great musician, and he's a little worried about his lyrics, and then you've got a guy who's got all kinds of lyrics but is not necessarily a musician at all. So, I just fell into that same situation when it came to 'A Million Vacations.' It was like, well, to make it legit Max Webster without trying to rock the boat, let's do a co-write, right? It turned out to be a good thing."

As Kim told Geoff Barton during the band's UK jaunt, "I think it works out well though. I'm not a good lyricist myself; maybe I was born under the wrong sign of the Zodiac or something. I read somewhere that Cancers make bad poets. I'm living proof of that. Terry can write lyrics, Gary too, but with me, well, I just get kind of stuck on the basic clichéd kind of stuff. Pye's unique though. He's been doing it so long."

"That was fine, absolutely!" says Pye, about watching the drummer get a song on the record. "Yeah, we loved it. How do you figure this? How drummers sing, we'll never know. How do you play... you've got a great band with two great singers, and then you get the camera on the drummer, and he's singing and he's really good! It doesn't make any sense; it doesn't (laughs)."

After a side-trip to blue collar boogie, the band is back to fussy pop with an intellectual edge. "Look Out" is as oddly configured as "Paradise Skies," a Master's level progressive pop rock, a deep album track that nevertheless underscores the cohesion of this rarefied record built of politely pulsating rhythm, not much guitar, and smears of deft keyboard gestures.

"Did I write that? Wow, pretty scary," chuckles Dubois. "Well, that's obvious to me. It's just a little bit of fear and trepidation about the world, the way the world was going. I don't know if we were at a precipice back then. But you better look out. Someone has just called 'Look out' on you, so your foot is over the edge of the cliff, but you better step back. I think that's a fair analysis of those lyrics. But you're putting me in a very odd position. I'll tell you why: people that are into it might read these lyrics and might have an interpretation of these lyrics that might be so far removed from the author's motive or whatever. I don't think that's very fair to do. It's never bothered me, but I think it's unfair with some people. That's why I never answer the question, what's your favourite song? Because it does prejudice the other songs."

"But yeah, 'Look Out' is a bit of an anthem, like, 'Look out, folks.' I think it's a universal statement but I think it's a personal statement as well, that you have a responsibility as a person to be looking out and call, 'Look out.' It's not just... you can't just wait. You can keep walking towards the edge and then all of a sudden discover that you're at the edge. I think there are obviously signs before you get to the edge, and I think you have a responsibility to be in touch with your environment. That's how I've always seen it. That's why, like I said the other day to you, one of the saddest parts about being with Max is that I seemed to be the one that was... not an intellectual, but burdened by some of the things that I would see on the news or see in our environment. These things seemed to upset me, but they seemed to be water over a duck's back with the other Max Webster guys. Nobody ever talked about these things, and I desperately wanted to talk about them."

Next up was another Terry track, with "Let Go the Line" credited solely to the keyboardist and sung by him as well. Helping out are a few members of the Toronto Symphony Orchestra. This one's also in that small class of pomp rock proposals the industry produced in and around '79 and '80, pomp being a genre practised mostly by a handful of mostly unsuccessful US bands (Trillion, Touch, New England, 707), but on this side of the border, also by Saga. But "Let Go the Line," which borrows from an earlier song called "Lady Let Me In," is so light and airy, it was actually damn near an AM hit, certainly a mainstream single, even if it hasn't lived up to the stature of its early fame, now eclipsed in the memory banks of classic rock fans by "Paradise Skies" and "A Million Vacations."

"I'll tell you a little bit about 'Let Go the Line,'" begins Terry. "Before we did the recording, in, I guess it was Phase One, before we did that, we did versions of all the songs on an eight-track tape, a pre-production kind of thing. I had a version of 'Let Go the Line' that wasn't working. Everybody said, well, we don't think this is good for the album. I actually begged them, I said let me go back to the drawing board with the song. Because I know the chorus is really good. So, I rewrote the whole verse in the way it's... all the instrumental stuff, I rewrote that, in a few days. Then when we went in to record the album, I said, 'Okay I got this together.' Sure enough, it happened."

"'Let Go the Line,' Terry and I recorded that song, right?" says Gary. "John de Nottbeck, John and Kim, they weren't even in the studio when we did that song—just like 'A Million Vacations.' Then what happened was, John, the producer walked into the studio the next day and hears 'Let Go the Line,' all finished, except for mixing and that, all recorded. His jaw dropped down to the floor. He says, 'This is a hit song here, buddy.' He had nothing to do with it—and he's the producer. But if anybody would be the commercial songwriter, it was Terry. But again, apart from 'Let Go the Line,' Kim wasn't ready to start doing Terry Watkinson albums. He didn't want to give him any more songs."

Adds Dave, "Terry would support Kim in whatever he wanted to do, but Terry had a voice. He had his own things he was capable of doing and did very well. Even today 'Let Go the Line' is probably one of the most played songs that Max did, over the airwaves. It's a fluff song. But it's a really nice song, it sounds wonderful, and it works as an opening for all kinds of radio shows, without trying to be controversial. Actually, when we did 'Let Go the Line,' I just couldn't get the pocket correct, and Terry said I'm gonna do it. I said no problem, go for it. Again, frankly, I was just grateful to be there, just to see all this going down. Terry was an amazing musician. But eventually, I could see after three years that Kim was going, I don't want you guys influencing what I'm doing anymore. He wanted to go it alone. Terry could see that. You look at 'Let Go the Line,' that is so far from what Kim is about. Those kinds of hooks, Kim would avoid."

"We would knock heads," agrees Kim. "I would knock heads with Terry a little bit, but with hindsight, this many years later, he was a very, very creative person. Terry's song, 'Let Go the Line' was a big song; it got a lot of airplay and did really well for us. To quote Geddy Lee, when they did 'Time Stand Still' with Aimee Mann, all of a sudden girls started coming to the shows (laughs). But at the same time, I always felt like I wanted to be a little more rock 'n' roll, punk, a little more aggressive. He was a little more leaning towards pop and accessibility. So, I knocked heads with him that way. Like, man, what the fuck do you wanna sell records for? Like, why do you wanna get on the radio? (laughs). I was one of those guys that I don't care for anymore, the guys going, 'What? Are we gonna sell out?!' (laughs)."

The Kim vs. Terry duality/dichotomy in the band was not an insignificant problem, explains Carla Jensen, as discussed last chapter, Terry's girlfriend at the time, and then married to Terry in June of 1987. "Basically, it was Kim's band, and he had a very sure idea of what he wanted the music to be like, right? Terry's music and Kim's music was very different. Most of Terry's songs were more commercial than Kim's, and I'm not sure how Kim felt about that. So, there was a tug-of-war. I could understand it from Kim's point of view, because they had a certain reputation for being underground and kind of cult—they had kind of a cult-ish following. Those were the people who were important to Kim, and the band too, to play to and to write for. I'm not sure it was really important to Kim to have those commercial opportunities. Although some of his songs became commercial successes, right? But I'm not sure that he liked the musical direction of Terry's songs. It was hard for Kim and it was hard for Terry. It was hard for both of them."

As for what was making Terry such an accessible songsmith, "Well, Terry was really influenced by a lot of jazz, although granted that didn't really come through in his songs too much," figures Carla. "In fact, he now plays a lot of sax and is finishing a new album, and there will probably be sax on that. I know he really liked the keyboard player that wrote 'Short People,' Randy Newman. But really, I think it came from inside himself, and I just think that's the way he wrote—in a commercial way. Lots of people loved it. It just may not have been the direction Max Webster was heading in, so it caused friction."

Asked whether Terry was comfortable being a singer, Carla says, "He likes singing his songs, but it wasn't as important as his playing. His keyboard was his main instrument, and his voice was the second instrument, whereas a lot of people, it might've been the voice first and then keyboards second. I think he really liked singing. He may not be the best singer in the world, but I think it comes through. It may have been that it just wasn't Max material." Full-time musician for almost ten years when she met Terry, the two never wrote together. "He was pretty private about it. It wasn't like I was shut out of it, but he would take advantage of the times that I was out of the apartment to do a lot of that. So, it was very private for him, and he really wanted no distractions."

A Million Vacations in totality turned out so keyboard-laden that *Keyboard* magazine, in 2004, took a closer look at the album from the point of ivories, explaining that, "Some of the polyphonic synths are hard to identify, but likely culprits include the Yamaha CS-80, Oberheim 4-Voice, and Sequential Circuits Prophet-5. After the pedestrian organ-laced opener 'Paradise Skies,' Watkinson takes it into serious rock territory with the galloping 'Charmonium,' playing Rhodes, ARP and organ through tricky time and chord changes. The songwriter and lead singer on this tune, the multi-talented Watkinson even lays down a bombastic ARP solo that must have been a treat in their live shows. The synth-soaked 'Night Flights' features thumping synth bass lines and plenty of polyphonic layering while 'Sun Voices' opens with a portamento-inflected synth melody over a melange of well-orchestrated synths. See if you can pick out the different keyboard used on the synth odyssey of 'Moon Voices,' one of Watkinson's shining moments in the Max Webster catalogue. The title cut rocks hard with minimal keyboards, but the following 'Look Out' makes it up with generous keyboard work that should set synth detective scrambling to identify its many layers of electronic keys. The catchy single, 'Let Go the Line' was sung and written by Watkinson, whose acoustic piano playing underscores his own synth orchestrations and the hooky electric guitar harmonies."

"There was always a lot of debate," recalls Deane Cameron, on the issue of picking singles, "and usually things came up like, it sounds like two different bands. I never got that. It doesn't matter. Look at The Kinks. Every single they ever had was completely different. So that always bothered me. Terry's voice wasn't as strong as it were, but to me it has a character and represents a contrast. He was cool. He was the guy that wrote more of the melodic material, and I think more for the average fan. That's the variety the fans want—to keep them a fan. There are some fans that want their bands to sound exactly the same record in, record out. But I don't believe that in all cases, that that keeps you alive for decades, or for albums."

"Certainly, there were questions about whether 'Let Go the Line' represented Max Webster as opposed to whatever," comments Tom. "But *A Million Vacations* put us through the roof. It's probably Kim's least favourite record, and the one we battled more on versus the making of any other record. But it had that Terry hit, plus 'A Million Vacations' which became radio staples. So that easily went platinum. But I don't think certain parties were happy. I think it probably ended up being a management call to just try and avoid inner politics with the band as best we could. I know Kim wasn't really happy with a bunch of that."

So, is the record somewhat more reflective of Terry's personality than Kim's? "Well, I think it depends on which corner you stand. There were three Terry tunes on it, but is there even a guitar in 'Let Go the Line?' I remember there being a certain amount of tension there. Terry wrote these—which is odd for Terry because he's such a left-field person, and I say that with love and respect—but he wrote more straightforward, slightly more commercial songs, than maybe the less commercial side of the band wanted to go."

"The way I look at it," continues Tom, "Max was this crazy group of guys that had this extra guy on the outside with a straighter management company that was always trying to bring it in line with what they thought should work. There were wars with Pye, because Pye was always trying to be the most creative guy in the room. So, there was obviously clashes between that kind of attitude and a straighter management type of attitude. It's that end of it I remember more than anything else. That and the fact that it had a lot of potential, and it just never really arrived at its fullest potential."

Next up was an outlier on this album and an outlier in the context of the whole Max catalogue. "Rascal Houdi" is nearly a parody of punk rock, but with Terry in the band with his bank of keyboards, it's more of a parody of skinny tie new wave. It's a sore thumb on an album that is the formal antithesis of punk rock. Zappa proposed a similar gesture—and probably for many of the same music snob reasons—with "I'm So Cute" from *Sheik Yerbouti*, issued the same year.

"Well, certainly 'Rascal Houdi'... Houdini is an escape artist," explains Pye, on this wonderful succinct, playful lyric. "It's a play on words with Houdini. And like I said before, I liked personal names. I like places with personal names, so I nicknamed this escape artist 'Rascal Houdi.' He was a rascal. He was smoking a joint, that sort of slobbering slovenly teenager at home with his headphones on not paying attention to his parents. But that world he went to was wonderful (laughs). That is 'Rascal Houdi.' The lyrics, I'm sorry I'm so cryptic lyrically, but that's the story."

Fair enough, and it even jives okay with what Dubois said thirty years earlier, in the *NME*: "I created a character based on Houdini; it's a freeform punner kind of seizure pancake mix happening not only in a concert but at home, where he has his headphones and he can retreat. It stays with 'a million vacations,' the idea of escaping."

Back to the present day, Pye recalls, "That's the song, when Max was on tour in England, they would set up a microphone backstage, and Geddy and I would sing the chorus, 'A.O.M.U., actual operating mechanism unknown,' which is certainly what the parents would say about 'Rascal Houdi.' What the hell is this kid doing? (laughs)."

"One time, they're playing the song, and the policeman, the bobbies came on, plainclothes policeman. The bobbies come on the stage and they got to Kim, and they stand between Kim and his mic, telling him to stop. These bobbies... I don't know if it was MI5 or Scotland Yard, but they stopped the concert and had a look. Because that was the time of the IRA bombings, and they'd just had a bomb scare. They told everybody to look under their seats, and then they said okay back to the song—very bizarre."

"Yes, yeah, that was me," admits Kim, asked about the strange vocal on the track, that sounds like none of the three singers on the album. "I was pulling my voice back, like, 'I'm going home, and put my headphones on, wave at my dad.' Ah, Jesus, stupid. That's just one of those stupid... I fuckin' wanna kick my ass so many times during... when I listen to that stuff back. Like, why was I singing it like that? Because that was a good, punky, fast, rock tune. Why didn't I just put it in a key that I could just fuckin' sing high like... Where was the producer telling me, or suggesting to me to do that? You know? If I was producing, if I was myself now, producing that, man, I'd go, 'No, no, no, you are not fucking singing it like that.' We're gonna put it in a key where you're voice is gonna sound rock. Because it was a good, rocking lyric. It was a good thing. As a matter of fact, once it was played for Keith Richards. The Stones were doing some session somewhere, and the engineer had that tune, and he was playing it on the playback, and the Stones were coming in. I guess Keith Richards sat there and listened to it and went, 'Man, that's some really far-out rock 'n' roll' (laughs)."

A Million Vacations ends with a jammy rave-up that hearkens back to the zanier days of the band. "Research (At Beach Resorts)" is a galumphing rocker featuring equal parts Frank Zappa and heavy metal. It's a lumbering and yet schizophrenic blues rocker, that without much effort required or expended becomes the heaviest track on the album, Kim strafing the thing with riffs, one of them a Geronimo riff that would make Soundgarden proud. It's got light and shade and much juvenile humour, with Pye writing true to nature, mentioning Wasaga Beach, which, for those who know Ontario, would quite simply represent the spiritual and sunburned beachhead homeland of this record. The song's roots go way back, but it was the last track recorded for the album.

"No, it's not; it was faux-live," laughs Kim, asked whether the band had recorded it in concert. "We added some audience stuff. That was a fun song to record and I always remember having a fun time playing that; it always used to go over great. Just because of the lyric, 'Take your dinky toys to Barbara; she sells hot dogs at Wasaga Beach.' People around Ontario could seriously relate to that. Even outside the province. When you mention Wasaga Beach, they don't know where Wasaga Beach is, but they know it's a beach, and hot dogs. Lyrically it was one of those early versions of 'I Am a Wild Party' and there's also 'A Million Vacations.' We had those summery things that we do once in a while. We were having a good time recording it and it came pretty quick, probably one of the first couple of takes we did of that tune actually. Just kind of banged it off."

One wonders if The Tragically Hip chalking up smash hits across the country by sprinkling in all manner of proper name Canadian reference... whether Gord Downie and those guys might have picked up that idea from Max.

"I'm not sure," says Kim. "I spoke to Gordon Downie one time and he never mentioned any of that. It's a good... he did give me a good compliment. I've always loved his singing, and I said, 'You know, I just wanna tell you, man, you're such a great lyricist and there's wonderful imagery in your lyrics, but I just love the way you deliver stuff too.' He was very complimentary coming back to me. He goes, 'Man, I think people don't praise you enough for your singing.' So that was a nice compliment from him."

In any event, the closing track on *A Million Vacations*, "Research (At Beach Resorts)," obviously put an exclamation mark to this idea that the record was a concept album—although subtly so, erudite, and then further underscored by the visuals. "Paradise Skies," "Night Flights," "Sun Voices," "Moon Voices," "A Million Vacations," "Look Out," "Let Go the Line"... there's atmosphere, motion, freedom, release. Doesn't that white cover art remind one of Pink Floyd's *The Wall*?

Indeed, both records emerged in 1979 and both were conceptual. Except Max wasn't writing about a rock star disintegrating into madness and isolation. No, like the Canuck goofballs they were, our guys were more concerned about getting in line at the beer store for a 24 of Molson's and heading north outta Toronto to cottage country, first long weekend in May.

So, in summery summation, Max had compromised, they had played ball, bringing to the table a record that could have crossed over, could have done well, and to a certain extent did do well, mostly in Canada but also in the UK, thanks in part to the label's efforts over there.

"That again is one of the links," begins Cameron, explaining the confluence of events that gave Max Webster a decent push in Great Britain. "Because EMI is based in the UK, I dealt with the marketing manager over there, David Munns, who was responsible for all North American repertoire. David was the guy who did the Pink Floyd pig at Battersea Station, that escaped, and then the RAF was called in to knock it down. At that time, for about six or seven years, I reported directly into the A&R department in Los Angeles. So, everything that I got signed was going to at least have an American deal. But because EMI was so internationally oriented, as are British business minds, we took Max to this marketing director, David Munns, played it for him and he really liked it. He knew that the management company was the same as Rush, and had felt, okay, we can get some support here."

"Because a band like this has to be seen," continues Deane, steadfast and dedicated to extolling the quality of Max Webster as a live act. "This isn't going to be getting on the Beeb; it's going to be getting them played and seen, and get them on shows like *The Old Grey Whistle Test* and *Top of the Pops*, which were very important at that time. Vic Wilson had lived in the UK, so he knew the market. He took care of Rush's touring over there, and the decision was made, let's bring Max Webster over there, and as we've talked about, in 1979, EMI in the UK supported a very substantial tour with Rush. Then of course from there, the way the European record business worked back then, anything that would get supported in the UK would certainly get a look-in in other countries. The EMI system was definitely geared that something coming out in the UK that was given a push would at least get released. In those days, because the business was physical, you could just send some British copies over to Germany and Holland and get the ball rolling with the idea that if we got something going at media on continental Europe, then we would take the band over there for a couple dates. We did do a little bit over there in the way of promotion. But it never caught fire."

There were deeper ties with the influential Munns as well. "Yes, David moved here. I talked him into moving here. He lived here for six years, and then he went back to England and eventually became the head of EMI globally. But he lived here for six years. He was part of the marketing team when we had Anthem. Plus, as I say, he and Vic became close friends."

"It is difficult to introduce Max Webster," reads the Anthem press release sent out with *A Million Vacations*. "There is so much going on in their combined musical mind that simple words always seem to fall short. When asked to give this writer some input for a bio, the Max Websters decided this time they would like to introduce themselves. So, I'll simply say that Max Webster is four musicians and one lyricist from Toronto who have gold records in Canada and put on an exceptionally exciting live party every time they perform. The rest is directly from the artists' mouths."

"The theme of escape has been an ominous nervous energy pervading the '60s and '70s. As the '80s approach, who would dare put their foot in the mouth in reply to the following questions:

Escape with what... escape to where? Well, we would! 'A foot in the kitchen, a foot in the door, but the foot in our mouths is so we don't get bored.' This is Max! This is us uninhibited and being ourselves, dealing with our past and our future, today."

"Our today is a new album titled *A Million Vacations*. This album is a consolidation and a catharsis of our histories. There's no better way to dissolve the nervous energy of the past than with the momentum and excitement of a new album, creating a new musical identity. It is an amazing feeling to witness all the variables surrounding this album slowly and surely falling into their rightful places. A confident past coupled with an acute awareness of our potential has been preparing *A Million Vacations* for quite some time. Our expectations in every respect have been reached on this album. We feel our musical diversity and integrity have been projected and protected in every song. Our instinct and insight say that this album should be celebrated. It is a milestone for us and we want to share it with you. We believe it is an appropriate escape!"

"So, from Max Webster, we send you *A Million Vacations*. We hope that soon we'll be able to talk with all of those who have read this greeting and to entertain all those who are about to embark on *A Million Vacations*."

Over to the actual press, smartly summing up *A Million Vacations* for the *NME*, Harry George wrote, "With keyboard player Terry Watkinson chipping in and Gary McCracken (drums) conceiving the 'Vacations' track with Pye, the results are homogeneous yet intriguingly diverse. Neither Kim nor Terry are seminal soloists, but the arrangements thrive on surprise, occasionally resembling the Floyd during their terse *Obscured By Clouds* period. Riffs dissolve imperceptibly into songs, while melodies twist and leap to Dave Myles' bass pulse and McCracken's nifty rolls. Instruments are layered with Abba-like skill."

But what George really wanted to know was, 'Who is Max Webster?' "We just wanted a 'name' name," said Kim. "At the time, there was all the one-word names—Rush, Kiss—and we wanted a Jethro Tull, a Steely Dan, somebody's name. Later we found there was a real Max Webster living really close." Adds Pye, "This guy was so wealthy—he's into horses or something—and he had this small town street named after him. Some kids found out about this and took the sign to Toronto."

Wrote the esteemed Geoff Barton, privileged as he penned this to have Max on his own turf, "*A Million Vacations* initially sounds flat and weak compared to its long-playing predecessors, and you begin to suspect that the band have adopted a restrained, slightly AOR stance in order to gain a touch of that ever-elusive commercial success. But upon repeated plays it becomes obvious that, yes, the familiar quirks and eccentricities are still there. So it is that *A Million Vacations* finally turns out to be a delightfully erratic album, the vinyl equivalent of a fun fair crazy house where you end up climbing steps instead of, as you might've expected, walking down them; when you turn a corner and find yourself walking on the floor slanted at a 45° angle... that sort of thing. Suffice for the moment to say that *A Million Vacations* finds Max Webster in a slightly more laid-back but no less weird mood."

In any event, quite purposefully squaring up to an AOR stance, Max Webster, had something of a hit album on their hands. Out on March 5, the record went gold immediately and platinum by summer (this is in Canada, mind you, and not America), while also rising to No.13 in the Canadian charts. On March 21, Max was nominated for a Juno award in the Most Promising Group of the Year category, as they were in 1978, winning neither time. There were no singles cooked up from *Mutiny*, but *A Million Vacations* generated two, "Let Go the Line" backed with "Moon Voices" and "A Million Vacations" backed with "Night Flights."

Thumping around the UK, Pye Dubois spoke with Geoff Barton about the album's promising performance.

"I think it's true to say that Capitol are pretty hot for the band at the moment. They saw the potential before, but the album we gave them, *Mutiny Up My Sleeve*, was not really something they could easily promote us with, not with tracks like 'Beyond the Moon' and 'Waterline.' Now suddenly they have *A Million Vacations*, something that's a little more accessible and straight-forward and they warmed to it because they want to break this band. *A Million Vacations* just turned out to be... well, less weird. Our next album will probably be totally different to any other and Capitol will probably groan, 'Oh no, they've given us one of those records again.' But we'll keep writing and writing because we're that prolific kind of band. Let them put us into a category. Let them sweat it out. At the moment we're happy that they're happy that they can see that we can come up with the goods. We're not alligators sitting on the toilet in Alberta trying to figure out God's gift to fucking pancake mix; we're just trying to create music and we just use what we got. So there."

LIVE MAGNETIC AIR –
"We delivered the pizza, right?"

Back from their triumphant tour supporting Rush in England through April and May of 1979, and then riding high off of the platinum status of the *A Million Vacations* record in the summer, Kim and the boys were staring at a career setback: the scotching of an expected return to the UK, this time as headliner.

As he explained to *Canadian Musician*'s Mad Stone, "This just doesn't make sense. I think there is more to this than what the band was told as an excuse. We went over to Europe and did great. We did phenomenal. So good that we got asked back. They flipped out over there. The whole thing when we arrived felt great. The interviews were together, everything flowed really nice... By the end of the English tour, when we were ready to go to the continent, they had pencilled in our own tour to come back in October, right? We had it all figured out, all the advertisements were ready to go up and everything and then Capitol US said, 'No. We are not going to give them the money.' Now if we bombed, I could understand. If we just went over there and blew it, they'd say forget it. But we were going over there with our first headline tour and we've sold three times the albums Rush had sold when they did it. The odds are so good for us to break out of Canada and not be so regional. They just say no. So that puts a big question mark over my head. Why were we even signed to them?"

"Max is going to be very, very big in the next two or three years, or it's not going to exist," added Pye, prophetically, perceptively. "It depends on Kim and I. I don't care what anybody says. You can really get screwed up in the head about all these people out there who seem to be against you and do not seem committed toward a goal. But in the end, I think it's the creative people who win out. You just have to stick with it. It was pretty well raw energy and raw innocence and just a healthy attitude toward writing that brought Max to this point. Now, as adult writers, more or less, we've got a different role to play, only because there are different people involved. There's more at stake; there's more risks that weren't there before. We have a responsibility to ourselves, the record company, the manager, and they are appropriate and realistic responsibilities."

"I don't want to put my foot in my mouth, but to me they don't hold a lot of water," continued Dubois, after just listening to Kim grouse about the state of radio in Canada. "I would never feel guilty about bumping out there with another really weird tune. Some people might. Some people might come to grips with those responsibilities and hold to them. Whereas I wouldn't. If the public can't accept what I'm writing now, fine. They'll probably come back to me later when I come up with a tune that fulfils their expectations more or less. I think that's what you have to do—you have to keep writing."

Seconding Kim's frustration with Capitol, Pye added, "They probably don't deal with me more because I may be a little more up-front. I may say yes or no very quickly and I don't think they would understand that. It intimidates them. But I think you have to go by your guts. I think that if you don't go by your instincts in the arts, you have no business being in the arts. Max is in a tough position. Kim is bummed-out and it's appropriate. Again, I'm putting my foot in my mouth, but it's a pretty good band and we've put out four pretty astounding albums for a Canadian band. And to not be more successful is a kick in the nuts."

The short answer as to why Max wasn't on their way back to England for a victory lap is along the lines that Anthem and Rush already knew all too well: it's expensive to tour Europe, and even if the crowds are impressive, it's pretty easy to lose money. Capitol knew that, and Ray Danniels understood it too, having counted beans for Rush. So, it was onto a different adventure for these frost-bitten Canadian boys, namely a live album, issued in October of 1979 after spending the summer and fall touring Canada, supported by the likes of Streetheart, FM, Zon, Teaze, Goddo, The Imps and Wireless.

One wonders what sort of classic for the ages Max Webster might have had on their hands if the powers that be had allowed them a double record (like Rush, twice). Perhaps there'd be a side comprising nothing but "Lily" and "Toronto Tontos," chops afire on a bed of jams? Maybe a pre-studio version of "Battle Scar" plus another chestnut from the band's considerable repertoire of non-LP tracks. A cover of some obscure prog classic from the early '70s? Maybe even a Captain Beefheart tune. After all, The Tubes covered the good Captain on their *Now* record from 1977.

Instead, what we got is an action-packed single record, sampling pretty much equally from the previous four records, plus a disappointing throwaway at 1:21 called "Sarniatown Reggae," over which Kim recites the opening lines to "The Party," a selection curiously not included on the record. Everything's got energy, about half the songs are faster, there's slightly less precision (how could there not be?), and Gary's celebrated tuned toms ring loud and clear. "Lip Service" and "Here Among the Cats" are performed a bit funkier, the latter lighter and more keyboarded, as is this casual rendition of "Waterline." In total, there are eleven tracks that together lean decisively into the heavy side of the band, creating a blue collar hoser rock party perfectly reflected in the Robert Reid-illustrated cover image.

Further to the cover story, the live photography was done by two famed and respected photographers, Philip Kamin and Fin Costello, with the overall design executed by Hugh Syme, celebrated for his iconic visuals for Rush. "No one ever really worked directly with Hugh Syme," recalls Pye. "I think generally he would have the album title. I think that was his process and then he'd just come up with something. I don't think the band really had much of a say whether they liked it or disliked it. Because you didn't have to with Hugh Syme—it was always pretty good." A nice touch was the addition of a couple of Pye quotes as well as the moon motif, but the highlight would have to be Reid's depiction of what constituted a Max crowd—that was us, you who are reading this, and as per Reid's math, that was six hosers to one girl.

Says Tom of illustrator Robert Reid, "He was a kid that came into the office and showed me a bunch of pictures, a bunch of his paintings, and he was a big Max fan. I thought rather than just put another live picture of a band on the cover of a live album, do something that had a sense of art. That was always Pye's view,

Kim's view, Pye's and Kim's view, in the main, probably, backed up by Terry, that there was an artistic element to Max. I'm not using the right words, but there was a sense of this being more than just a rock 'n' roll band. It dressed itself in more interesting stuff that just pushed the boundaries of thoughts and ideas and art along with being a great live band coming off the stage. So, it made sense to me that that's where we'd go."

"It's pretty big, as I remember," continues Tom, about the final painting. "It was on the wall for years in the office in Stouffville. It was four feet across by six feet. It was big, and everybody liked it. As for the Max fans, I'm sure that that was his idea and that we all agreed with it. It's funny, he captured it pretty well, because that was the audience, right down to the hats and stuff. It probably was four to six weeks it took him to do it."

The sensual concept of "live magnetic air" was sent down another cheeky creative pathway as well. "Yeah, we went to a cannery and got 8 oz cans of tomatoes and made up labels for cans of *Live Magnetic Air*, that we used in promotions. I have one sitting here on my desk—lots of fun. It says: 'Max Webster *Live Magnetic Air*, non-toxic, highly volatile,' using those logos. Then on the side it says in quotation marks, '*Live Magnetic Air*. A highly volatile formula extracted from a Max Webster high class curiosity rock 'n' roll performance. This product is especially useful for instant relief. It contains rock 'n' roll additives and gaseous cranial lubricant which guarantees orgasmic stimulation of the central nervous system. Simply place this can in any convenient room, place the new Max Webster *Live Magnetic Air* on your turntable loud'—in bold—'and get ready for instant party. Danger. 1) Keep away from open spark, flame, or the lackadaisical. 2) Product can be very addictive. First aid treatment: If rock 'n' roll frenzy occurs, *A Million Vacations* or *Mutiny Up My Sleeve* is recommended. If symptoms continue, contact your local record dealer for further Max advice. Caution: Contents under extreme pressure. Do not place in public libraries, hospitals, old age homes, or middle-of-the-road stations. May cause terminal hyperactivity. Must be stored in an open environment, preferably on one's desk where it can be handled. This package will feed off human energy.'"

Very little needed to be done to the tapes to bring the record up to snuff. For sure there was some manipulation of crowd noise, and maybe a few vocal tweaks but this was no Kiss *Alive!* situation. Max could execute.

"It was at the Lyric Theatre in Guelph," recalls Gary. "I don't know if the place is there anymore. But we did two nights, Friday and Saturday night, and a sold-out crowd and everything, and we recorded it all, and I thought it ended up being a pretty nice live album. There might be some vocal fixes and stuff, but as far as, again, when you're actually listening to that album, it actually did happen, all that stuff."

Research didn't scare up a Lyric Theatre in Guelph, but there was one in Hamilton. Adding to the confusion, Tom Berry says, "It was either Guelph or Waterloo. I thought it was Kitchener/Waterloo. Kitchener was a really big Max town. I can't remember the name of the room, but I remember it was one of those scary bars to go into. But just packed. We didn't put that in the credits? That was stupid (laughs)."

DJ Steven "Dr. Flippy" Richard confirms that it was in fact both: "*Live Magnetic Air*, I was at Guelph University, Memorial Hall for the recording of half of that album in the front row, the other half of which was recorded somewhere in Kitchener, Ontario. In between tracks I am sure I can hear a friend behind me in the audience yelling, 'Hey Flippy!' trying to get my attention."

So, to sum up, the band would record two shows in one night at the Lyric Theatre in Kitchener, September 13, 1979, and then two shows in one night the following day, at the War Memorial Hall at the University of Guelph. As for the liner notes of the album, the scene of the crime is specified only as "southern Ontario."

In any event, Tom, much like Pye, reminisces fondly about how torrid the band could be live, so they were a natural for the making of a live album. Asked about pinnacle moments, Berry figures, "Well, the Genesis gig, because it was at the CNE. But the Rush New Year's Eve gigs at Maple Leaf Gardens were... they were our gigs. Both bands were our bands, New Year's Eve, and they were sell-outs. Then everybody that was there to see Rush absolutely adored Max, so it was two headliners in terms of audience appeal and stuff. It was CPI supporting the shows, who were hugely supportive of both us the management company and the artists. So those were always fantastic. Those were big concerts, sold-out, with huge parties afterward (laughs), where you found yourself staggering out at 7AM the next morning."

"So those were great," continues Tom, "but so was going to the Knob Hill on a Friday, Saturday night, and being 23, 24, and going out to the innards of Scarborough and with bikers out front and strippers upstairs, the room just packed and sweaty, and the band on stage just on fucking fire. Really, to this day, some of those shows at the Knob Hill are some of the hottest shows I've ever seen. Plus, Max owned Yonge Street for a lot of the '70s. Max was the Toronto band for a couple of years there, when there was the Piccadilly Tube and the Gasworks and the Abbey Road. There were these real rock rooms in downtown Toronto, and Max was the band that brought all the girls out, and all the interesting rockers out."

Dubois also zeroes in on Maple Leaf Gardens as the pinnacle of live achievement for the band. "I always referred to that as Max peaking, those Maple Leaf Gardens kind of years. I remember one where they headlined, Kim wore a white shirt which I found very disconcerting. I remember I had a cerebral collapse during that concert. I don't know what was happening with me, but all of a sudden, I couldn't hear anything except I could hear all the audience singing. What would you call that? A stroke? It was this beautiful... not serendipitous, that's not the word, but there seemed to be a serenity. Because all I could hear was the audience singing. I couldn't hear anything else. It was very weird. It just shows you that I am weird. Then the song ended and I just seemed to drift off. I wasn't daydreaming. I just seemed to drift with the audience singing the song. It was very pretty, very nice. Very, very nice."

"I remember it being a lot of fun," notes Terry Brown, brought back as producer for a Max project, even if it was the quick work of a live album. "I remember one thing specifically, pretty trivial, but I used to smoke Gitanes Lights cigarettes. Mitchell was insisting on having one of my cigarettes. I said, I don't think you should you do this, you've got a record you gotta make. 'Oh, come on.' He had the hardest time vocally on that session we recorded—well, it was live—because he smoked one of my cigarettes, or two of them. But those sessions were fine. We used Guy Charbonneau's black truck, I think. I don't think we did many touch-ups. If memory serves me correct, it was pretty much just live off the stage. The guys were good and they played well. Mitchell is an exemplary player. I think we just did two nights."

The black truck that Terry is referring to there is a Chevy that Charbonneau had retrofitted into a mobile studio called Le Mobile, officially in the album credits as "le Mobile Filtroson Ltée." Further to the credits, Terry is listed as live engineer and mixing engineer, with Tom Berry taking an executive producer credit and the band and Terry taking the regular production credit.

"We always just went right for it," says Gary, of the shows. "It's either good or it wasn't. These were just two, regular 90-minute concerts, and again, we would obviously zero in on certain tunes that we knew were going to be on the record. Then the rest of the time, it was like, we'll just start preparing takes, whatever the best take is, knock 'em out. Okay, Kim, the guitar might be a bit out of tune. Oh, okay, we'll get that fixed up. Little stuff. To my knowledge, if there was any vocal repairs, they were very minimal."

Live Magnetic Air was recorded sober, confirms Gary, as was the norm for Max playing live anyway. "For sure, I know when we played, for starters, no one ever drank on stage. I know that. We always kept it pretty good that way. I am still like that today, right? I like a beer like anybody, but when I'm playing, it's all water, it's all business. Then when I'm not playing, then I'm off work, so to speak. But with Max Webster, same thing. Any drinking and partying or carrying on was always after the gigs. It never got to the point where the band was like hammered (laughs). If there was any excess, it was always on off hours."

In fact, increasing sobriety on the part of Kim, according to Gary, was one of the factors that was gradually leading the band toward break-up. "I'll tell you, at a very crucial point, maybe around '78, Kim quit drinking. He never did smoke pot. Well, he did, when we were twenty. During the professional years, he was just anti-drugs and he used to not be an alcoholic or nothing, but he would have a few beers here and there like everybody. But at one point he decided to quit drinking. Everybody noticed it, but I really noticed it, because I know the guy. Well, he just turned... all of a sudden he started to not hang around with everybody else. Because everybody else was having a drink, a lot of times. Over a period of time, he just ended up being a bit isolated. He didn't want anybody... If you were smoking a joint, he'd get mad and freak out, because he was just career-conscious. He didn't want to tolerate it."

"It was no big deal. He used to smoke Rothmans cigarettes. Eventually he quit that too. He wanted to sing better, so he had to quit. But we'd just sit and smoke cigarettes and black hash and drink beer, and be fucking typical boys from Sarnia, right? Like everybody else. But as I say not ever before playing. That's my big rule, eh? I play better, right? I don't get tired and it's all good. So, you drink your water and have a Coke or whatever, go on and kill and then at the end you can have a beer. Well, for all that time, Kim wouldn't have the beer. Everyone else did have a few beers and a couple of drinks, whatever, but Kim would be, 'Oh, let's get going. I don't wanna hang around here.' So that became... that wasn't a rift per se, but it was just Kim kind of separating himself from the rest of us."

Tom doesn't buy Gary's assertion here at all. "Well, number one, Kim never drugged. So, there's that, and as a drinker, he wasn't a hard drinker. He was, on a Friday night. I don't know whether anybody's brought up Heath Street and when they all lived together, but it was the best party place on the planet. You'd go to a Gasworks show, and everybody, including everybody at the Gasworks show, would go to that Heath Street house and party till the wee hours of the morning. But Kim did not party that hard."

"Well, the road is tough," answers Dave, asked about Kim's known dislike for touring, stone sober or not, the rigors of the road being another contributing factor to Kim eventually wanting to knock it on its ear. "It is tough unless you're traveling first class. Even then it seems tough. It takes part of your soul away, when you're out there. You know, there's all kinds of things you probably don't want to tell people that you did. Whether you're talking about women or you're talking about drugs. When we were out, I have a son, he's in his twenties, and he's talked to me pretty frankly. He was going, 'What drugs did you do, dad?' I said hey, I freebased cocaine. He went really? I said, 'Well, that's what those big road machines ran on, stuff like that.'"

"That doesn't work either," replies Tom to the oft-floated idea that Kim couldn't hack touring, "because Kim has spent his whole life on the road—to this day. So no, if somebody said that to you that's just incorrect. He's a road dog."

"If you have roadies, that makes a big difference," continues Dave. "We had a great road crew (laughs). All those guys went on, it seems; Gary's drum tech, Lorne Wheaton, he became Neil Peart's drum tech. So, all those guys moved up the ladder after us. But with Max, in the beginning, it was really an adventure. At least for me it was. But we had these wonderful songs that we loved to play. We really did. We had, at least in Southwest Ontario, this very appreciative crowd who just wanted to cheer us on. So it wasn't that bad. But when you went out and started to tour in America, then we were opening for whoever we could open for. It was a pretty bizarre and dark thing you go through out there. A very tough thing. I am so glad that I don't have to make money in music. I have a studio at home, I still play jazz—I think everybody ends up playing jazz after a while."

"But Max, the first couple of albums, it was wonderful stuff. We actually had sincere interest from the press and the rest of the musical community. Max was really something. Everybody thought we were really doing something that was different and new and exciting, which did wonders for all of our egos. I tell you, it did wonders for mine. It's a wonder that my wife took me back (laughs). But Max was a wonder, it was a gas. I would not have traded it for anything. I'm sure the rest of the guys would go, sure, well, you didn't have to play on the dumpy gigs in the beginning, and you just jumped on when we were opening for Rush and we were having a good time. But I go, well, that's how it worked out."

Across Canada, the band could pull their own weight, assures Dave. "Sure, well, we were doing 2000-seaters, a thousand, down to 500-seat places. We were not huge by any means, but the promoters could make money with us. We were always looking for something to happen with the records. Of course, we're looking at England, we're in great hands with Ray Danniels, he's got connections everywhere. We have Rush, you can't tour for a bigger act in the world than Rush. Or a bigger band that are that professional and know what they're doing. So, everything was put in place for us, it really was. Everything was lined-up and we all thought that it's going to happen soon. It's gonna happen. Unfortunately it didn't."

"With the live album, again, the conversation was simply, okay, it's time to do another album," says Gary, back to the record at hand, *Live Magnetic Air*. "What do you think about doing a live album? At the time, there was some discussion we could record it for little less money than a studio album. But we were still going to get the same amount of money from the record company for, let's say, $100,000, or maybe between $80,000 and $100,000, although not too sure on these numbers."

To clarify, Gary means from the US, not from Anthem. "Yeah, well, at the time, we were on Anthem Records, but we were getting the money from Capitol." Who, of course, weren't seeing much of a dent made by the Websters in their sphere of concern, the wide expanse of America. So even though we're not exactly talking about some sort of comical situation where the band is coaxing large sums from their in-house label—who is also their manager etc.—the whole business set-up of the band smacked of being just a little too cozy.

"That's correct, and our manager is also the publisher," explains McCracken. "Which is wicked. Of course, we're thinking, we don't know any of this, see? We know that it's the one guy running everything. We know that, but we don't realise at the time how not correct that was. Because you've got three... usually it's three individual people, all representing you in each of those areas. Then when it's time for any negotiating or whatever, the three of them duke it out and you find out about it later, kind of thing. There's always your involvement, but again, back then, it was like, well, obviously whoever's the record company is going to decide in the best interest of himself—not us. The same with the publishing and the same with everything. So back then it was called a three-hat deal. We find out that it's illegal (laughs)."

To management's credit, *Live Magnetic Air* would go gold in Canada, an impressive feat for the band, given that we are essentially talking about re-released material here and not from a monster act, even within the borders of Canada, where tallies concerning certification were one-tenth that of the US. The album actually shipped gold, certifying on its October 22, 1979 release date, even if it never reached platinum. It got to No.17 on the Canadian charts and generated a No.21-charting, gold-certifying single (non-picture sleeve) in "Paradise Skies" backed with "In Context of the Moon," both from the live album.

Three years later, Kim had a litany of regrets over *Live Magnetic Air*. "The label wanted us to record a live album. I kept saying, 'Well, I don't want to record a live album. I take tapes home every night—I don't know anyone who can pull this off, engineer-wise, facility-wise...' Okay, you get drunk at a party in England and your manager talks you into it. You do the thing in a 1700-seater and take them the tapes and they say, 'We want it to sound like 15,000 people!' Sorry, that's impossible. It's funny. I was so dead-set against doing that live album, at that time. I came down with laryngitis for the first time in my life. It was almost as if something inside me didn't want to do this so much, my voice refused when it came down to the wire. Totally kacked. Most of the vocals on that album had to be redone again."

"It was definitely felt by anybody, including our American team, that you had to see and hear this band live to get it," says Deane Cameron, on the rationale for the live album. "So, it became, if you will, a legitimate marketing approach, based on anybody who had seen the band. But live albums traditionally aren't big sellers. If you're dealing with an artist that isn't working on radio because you were more of a live attraction, then why not try that?"

As for issuing *Live Magnetic Air* as *Magnetic Air* in the UK, half live, half studio tracks from the first two records, Deane figures, "We were still trying to break. So, you were trying to get the best of the best combined with the best of what we thought the artist was over there, which is a live attraction. It was a calling card. We just kept trying ideas that we thought made sense hoping that sooner or later it would click. I remember trying to sell the band to all of our countries around the world, but, you have to see them live. I remember one of our guys from Germany and from Australia, who, I think, went to one of the UK dates to see them, because I was constantly pushing, trying to get the EMI world to really step in on this. But it was always, 'You gotta see them live.'"

Boni Johnson from the esteemed but short-lived *Record Review* magazine tried to help the record's prospects stateside, writing in her review, "I've been dosing this Canadian-crazy music for a couple of years, but it's only now that I'm liking (rather than resenting) it. I'm saner because I've stopped struggling and finally admitted to myself that Max Webster music belongs in that rarefied category with yellow cake, double cheeseburgers and *Bewitched* reruns! I gotta have a taste, at regular intervals. Naturally, the uninitiated should approach *Live* with cautious anticipation. On the first or second sampling, it just sounds like goodtime music. Well, maybe it sounds like uncommonly well-played goodtime music. But keep an ear cocked for the landmines. The superbly orchestrated arrangements, the clever turnarounds, the economical solos from guitarist Kim Mitchell and organ master Terry Watkinson, and especially Pye Dubois' evocative nonsense words can turn a good brain to tapioca. Hell, somehow these clowns have got me convinced that side one of *Live Magnetic Air* is among the best live rock tracks that I've heard. And side two ain't exactly pig slop. Sounds ridiculous, huh? Well, bug your local radio station to play the stuff and you can be the judge."

Surprisingly, hometown music newspaper *Music Express* was less kind to the record, although the general point is quite accurate—*Live Magnetic Air* is not a particularly exemplary or explosive live album. "Max Webster's main forte has always been their live act," began the uncredited 5/10 review. "So, it makes sense to attempt to capture that spark with a live album. This they have done with a single-record release that steers clear of being a greatest hits package in that Max Webster have included a few of their more obscure tracks. In a way, this is a mistake. Songs like 'Paradise Skies,' 'Night Flights' and 'Waterline' aren't strong enough to carry the album, which becomes somewhat tedious for a supposed 'live' release. *Live Magnetic Air* is a faithful reproduction of Max Webster in concert but the album lacks that certain spark to raise it above the studio work."

It's true concerning the track listing—not included on the album were renditions of "Toronto Tontos," "High Class in Borrowed Shoes" or the biggest song from *Mutiny Up My Sleeve*, "The Party." Also missing in action was "A Million Vacations," no less than the hit title track from the most recent record.

"Oddly enough, Buffalo, right across the border, turned out to be Max territory," continues Gary, asked where indeed the band did get any love in the US. "We always did well there. We weren't too known in many other places, but we could win them over. There was something about it, right? Even though if you're looking at Max Webster for the first time, pretty weird-looking band, I'll grant that. But once we started playing, we could play, eh? We delivered the pizza, right? You could be in Texas, and it doesn't matter. If no one's ever heard of you or not, once you start letting them know who you are, and they find out that hey, these guys can play, that's what happens. People would just find out that we could play."

Yet given the band's goofy hippie wardrobe, how did the guys not get the hell beaten out of them in places like Texas and all across the south?

"No, actually not. We usually made friends with the biker gangs and stuff as we went along. So no, there was never any problem like that. Because again, once we started playing, there was no... well, just imagine, we're down there, we start doing 'High Class in Borrowed Shoes,' they're not thinking anything other than holy shit, these guys are rockin'. We just proved ourselves through on-the-job training. But, sure, Kim used to get these pyjama things that he'd wear ('I used to buy all that stuff at a place called Willy Wonderful's up in Richmond Hill,' says Mitchell). For a top, instead of sleeves, he just had a portable sleeve you could put on. That was weird at the time. Plus, the funny hat that looked like an umbrella. Because again, he was getting some of the stuff made for him, right?"

Pushing the envelope further, Terry often adopted an effeminate look, underscored with the use of makeup. "Terry just wanted to show that his personality is a little different than a lot of people, and different from Kim," reflects Carla Jensen, Terry's better half. "Rightly so, because Kim formed the band, it was Kim's band, and he wanted to be an individual in this band. But I think all of them did. Terry just had a lot of fun with his wardrobe. I really liked the leopard scarf that he used to wear, and I like that he wore makeup, and I liked that he was androgynous. Lots of people would question, is he gay, is he straight? He liked to be a mystery, and that's the way he showed that side of him without talking about it, because as you know, he certainly doesn't like to talk much or do interviews. He's not a good communicator and I think he feels that, and as a result, doesn't talk much."

Arguably, Kim and Terry weren't portraying radically different characters from each other, partly by virtue of them dressing more flamboyantly than any members of the Max rhythm section... "Well, they were the focus, really," notes Carla. "Because they were the two that wrote the songs and sang the songs, right? So, from the audience point of view, they were the focus of the band, although the others were just as important. But Terry, although he just made it up as he went along, the lab coat was very much a big statement for him, because I think he would have been a scientist if his artistic side wouldn't have been so strong—I think that was a very clear picture into him."

And as we know, in the early '80s, Terry would go back to school and become a medical illustrator, briefly flirting with the idea of completing the architectural studies he had began at University of Toronto, pre-Max. Through the ensuing decades, as things went digital, the medical illustrating career would drop off, just as Watkinson's fine art career became steadily more successful.

"He always loved colours," continues Carla, "you could see that in his stage wear. He may not have told you this, but when he was two, I think, his mom used to find him on the front porch just staring for hours into his box of crayons (laughs), looking at the colours, just transfixed by the colours. Basically, what she did was just leave him to develop that artistic side of himself; she encouraged that. The music really came from him. I think, they had a piano and she played, and I don't remember whether his father played or not. So, he learned to play, but I think the music was really his own endeavour, whereas she was really more encouraging and supportive of the visual arts aspect. So, he was always captured by colour, and I think that played out in a lot of areas of his life."

Besides the memorable visuals, another reason Max was so captivating live, says Gary, is that the band really worked at getting the music to back up the daring theatrics, with Kim known to be a harsh critic post-show. "We used to record ourselves every night. But, I'd say we were all as critical as he was. You know what I mean?

But you'd make your tape and then you'd drive to the next gig. You listen to yourself play, and you go oh, we sped up there, or, oh, this singing was horrible there. So, we were our own worst critics. But Kim was no worse than the rest of us. We were all like that."

Ask if the guys in Rush disseminated any particular pearls of wisdom to them in terms of the music business, McCracken says, "Well I can't say we got much advice. I think we were just happy to be out and getting all the exposure we got from being on their tours. That's where it came from. When you put the two bands side-by-side, they're quite different, right? Then any advice would be business advice. As far as music, we had respect for them and vice versa. They liked our band, we liked them. Neil used to always compliment me on my timing. Like, he always liked that I kept a nice time, the groove going. That's about it. We got to know them quite well as people, as friends. It wasn't all business."

"Rush was the only band I've ever seen that could play in 7/4 in front of a crowd and the crowd liked it," laughs Dave. "Didn't even realise you were in an odd time signature. Which speaks to their musical prowess. Again, us with SRO and Anthem, it was just a magical time. Just a bunch of stuff came together, although it's a shame that it didn't click. It really is. Just because of the common management, I got a close-up look at what happens in the big time. Of course, those guys were always very, very cordial to us. 'Come on our bus!' kind of thing."

I asked Terry Watkinson if there was much concern that all the management attention and brainpower might have been expended on Rush, with little energy left for the baby Rush... "Well, obviously they were going to work with Rush, maybe a little harder than they would with Max. Because Rush had that American appeal, which was not as easy for Max Webster to do. So, they ran with that, but they worked hard for us. They put us on, what? Five or six American tours with Rush? Plus Europe? That was all great experience for us. It's not their fault if we didn't succeed, really."

Pye is pretty emphatic that there was no resentment of Rush. "Absolutely not, I never saw that at all. No, never. We had a great time. They had a gas. They loved Max. They really enjoyed Terry. It was fun. We were the only two bands on that label, and so we became friends, you know?"

Adds Dave on the jewel of the SRO crown, "I remember the guys in Rush used to try to encourage us and say, 'Hey, we used to go out in this little Travelcraft van, and we'd be opening for whoever we could hook up with.' They said you just have to keep pounding and doing it, you know. But when they did it, it was like 1974, and it was a different time. Things were changing in 1979. The '80s were about to come in. Kim, I think his marriage, or his relationship was having trouble too. It's just the road eats people up. It eats them up."

"We were quirky," cautions Dave. "We did interesting things disguised as rock 'n' roll (laughs). It was not your average stuff. So, Lord knows, when we were touring with Rush, there were a lot of times where crowds would yell, 'Fuck off, get off the stage. Rush!' They didn't want to listen to us. I can fully appreciate that Anthem had, or Danniels had, problems trying to get us hooked into America."

As discussed, all the while Pye is on the road with them soaking up an extra body's share of the dollars that were hard to come by. Add this friction to the widening rift between Kim and the rest of the band, and the celebration of crowd communion that was *Live Magnetic Air* begins to look a bit more rose-coloured than what was happening in real life.

"I was shocked that they let me go on tour with them," says Pye. "It wasn't a problem, at least not initially. There was a tour later that I didn't go on. Maybe the last tour, when Kim broke up the band. So, I was just stunned that they would do that. But as I said, it really worked out well for them, because all I would do was write. Absolutely. That was just a gas for me, to be in the dressing room or the tour bus, or on a plane anywhere, and I would just write. Or in the studio. You know, in the studio, I'd be onto the next album."

As we've also stressed, there was subject matter to be had, and no shortage of it across America. One wonders, given the lack of success in the States, given the grind of playing the States, do we therefore find an anger at America in the music of Max partly for that reason?

"No, no, that would only be me," figures Pye. "That's an odd way of saying that, 'mad at America.' That would only be me. Thematically, poetically, lyrically, it would be something that would get into the lyrics. You think about 'America's Veins,' 'Battle Scar,' 'Oh War!'... it's not that I'm... I'm very political, but I hid it well, I think. I remember sometimes getting off the freeway, trying to get gas, and seeing a beautiful colonial house in the South and you get off, and all of a sudden, you get a little closer to the house and you see that there's no screen door and you're in the wrong neighbourhood."

More on the topic comes out in the following excerpt from a Dubois letter to the author, but what also falls out of it, yet again, is just how much Pye thrived on watching Max perform live.

"I am conflicted. I want to 'do good by you.' But I contend your focus must be how great the band was live! Why do you think I tried to never miss a concert? Many Max Webster songs would not exist if I had been off the road or out of the studio. I was a glutton—I wanted it all because I knew I would write, write, write… write for the band, not for me! Yep, years ago, on tour with Max I would drool upon arriving at the venue—so much material for me."

Back to regular conversation, Pye responded to what sort of sick and twisted person would want to see the band over and over again, every night, as Pye pretty much did. "Because I'm sick and twisted (laughs). Haven't you figured that one out yet? With Max, you couldn't… every concert was different. Yeah, they had some off nights, but 'Toronto Tontos' was not the same every night—it just wasn't. And Kim's guitar solo and Gary's drumming, it was just such a treat and just so entertaining—it was really a great band to see live."

Terry Watkinson most definitely remembers being ticked-off about the arguably unnecessary road expense of having Pye there, as well as how it extended beyond the road. "Actually, the situation was that Kim and Pye, of course, worked together all the time on music, and Kim said he wanted Pye to be a paid member of the band, just like everybody else (laughs). We said, are you kidding? We're out there working like dogs every night, traveling all over the place, and he's sitting at home writing lyrics, which he's going to get royalties on. Why should he get a salary? Because we weren't making very much money, right? So that was a little discussion that went on."

"Well, Pye wanted to be on the road," laughs Tom. "We all went, 'Really? Do we really need you?' He'd answer well, look at Procol Harum; that guy's always on the road. If I'm not out there on the road, how am I gonna get inspired for lyrics and stuff? It was just all very odd. It was, how do you handle this? It wasn't like anything else that any of us had dealt with before. There was support from the band, and then lack of support from the band. This week we like Pye and this week we don't understand Pye and this week we don't like Pye. Oh well, we gotta have Pye. So, there was no book written on how to deal with this one, you know? He didn't play guitar and he didn't lift an amplifier. He just travelled around. He wasn't expensive on the road because, Pye just lived like a hermit—he was not one to spend a lot of money. But there was certainly the cost of being in the band and on airplanes or wherever we went."

It's refreshing to see that Deane Cameron—label guy, no less—

could see the value of Pye being on the road, despite there being concerns that, "In certain instances, we were paying for it. Yeah. Not in favour would've been bosses who have to approve tour subsidy. You have to remember, the Max Webster years, I was an A&R guy. I wasn't president of the label yet. So, I thought it was a great idea and I thought we were creating cultural history having a poet/lyricist on the road. To me, this was, oh, we're going to be the new Dylan Thomas here. But the people who had to approve the money... the cost of UK touring is expensive. Back then, it was still ridiculously more expensive than touring the United States or Canada. So those expenses are like, 'Are you sure we can't do without this? Could we put it into another guitar tech or towards the bus?'"

"The issue was with Pye, not us," offers Gary. "We didn't want him to go. There was no issue. Just because you wrote the lyrics doesn't mean you're gonna go on the road with us. It was ridiculous. That was all like that through the band, too. Pye always felt he had some kind of outside influence on the band because he was the lyricist, right? We would think, well fuck, if you didn't... Without Kim singing those lyrics you wouldn't be anything, so quit thinking you're anything more than anybody else. You're just part of the big picture, dude. Then, 'Well, I think I should go on the road with you guys.' Kim goes, 'Well, let's see, we got thirty dates we're gonna play. Let's see, hotel room, hundred bucks. You're gonna need some money, right? You'll need some dough when we're out there. Okay, for you to go on the road and just hang around and be on tour with us and really not do anything, just hang out, it's going to cost so much money, and that's why we're not doing it.' Well, when we did the reunion, we ended up bringing him out anyways. He came out, and we ended up getting him on stage. He did a little five-minute rant on his own, which nobody understood. Not a word of it. But there he is, and so it's like, okay, as long as you're happy, kind of thing. There was a lot of... Max Webster was funny. A lot of appeasement went on, just to keep you happy. Okay, now quit fucking bugging us about this shit."

You couldn't put him to work?

"What, like lifting cables? No, he wasn't that kind of guy; he was a writer. We had guys doing that already. He just went. He just went along, and he would sit there constantly with his notepad writing lyrics. That's what he does. His house must be just wall-to-wall paper. I'm sure it is. I don't know how many millions and millions of words he wrote."

The Bluesmen Revue, with Paul Kersey, third from left.

Music Shoppe promo photo circa 1973. From left to right, Paul Kersey, Mike Tilka, Kim Mitchell and Jim Bruton.

Early days Pye Dubois, in Sarnia, Ontario.
© Scott Feeney.

Paul Kersey, 1976. © Scott Feeney.

Mike Tilka, during the *High Class in Borrowed Shoes* sessions, Toronto Sound. Early 1977. © Scott Feeney.

A relaxed Kim Mitchell, 1976. © Scott Feeney.

Terry, recording *High Class in Borrowed Shoes* at Toronto Sound. Early 1977. © Scott Feeney.

The dream team: Pye and Kim, at Toronto Sound. © Scott Feeney.

With the special backup singer duo of Judy Donnelly (far left) and Carla Jensen (second from right), at Massey Hall, Toronto, June 9, 1977. © Scott Feeney

Announcing the formation of Anthem Records

The New Yorker Theatre, Toronto, March 26, 1977. © Scott Feeney.

Laminate from 1977. Left to right, Mike, Gary, Kim and Terry. © Scott Feeney.

Kim and some "stubbies" (if you're Canadian, you know). © Scott Feeney.

The mad scientist. © Scott Feeney.

Another shot from the New Yorker Theatre show. © Scott Feeney.

An ad from Bigland Advertising congratulating Ray for putting together Anthem.

A classy ad for *High Class in Borrowed Shoes*, including Western Canada tour dates.

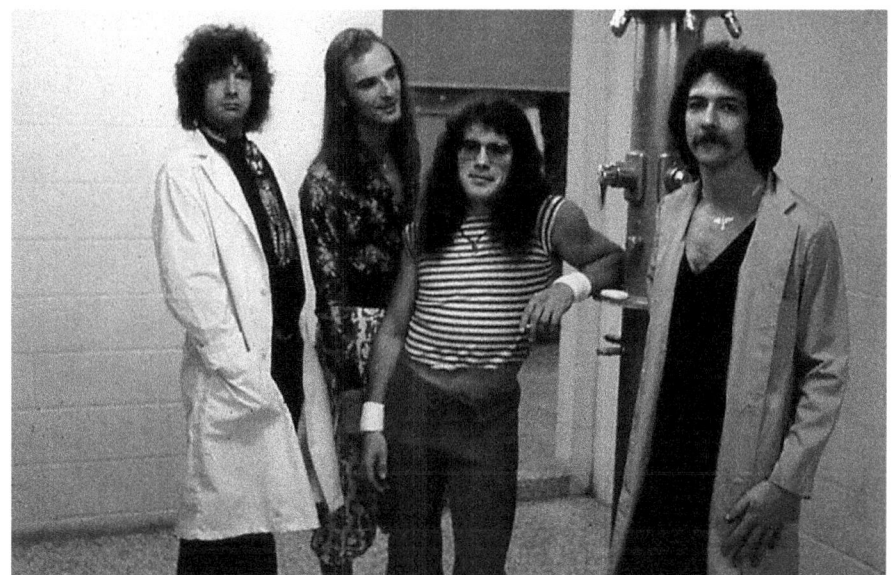

Terry, Kim, Gary and the new guy, Dave Myles, at Centennial College, early 1978. © Scott Feeney.

First page of the *Mutiny Up My Sleeve* label bio, along with a *Mutiny* button and a shirt for the Genesis gig, which also mentions Max.

Kim, Ernie from Sesame Street and new bassist Dave Myles. © Philip Kamin.

Kim, Gary, Terry and Dave, circa 1979, plot their next move. © Philip Kamin.

Kim looking wiry and Gary looking angelic, 1979. © Philip Kamin.

A couple of singles from *A Million Vacations*, along with a breezy button.

Slight variant of esteemed Toronto photographer Philip Kamin's iconic shot used for the inner sleeve of *Live Magnetic Air*. © Philip Kamin.

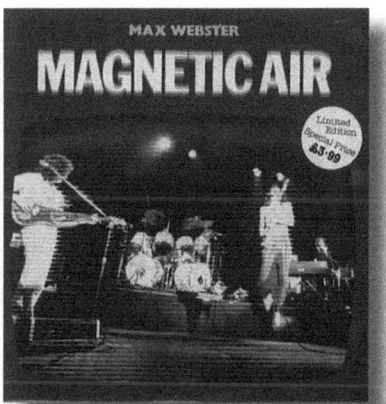
The UK-issue *Magnetic Air* album, along with an ad for it.

Two "battle-scarred" veterans of the Canuck music scene, Kim Mitchell and Geddy Lee. © Philip Kamin.

Terry Watkinson in Max's final days. © Philip Kamin.

The post-*Universal Juveniles*, 1980/1981 Max Webster lineup. Left to right: Steve McMurray, Mike Gingrich, Kim Mitchell, Terry Watkinson and Gary McCracken. Sadly, we lost Steve McMurray in 2014. © Philip Kamin.

1981 promo shot, with Mike and Steve.

Kim plots his future. © Philip Kamin.

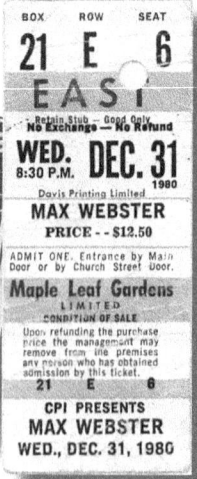

Ad for the new single along with UK dates, plus a ticket stub for one of the band's shows headlining Maple Leaf Gardens in Toronto, the top of the heap, as far as Max Webster's career went.

In the end, there's just Kim, singer of songs. © Scott Feeney.

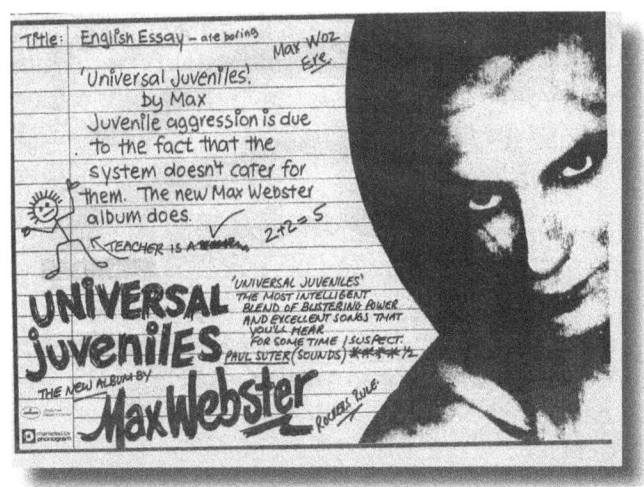

UNIVERSAL JUVENILES –

"Are the drums loud enough for everybody?"

Up the food chain at SRO there was Rush, doing very well indeed as 1979 swung into 1980. *Permanent Waves* found that band moving from strength to strength, and then *Moving Pictures* would mark the band's biggest of all these incremental steps yet—I was gonna talk about smash hits and breaking of the bank, but... no, that previous description is more accurate: Rush had been growing in stature surely and steadily since the nadir that was *Caress of Steel*, and *Moving Pictures* was simply another sweet spot of progress upon building the band into the legendary powerhouse they would be until the end in 2015.

For Max at this time, unfortunately, comparisons made to Rush are embedded in another era and chapter in Rush lore. For what Max Webster were to do, less consciously and deliberately than Rush, is that they were about to plant their *2112* flag. Or Kim was. And not with much joy.

For Rush, the idea was that 1975's *Caress of Steel* marked a drop in everything—record sales, tickets sold, quality—and if Geddy, Alex and Neil were going to flame out, they were going to do it on their own terms, with an album just as lacking in a hit single, with an album more conceptual than the last, with an album not even set in reality.

Max, on the other hand, well, they were coming off of a considerably successful record, as it turned out, a poppy and commercial one, but one that did not set sales records stateside, which is what the guys all felt needed to happen—just so they weren't so God-damned bored with the cycle of life as a working class rock band, more than anything.

Max Webster's *2112* would be called *Universal Juveniles*, and although it's not a half sci-fi concept album about music being banned, the wardrobe was just as silly. More to the point, the *2112*-ness of *Universal Juveniles* was represented by the album's piles and piles of guitars in construction of a near stadium rock sound, but one pocked all over by the bullet holes of quirk. Ergo, just as *2112* was seen as obstinately anti-commercial, *Universal Juveniles* was a guitar-charged slap in the face to a formula that had worked quite well, thank you, just last year.

If one could argue, in broad strokes, that *A Million Vacations* is a Terry Watkinson record (the band's *In Through the Out Door* as it were, to keep it in 1979), with enough of his writing and singing, but also with songs that sound written by him and keyboards everywhere, then *Universal Juveniles* is very much Kim fed up and taking the reins, now that Watkinson had indeed left the band (more on that later). After all Kim's the only Max on the album cover, resplendent superhero in yellow jumpsuit racing through these songs with his guitar. Then if we didn't get the point, well, flip it over and there three more Kims on the back and no one else.

"Yeah, well, you know what?" figures Kim. "At that point, Mike Tilka wasn't in the band, Terry Watkinson wasn't in the band. It wasn't my idea. Nor was the outfit even my idea. That was all the record label. I remember Tom Berry, just recently apologising for that. He goes, 'Man, I'm really sorry we suggested you wear that on the cover,' because he thought the cover was a disaster. I agree with him. I don't remember catching any flack from any of the guys. Dave Stone was a side-man. Gary was always cool; Gary didn't care. He was fine. He was just a mellow dude."

Comments Mike Tilka, still working back at the office all this time, "That whole idea of just Kim on the cover, I kind of know what they were going for. There was no Max Webster. It's not a cover I would have done, although it's interesting, and it obviously worked. Wasn't my decision. I had no part of it. By the time they did *Universal Juveniles*, Terry was in and out of the band. Like he would quit and come back. The band went through so many weird little permutations and combinations, they weren't really a band."

"Well, that was me, Kim and Rodney Bowes," explains Tom on the slapdash sleeve. "Rodney's in Los Angeles today doing graphic art. He was one of my best friends and he was a photographer/graphic artist. I don't know how we got to the point of having just Kim on the cover. I think it was seriously obvious that that's what was going on. But I don't know how that ended up happening. When Kim, Rodney and I sit around, to this day, that jumpsuit always comes up. I cannot remember how we got there, except that Kim was into this flamboyant crazy stage clothing, and somebody obviously said, 'Try this and do a guitar jump,' and Rodney photo'd it. I was the guy that was there from the record company and had the relationship with Rodney and walked us all the way through it, but I can't remember why we went with that."

"Willy fucking Wonderful, that's right!" laughs Tom, with the subject turning to Kim's weird wear. "He'd just go into that place and find the strangest, craziest thing and put it on. Man, some of the times he would come out on stage, you'd go holy shit, man, that is the craziest thing I've ever seen. By the end of the night, after it was all sweated out, it made perfect sense. But when he first hit the stage... I remember the first time he came out with that rain hat, whipped it out of its little circular package and put it on, the audience went absolutely nutty."

Asked what kind of a statement Kim was attempting to make, Tom says, "I think it was just rock 'n' roll. You know, his heroes were the Zappas of the world, people pushing boundaries. Certainly, nobody else was doing anything like that in this neighbourhood, so it's not like he was copying anybody. He was just this wonderful, crazy character that came from small town Ontario, Sarnia, and was just breaking out."

One of the more amusing descriptions of Kim came from *Georgia Straight*'s Tom Harrison: "His thrift store leisure wear, barbecue aprons and harem pantaloons usually cause a remark or two to be passed among Webster audiences, while he has a frame that looks like a collection of chicken bones. The way it snaps around the stage, you'd think they were held in place with rubber bands."

Adds fellow Vancouver presser, Vaughn Palmer, upon witnessing the same Commodore show on the left coast, "Mitchell is the leader, writing most of the music and handling much of the singing. He is also unusual. Here's this long-haired string bean, six-foot-two, 120 pounds, dressed in preposterous tights and vest, looking like he just came from a Salvation Army sale on the planet Saturn. But for an hour or more, he is also the hardest working man in the country, gyrating, cajoling, chording, and flailing—pushing the music, the band and audience farther than either appeared willing to go. Madcap and reckless it was. Max Webster is shaping up as the country's most unusual band, with a combination of outlandish lyrics and superheated rock."

As for the other guys in the band, Berry relates that, "Gary had the classic barrel-chested drummer body, and so it was always abstract watching Gary put anything on that wasn't kind of local Canadian hoser world. Terry is just the most artistic, wonderful character on the planet. Terry just wore everything and anything, including at one time, a codpiece. And Mike for a long time had a white judo suit that he wore a lot."

Was there something new wave about this approach to wardrobe? "No, absolutely not. It definitely wasn't that. And it only came to me years later that Max was probably one of the original Toronto punk bands. I hung out with a lot of original punk bands, at Dave's Bar and all that shit; Rodney was also seriously into that. I don't know if they would agree, but Max could just be vicious coming off the stage in that very punk way. Some of Pye's lyrics would easily qualify. So, I think that they were more one of the original punk bands than they were a skinny tie band, which was one of Terry's looks for a minute-and-a-half."

"If I have to give talks or anything, I use it as, this is exactly what you don't do," laughs graphic designer Rodney Bowes, who goes on to reveal much of the back-story of the *Universal Juveniles* jacket, and in the telling, the psychological state of the band and the office and why the characters therein were about to scatter this way and that.

"This is right in the heyday of punk rock. I was photographing all those bands and doing all that packaging, right? So, I get this gig with Anthem. I'm doing Aerial, Wireless, Zero-One!; did a bunch of bands that they had, right? So, then they put me onto their biggy, Kim. But with Wireless, I did it without the title. I didn't put their name on the cover. Ray freaked out, right? He was like, what the fuck? Who would put out a fuckin' record with no band name on it, right? We did a sticker on the shrink-wrap."

"Anyhow, nevertheless, so when the Max Webster thing came along, Ray was really involved. Hugh Syme had done *High Class in Borrowed Shoes*, and I was actually excited. Because these guys are wonky. They're like, I don't know, Pretty Things meets New York Dolls. They had this strange hybrid of what they looked like, androgynous shit, and I thought this could be great. They were almost like a glam band. You could've done that with them, made it T. Rex-like, although they were more complicated than that. And *Universal Juveniles*? How fabulous is that? What a great launchpad, right? But what happens with record companies, which I always find amazing, the more important the record is, the more they get involved and fuck it up, you know what I mean? You end up doing your best work on some indie band or something they really don't give a shit about. Then they go, 'Oh, whatever, Rodney, just do something.'"

Ergo, we're back to Ray Danniels being involved, by Rodney's own hypothesis, however, because he didn't want to see another Wireless cover!

"There was a feud within the band," continues Rodney, who knows all this because he was best friends with Tom Berry. "I think Max Webster was just about to break up, right? So, there was all this politics. And nobody could go on the cover except for Kim, right? There was a lot of bad blood. But Pye and Kim were bonded at the hip, right? So, Kim wanted Pye on the cover with him and so did Pye. Ray was like, absolutely not. There was a major rift between him and Pye, right? So, then it's, well, what the fuck are we gonna do? We got one guy. Ray said, you gotta make it action-like and all this shit. So, the only idea I basically came up with, I was gonna get this guy to jump off... I had a black background, I had a black covered box with velvet so you couldn't see it. The poor guy got shin splints from it. I made him jump about 2000 times, doing these leaps with his guitar and stuff. Kim shows up, and this is right in the middle of the whole punk rock era. We were very fashion-conscious. We're at my studio at Queen and Broadview. He shows up in this yellow jumpsuit. I couldn't really relate to Max Webster, so I was just like, this is what they do?!"

The ragged hand-written text for band name and record title was a nod to Rodney's punk preoccupation and was one of the areas Rodney had a fair bit of control over, within the process. Additionally,

Rodney "put those lines in the back, those perspective lines, to try to do something, and then we put a flame in his hand to try to make it do something. It was just one of these wanks."

Bowes had actually just won a Juno award for his Battered Wives cover, so he had rolled into Anthem on a high horse. "So now I can make some money," thought Rodney. "Finally. Because I was making nothing. So then, Anthem and Tom, they grabbed me and brought me in. Ray will still introduce me and tell people that this is the guy that did a record cover for me and did not put the band or the record title on the record anywhere except on the spine of the record. Then I go, 'and this is the guy that made me do the worst record cover ever.' Then Ray laughs and goes, 'We're even, right?' Ray would always say to me when I go, 'What the fuck, Ray?' He'd go, 'Dude, I signed Rush and I love Rush. You know I have no taste.'"

Asked how he put the flame in Kim's hand, Rodney says, "How we do it? Oh, after the fact. I took a picture of a burning match, because it's on a black background. Today in Photoshop I could do that in three seconds and make it really great. But I just shot a match. I had a four-by-five camera, shot on a black background, and we went to Colour Image and they swapped that in. But it was one of these things like, you've got shit, you know? Well if I shine it up enough, it'll turn into Shinola."

"Here's what happens," continues Bowes. "Big lesson. I end up stuck with it, right? At the time, that record, because of the Geddy track, that was a great record, actually. For a Max Webster record, that's one of my favourites. What always happens is that when you do something that you hate, and you go, Jesus Christ, it's like Wireless sold one record. So, I was blamed, right? Then I do the worst record cover I've ever done in my life and it sold more records than anything. So, then it's like, 'See Rodney, you don't know what the fuck you're doing.' That's garbage. Stupid. So, covers contribute to maybe 2% of sales—maybe. A lot of my old covers bother me now, obviously. But what happens is that you have a cover, you do it at the time, you love it. Then you hate it a month later. Then you hate it four years and then five years later, and you go, you know what? I like that now. You end up with this love/hate relationship. *Universal Juveniles*, I gotta tell you, is the one that I hated and hated and hated and hated (laughs). Just never, ever embraced."

Rodney went on to do covers for Kim as a solo artist, including the live album, the greatest hits and *Aural Fixations*.

"See here's the thing about Kim," relates Rodney. "This is really important. He said something that I've used forever. Because I always feel that, why the fuck is the head of sales telling me how to design shit? I don't know if I was doing *Universal Juveniles* or another one, where Kim was in the studio and I was, in those days, there was no fax or anything. I kept calling him, saying, I want to come to the studio and show you what I'm doing. Just out of courtesy, and because you're used to the artist contributing, right? It's their jacket in the end, not mine. So, I just want to make sure that I've nailed what their vibe was and how they feel, and their passions. It was amazing, man, I'll never forget this. I was on the phone with him and he said, 'You know what Rodney? Here's the deal.' He said, 'Do you play guitar?' I said no. He said, 'So, how would you feel if I kept calling you and asking you if this is a good riff or that's a bad riff?' I said, 'Ooh, I'd feel like, why are you calling me?' He goes, 'That's exactly how I feel about you calling me.' I said, 'So you...' He says, 'Dude, like everybody who works around me, I don't tell the T-shirt merch guys what to do. Because I don't know anything about it.' He says, 'So I'm just gonna do my guitar and do my vocals, you do the cover, and it'll come together in the end.' He wants nothing to do with it, right? Not out of nastiness. He just said this is not my thing."

"Now Pye on the other hand was all over it," says Bowes. "He was just meticulously involved. Probably because of his loss of power, and Ray dissing him. Feeling insecure, feeling that Kim was gonna abandon him. So, he was not pleasant, on that whole thing."

At this point, Bowes is talking about the inner sleeve, with the lyrics and little monsters, and, tellingly, photos of Pye and Gary and no one else. "Yeah, Pye really controlled that, where all the lyrics were and how it was laid out, his writing and all of that stuff. I just remember it being a major pain in the ass. That was all Pye. That was all delivered to me. Pye was a control freak. I really liked Pye too. He's a very neurotic, vulnerable little dude. Extremely talented. I wasn't displeased with the inner sleeve, but it was really neurotic and overworked. Like that's probably because that was all he was allowed to touch. Such an odd, humourless guy, and just very, very insecure. Brilliant but just... a little mad, you know? I did not enjoy working with Pye. It was just a bad vibe. The whole thing was just fucked. Just a huge disenfranchisement of the band. You know, which I've seen a billion times."

Recalls Pye on the workings of the inner sleeve, "Well, we were at CHUM doing this interview, and this letter came, and I still have the letter, actually. From this kid. All this stuff and all this lettering and these cartoons figures—wonderful! I don't like cartoons, but I was dazzled by this kid's little gift. I responded to him and just said look, if we do a lyric sleeve, you've got to do it. So, this kid just sat down and I told him the only thing I wanted, was I wanted personal handwriting for all the lyrics and then he set all this out and he was just dazzling. It was great, really good. That was it. I don't even remember his name. But then I saw him about fifteen years later at MuchMusic."

Offering more on the inner workings of the office, Rodney explains that "Tom is one of my dearest friends in the whole world and we've been friends for a million years. Tom came in there, and he was really, really into Max Webster. He was totally their guardian saint over Ray. Because Ray's whole thing was Rush. Obviously with the success of Rush and stuff, Tom tried to get involved with that but he was basically eschewed by the band and by Ray. Stick to your shit, right? I don't think they were particularly nice to him with that. Kim and Tom… he has taken Kim the entire way. But he thought Max Webster was the greatest thing in the world."

"But Pye was so pissed-off that he wasn't gonna be on the cover. I've even got shots now, to this day, that when I was poring through all this shit, that I found, where I did portraits of Pye and Kim together. I had no idea whether that was like the original idea for *Universal Juveniles*, if that's what we were gonna do. I don't know whether it went that far. I think that's what Kim and Pye wanted to do, and Ray was like abso-fuckin'-lutely not. All I know is that I've got hundreds of 4" x 5" slides of this jumping shit. And then those portraits of Kim and Pye."

"Ray and Kim… there was weirdness there, right? Possibly some competitive shit going on with those two. Although I always felt things were really good between Max and Rush. Rush is just really, really nice, so they, Geddy and Alex and Neil, I never remember anything bad there. Dissension within Max Webster came from Tom being the bastion of Max Webster, to Ray being lukewarm and not really… Ray didn't get along with Pye, and Kim just dragged Pye along and split everything with him. Almost like an insecurity. Almost like Pye was the Svengali, 'Without me, you're nothing.' So, there was real weirdness there, a strange toxic, love/hate relationship."

Reminded that much of the Ray/Pye division came from Pye not being afraid to ask where the money was going, Bowes agrees, "Yes, big time. Big time. Protecting Kim, who was just like, 'Dude, I'm just a guitar player and a singer. That's all I wanna do,' you know?"

Hugh Syme represented another complication. "Hugh is great. Hugh was a really good friend of mine for years and we still talk every so often. Hugh was a great ideas person. I worked with Hugh on a bunch of different things. The guy is really creative and really fucking technically great at what he does. I think his Max Webster stuff was mainly disappointing, compared to what you see he's done with Megadeth and Rush and all that, which is all very conceptual. Tom and Hugh... Tom was like a newcomer and Hugh was well embedded in there. Hugh would do this shit of not showing anybody anything he was doing, except he'd work with the band. So, the first time Tom or Ray or anybody would see what Hugh was doing for Rush, would be after Rush approved it. There was a lot of that."

Having lived in Chile, London and Toronto and now doing well in Los Angeles, Rodney offers the interesting perspective that one contributing factor to Max not making it in the States has to do with all the baggage of being Canadian.

"Yes, it's unfortunate, but I think so much of it is the Canadian condition. I really try to get my head around it. Like Cowboy Junkies, Blue Rodeo, The Tragically Hip and stuff, you just go why aren't those guys huge in the States, right? You think, was this a conspiracy, that the States were like, 'Fuck you, you're Canadian!'? I think there's that. Plus, Canadians not feeling that they deserve, which comes from that kind of puritanical, almost Calvinist background of like, it's not fair to get a big piece of the pie. 'Yeah, sure, you can fuck me in the ass. Sure, no, no, no, fine, thank you, thank you.' I think that really gets in the way. It was funny, okay? So, I'm twenty something years old, right? I win a Juno, which was absolutely the biggest surprise of my life. What?! Are you kidding me?! I've only done three record covers in my life. This is crazy. Of course all my friends were like, 'That's awesome, good for you. You deserve it.' But I also had a lot of, 'Oh, you think you're so fucking... oh yeah, little whippersnapper. Now you're really something.' I almost felt embarrassed about it. Then I had my fraternity of punk rockers who were like, I sold out."

Just by winning, right. That's the Canadian mentality. It's interesting, isn't it?"

In any event, whether it was signalled by the messaging on the album jacket that Rodney Bowes so entertainingly dismisses, the under-achieving Canadian band known as the baby Rush was indeed about to fold in on itself, having failed to conquer America.

"I was with Max for three years," says Dave Myles, setting the stage for the collapse of Max Webster to come. "In the three years I played with them, we were quite busy. There was a lot going on, and a lot of ego was happening, especially at the end. In the final year of Max, I knew things were gonna blow up. I could see it. The band was coming apart at the seams at that point, it really was. Things changed, people changed, Kim changed, Gary changed, although Gary was just totally supportive. He just wanted this thing to work. Really, anything that would make it work, he supported. But that cover, I only saw it after it was done. Of course, don't shoot me, I'm just the bass player. Stuff gets handed off to other creative people."

"It was mainly between Terry and Kim," relates Myles, as to the main ego battles at this point. "Essentially, it was Kim's music. It was his music. There was a real band thing happening when we did the first couple of albums, but by the time it got to *Universal Juveniles*, Kim was really feeling restricted. We were all encouraged, or we said, well, we should all get a song on the album. I'm not sure that was a good idea. So, we all worked on each other's tunes, and everybody had a tune. I did 'Chalkers,' or at least wrote the bass line, which was a pretty busy bass line, if you think about it. But when I listen to it now, I'm going, I've heard that kind of thing before. I've heard it with other bands, use that kind of groove. Like even today you hear it. Of course it was necessary that we used Pye's lyrics, which was fine, because I didn't have lyrics for it. I'm certainly not a singer. So that was good."

"But when Terry left, I could see what was going to happen, but I wanted to make sure that we were gonna have a good keyboard player, to replace him. I really liked Dave Stone; I really thought he was good. He worked out really well for us. I think we moved out to a bigger sound when we got Dave Stone. But I could tell that this was not going to last."

"It was such a crazy time, because we were gonna break any moment," continues Myles. "We had this following around southwestern Ontario, and we were, stars. We would ride in rented limousines and drink champagnes sometimes. But I was on a per diem of $125 a week. We all were. We were all poor. When we went to England, again on Rush's coattails, I was trying to support my wife back home, and she was pregnant with our first child. Here I was running around England. Again, because we were with SRO and Anthem, and Rush was becoming so huge, we were just along for the ride, kind of deal. At the time I came into Max, I didn't have to do any of the really tough work that they had done. They had already played all the stupid gigs. So, I just went, well, great for me."

"As I said, at the time, my wife and I, we were expecting our first child. And I just made a promise to myself—this is 1979—If I'm not well-off or going somewhere in a year, better than where I am now, I'm leaving. So that's exactly what I did. I ended up recording the album, but I knew I was not going to go out on tour with it. When it was done, of course, at this point, Terry was gone, I think, at that time. I just said to Kim, this is it, I'm getting off. He went okay."

Asked about the curious happenstance of the Kim-only cover, Dave says, "Kim was on his way to being a solo act, like if you look at the front of the album. There it was; that's what it was. It was like, well, we'll do this one more time and see what happens."

The album that was to be the band's fifth and last, *Universal Juveniles*, opens with a flurry of guitar, then drums, and we're into the near heavy metal gallop of "In the World Of Giants." It's almost as if the band is singing 'Hail To England,' in ardent hopes of getting back there so that they could participate as landed aliens within the milieu of the New Wave of British Heavy Metal.

"We had all learned more about rock, how heavy we could make it," says Myles. "It really became this idea that we were growing up as players and artists. Kim in particular is moving forward. He's going, no more of this Mr. Nice Guy; let's make some noise here and get people to notice us. I have to say, playing with Rush taught us a lot too, about 'this is what this is about.' If you're gonna go out and do shows, you gotta get hot or you better go home. You gotta be in their face."

Adds Berry on the subject, "I think that was in response to *A Million Vacations*. It was, okay, that's not going to happen again (laughs). It was a reaction to the softer sounds of *A Million Vacations*. That was a pretty odd record. Things were starting to deteriorate at that point; it was a difficult record, although I think it went gold really fast because of 'Battle Scar' and the hype around that."

Balled up in that is the idea that a "get tough" sound was in fact a different way to try be commercial, to get noticed by getting loud, getting competitive by being faster and more outspoken. After all, look what Kiss did at the time with *Creatures of the Night*, not to mention the bulking up of Budgie and Uriah Heep, but in direct deference to the NWOBHM.

The bonus falling out of material that plays that card is the fact that it has the potential to explode off the stage more so than a "Charmonium," "Night Flights" or "Let Go the Line." "In the World of Giants" is certainly that type of song, a cracking show-starter and a platform for Kim to shoot sparks from his guitar. The track features Rainbow exile Dave Stone on synthesizer and Canuck legend Doug Riley on piano. As for the swirling, triplet-feel guitar intro, that's in fact Kim playing rapid-fire notes in unison with Dave on Oberheim. On the back cover, Terry Watkinson indeed is not listed as a band member... but Pye is! Along with Kim, Dave and Gary.

"What's that word, inchoate?" queries Dubois, asked about the lyric. "It's the anti-corporate, anti-culture... I can see seeds of that in 'In the world of giants, candy stores.' These people are always dangling candies in front of us like we are children. It's just not comfortable. It's like a hangover, and you don't sleep."

Back to the cover, sure, stalwart drummer Gary McCracken is glad to still be part of the band, but the visuals were most definitely sending crossed messaging out about the future of Max Webster. "It was obvious, yeah. There wasn't even a question mark. It was like, oh. (laughs)."

Asked whether the message was that Kim was going solo, Gary figures, "Well it sure looks like it. Again, who was in the band? I'll tell you a little story. We were doing the album, and we had liner notes, and that album was coming out. I had to actually fight to get my picture taken and put on the album. They weren't going to put my picture on it. It was just going to be Kim Mitchell and then the liner notes was a picture of Kim and Pye. Him and Paul Woods, the two of them. But no band guys. I'm going... I didn't know what to think. To be honest with you, I was going, well, fuck, can't you at least put my picture on the damn thing? I ended up getting it on there, but I knew then, okay, I said, I should've quit."

As it turned out, Kim's on the front cover once, Kim is on the back three times, and Pye and Gary get pictures on the inner sleeve, and there's no Dave Myles shot anywhere.

"And it turned out I didn't have to quit, because Kim did it for me," continues Gary. "But see if I would've quit, I would have got my money. I would've had to absorb the losses, the debt. Right? I just said, again, when I agreed to stay on and not quit, I thought I would get the sort of honourable reaction of, okay, I won't quit on you, thing? Okay? We'll try to work this out. But it was just a matter of delaying it until Kim was ready to give it up. It wouldn't matter what I said or did or anything. He was quitting and starting a whole new thing with his own deal. Which, right, fair enough, off you go. For me, apart from losing the money part of it, apart from that, it's like the 11th commandment. Your band will break up. Bands break up. So, no problem, I've done okay on my own. Not as a solo singer guy, but just as a drummer. I got voted on the Top 40 all-time classic rock drummer list at No.32 by Q107's listening audience. I'm going, well, it's cool only in the sense of somebody knows who I am."

"I was the one who was really pushing for Dave Stone," says Dave Myles, on the hiring of Ritchie Blackmore kicking post Stone, actually a Torontonian, first making waves with art rockers Symphonic Slam. "We were looking for a keyboard player, and I listened to him play in Toronto somewhere. I said, this guy is the guy; this guy's got the chops and he did. He could play and he could do the songs justice. He really could. Very shortly after we worked him into the band, we taped a show for *The New Music*, somewhere north of Orillia. We were hot that night. It was really, really hot. I don't know what they did with the tapes. You can see parts of it on YouTube. It was the passing of the guard. Terry just said I'm not doing this with you anymore, Kim. It's sad when stuff like that happens, because the two of them were... I'm sure are still really good friends. That's when we look at Rush and I go, wow, that's amazing that those guys were able to do that and stay together (laughs). Because they were out there in the corner doing their own little thing and not compromising at all anywhere. As Neil would say, if you don't like it, tough."

"My dad is a great piano player, and went through the Conservatory," explained Stone, by way of introduction, speaking with Jeff Cramer. "So, they started me in the Conservatory when I was five years old. It was the greatest thing that ever happened to me. I got all that technical ability. The old 'practice an hour a day;' next thing you know, your hands can do anything you can think of if you want to play, you know? I knew at an early age that my father was improvising when he was the lead. He would do that for jazz standards and things like that. But basically he took the theory of music and applied it to his job, like all jazz musicians. So, I just couldn't wait to start doing that myself, improvising, taking the form of music and playing around with it. Getting off the curriculum from the Conservatory and following your own path of what you want to learn."

"I got the call from SRO that they would love me to play in Max Webster," continues Dave as his stay in England was falling apart due to contractual and immigration issues. "I just thought, oh, this would be great. I'll go back home to Canada, I'll play in a top Canadian rock band, we'll get into an album right away, I'm gonna do the first national simulcast. Again, I thought Max Webster was this great band. All the guys were really talented there—great drummer, great guitar player, that kind of thing. So, I just told Ronnie (James Dio), I said, 'Listen, I gotta go home. I'm gonna go play with my hometown boys.' I just packed up and joined Max Webster. Literally the end of my international career was that day."

So, Dave joins Max... "Yeah, which was great at the beginning. But what I didn't realise was what a horrible, horrible contract Mitchell had with Ray Danniels and Vic Wilson over at SRO at Anthem Records. It was just a nightmare contract. I think by that time, Max Webster had five golds, two Canadian platinums. I thought they were considered a, say, top five Canadian band at the time—and we're broke. We're freakin' broke. I can make money on the side doing session work and all that, and I was comfortable. I'm fine. I had money from Blackmore too. But Kim, he's living in a crappy little house down on east Broadview there. He can't even make his mortgage payments. Kim and I lived in the same neighbourhood near The Beaches, and so we would stop at a hotel and chug a beer and talk a bit. He started slinging all this stuff to me and I didn't realise, 'Oh, this is just a horror story. I just made a huge mistake.' Thankfully, I didn't sign anything long-term with those guys."

"By then, the band, for all intents and purposes, was dead," offers Dave. "Ray Danniels got the guys from Rush to work with us on a couple of tunes. That was a lot of fun. No one told us what to do in the studio, so Kim and I got to do what we wanted to do. We were working out of Phase One, and it's also when I got to work with the legend Jack Richardson. Jack Richardson was the chief engineer, and then the other guy was Dave Greene—I'm sure these guys are legends. I know Jack's dead now, but I know Dave Greene went on to do major international things. It was totally professional. The sound was great. Those guys totally knew what they were doing, and I wasn't under any specific... I wasn't under any contract, so I thought what the hell? I started working on B.B. Gabor's second album and I was gigging again, making sure I'm solid in the Toronto scene."

"I would go and do all the session work at Phase One at 2:00 in the morning. After I'd play, I'd just go play somewhere and then drive to Phase One at 3:00 in the morning 'cause that was the only time I was available, and they would be there. So, I did that for two weeks. Then I guess they tried using Doug Riley on some of the stuff, the Dr. Music guy? They weren't happy with some of the stuff he was doing. So, I'm pretty sure I pretty well replaced everything. I just basically did all that stuff I wanted to do when I was rehearsing with Kim three months before that. We did one national tour, before we got to the album stage, and that's when Kim and I got to work on the stuff that's on the album. So then when they put me back in the studio, Kim and I went back and did all the stuff that we were recently doing three months before that. So, that was cool."

Once having passed through Max, Stone says, "That's when I realised, it's like, this business sucks. I was never a major songwriter. I work more on songwriting now than I did back then. I consider myself a player. I just thought I'm in my middle-late twenties now, and getting burnt-out on the whole thing, and maybe I'll just try and find a different kind of lifestyle. My wife got offered a posting in Vancouver with Canadian Press. She was a graduate journalist. She had a career, too. So, 'cause I'd been touring since I was eighteen across the country, and Vancouver's such an amazing city, any chance to move out to Vancouver, Christ, just blow Toronto off and move to Vancouver. I did a few albums out here, and then I just basically packed it in after that. I did Doucette's third album, Prism's third album. I got asked to play with Loverboy."

Which Stone turned down, calling it a "six-million-dollar mistake." Then? "Played country and western. Lots of money in that. Spent the next ten years playing live, playing country and western, did some session work. I don't know. It's all pretty hazy. I became a heavy-time drug addict then, too. In Vancouver, the drugs are everywhere, and they're so cheap, it's crazy. Toronto was pretty... had probably respect then for rampant drug use. A lot of the guys I worked with in Toronto are dead. So, drugs were a real problem back then. For me as much as the next guy. I'm 60 years old, and largely because of drugs and rock 'n' roll, I'm pretty burnt-out. I just want the rest of my life to go okay, and that's basically it."

On that note, back to the record; next up on *Universal Juveniles* is another hard rocker, in fact one of the catalogue's heaviest songs. "Check" is a party-hardy stadium rocker drenched in distorted guitar, but for a song this guitar-charged, it's actually quite cheerful.

"I had no problem stealing words and phrases from everyday life and turning them into lyrics," chuckles Pye. "I can't tell you how many concerts I heard, at the sound check, 'Check, check!' I just thought that was great (laughs). This is what we do and that's that."

"Those tunes were all played for six months," adds Gary. "Those were all in the show, especially 'In the World of Giants' and 'Check.' Yeah, 'Check' was our opening song, right? In the studio, 'Check' was something like second take. We just went in, here's how it goes, play it. You know, it was very obvious when we went to do *Universal Juveniles*, how it was, holy shit, there's all this heavy overloaded guitar. Even I noticed it. But I wasn't complaining. I was going okay, that's the way you want to go, fine. Are the drums loud enough for everybody?"

As for Kim's conjecture on why there were so many crunching rock numbers like "Check" on the record, he figures, "Well, it's because that was the exit of Terry, and into more of an aggressive sound that I was always wanting. Dave Stone was the keyboard player on that. We stole him from Rainbow, Ritchie Blackmore's Rainbow. Yeah, fuck him, eh? Sitting in a pub next to him, and he goes, Ritchie Blackmore, we're doing some dates, and all he says to me is, 'You know what I don't like about you?' That's what he said! I go what? He goes, 'You play a Gibson Les Paul. You should go buy a Strat.' So, the next day I went and bought a Strat, and then we stole his keyboard player (laughs). But yeah, it was just the stuff I was writing at the time. 'In the World of Giants,' 'Drive and Desire.' I used to like some of that stuff. The album's drum sound I never was a fan of. There was a thing that Jack Richardson and his engineer Dave Greene used to go for, with the dumpy snare, and I just thought it wasn't right for the record. To this day, God bless Jack, but I just thought this is the wrong drum sound. You should've just left the drums as natural as possible. Because I thought they were way more aggressive. Anyway, it ended up being okay."

Deane Cameron has an interesting perspective on why the guitar charge of *Universal Juveniles* might not have been as much of a commercial suicide, on paper, than one might conjecture, even if his timelines are, with the Maiden reference, a little tight, and with the Helix reference, a little loose!

"I'm speaking on the artist's behalf. I will say that there was a developing frustration of, what will it take to get to international markets, combined with what will it take to keep our fans interested here in Canada? By the time that album was made, there was a much stronger move made towards a heavier sound at radio. I think in and around there was when I signed a band from Kitchener called Helix, which was a pretty heavy band, song-oriented. So, it was a combination of everybody trying to tell you what it takes to break in America, and there was a move at that point to a slightly heavier sound. So, it was a combination of those three things, that this would be good for the band. I'm not saying that Kim or the band, or Pye, chased anything to happen. I think that would be wrong to put it that way. But I think once you get exposed to the global market, you can sometimes be influenced by what's going on in bigger markets too—what would be the way to help this break?"

"There was the whole Maiden factor," continues Deane. "That was in everybody's life. But for whatever reason, we prefer things that are a little more melodic. Nickelback, AC/DC... even The Sheepdogs right now—it's much more psychedelic and melodic than really heavy. I know Maiden was a huge influence on the company. The one thing I was trying to say to people is, come on, we have Kraftwerk, and we turned Kraftwerk into something commercial. Even though Max Webster and Kraftwerk were nothing alike musically, there was the notion that we were taking something like Kraftwerk and making it successful, at least around Europe and Australia. Like Max, we never broke them in America either."

Kim's solo on "Check" is quintessential Kim Mitchell, a mix of chops, humour, and in this particular case, an amusing blend of Frank Zappa, Robert Fripp and proto-'80s heavy metal guitar hero. Kim will usually take the listener on a little trip, a little treasure hunt and that's most definitely the case here, stringing you along to the point where you can almost envision bits of silly string shot about the cold Canuck motel room about to be abandoned in a hurry. Structurally, the verses are dispensed with fast, and all told, there was a bit of a battle with the label in terms of getting the song on the album. Kim put his foot down, however, arguing that the song had been going over a storm live.

"Zappa was a really big deal to him," relates Dave Myles. "Really big deal, and in fact you can hear that in a lot of the lines that Kim would play and that Kim and Terry would play in unison. Those are Zappa-like for sure. When we were on the road and we would listen to stuff that wasn't our own, I was a big fan of Weather Report, as was Gary and as was Kim. We used to listen to Weather Report for some reason, which was pretty crazy. And one time we were in Chicago playing a festival, and who do we get into the elevator with, but Joe Zawinul and Wayne Shorter. It was like, oh my God. I didn't even realise who they were. And we got out of the elevator and Gary says, 'You know who that was?' They were playing the same music festival we were."

"I do like *Universal Juveniles*," continues Kim. "I like the memories of the recording experience. The sound of the recording isn't that great; it's dated now, so it's hard for me to listen to."

Comparing Terry Brown versus Jack Richardson, Kim says that

"Terry Brown was more cerebral, more into getting things a little more perfect. Jack Richardson was more into the song, just the performance. I think that's a difference you can spot between Rush and the Guess Who, even. Jack Richardson's thing with The Guess Who, some of those songs are far from perfect. You hear tempos speeding up and slowing down, that kind of shit. But it's the song; there's a performance going on. Terry Brown, Rush, it's more like maths rock. This has to be in time, this has to be like that. That was a difference I found working with him."

Speaking to Elliot Lefko back in '81, Kim had framed the collaboration with Jack this way. "Everything was so crazy; we went into the studio as a three-piece band and just locked right in. It was such a great feeling. I really feel we captured some good stuff. Whatever people might say about him, he's still a great producer. If anything, what people might fault him for is that he just lands into the wrong things. He does such a wide variety of music, from classical to jazz to everything. We didn't know if he'd take the production gig with us. We didn't think that, in his eyes, we'd be marketable enough for him to make some money off of us. But he grabbed it right away. We played him the pre-production tunes and he liked them."

"Jack was wonderful," adds Dave Myles. "Bless his heart. He was a great guy. He says, 'Hey, I can rock with this; let's get it on.' But no, Jack was a wonderful guy. And what a history this guy's got. He knew… he brought in his guy that he liked to have mixing, and at one point, I don't know if it was Gary's idea or their idea, but he wanted a deeper bass drum. I don't know whether they put a piezo trigger on the drum, but they ran it through a low sine wave generator, and loaded in maybe eighty cycles, forty cycles on the bass drum, rather than do it with EQ—they actually gave it an electronic low end that wasn't actually there."

As for loading up the record with all these rockers like "Check," Dave says, "We were looking, really, at trying to have something that we could use live that would support us, that we could go on tour with. So, a lot of the tunes, it was often we thought about whether the tune was going to make it in a live performance. Whereas when we did *Mutiny Up My Sleeve*, we did… what was the tune? It was the quirky, 'It's morning in the sun.' I mean, that song is not going to work live (laughs). But in the studio, we did it. For example, that song was totally spontaneous. Let's do this and see what happens. Terry Brown just went, 'Are you guys kidding? Okay, roll tape, let's go.'"

"April in Toledo" was one of the quieter compositions on the record, but it was still worlds more punchy and rhythmic than the sum total of *A Million Vacations*. It's almost a hard rock funk but sweetened by a melodic chorus switched over to a "snare on one and three" beat from Gary. Kim turns in an exotic guitar solo on this one that evokes both the blues and fusion. Notes Gary about this magic moment to the thing, "'April in Toledo' has double bass, although you can't hear it very good. But they're in there rumbling away. Then on any other things, there are little drum licks with the double bass in there, combinations. But there's no real meat-grinder double bass anywhere in the catalogue."

"'April in Toledo' was another one of my favourite tunes," adds Dave Myles. "Kim came up with so many great hooks. But the way Kim had to try and deliver the 'April in Toledo' lyrics is like... nobody does that. No one does stuff like that. That was Pye! That made Max the quirky cult band that it was. People thought it was really something bizarre. I guess knowing Paul from so long ago, and seeing him before he became who he is, it was like, okay, these are crazy lyrics but I know who you are. Pye would go, 'What do you think it means?' That was his whole thing. It was the real creative stuff is when you get to fill in the blanks, when you make it into something that's more than what it originally is."

"Great tune. I love that song, love the guitar work," figures Dubois. "The guitar work is fabulous in that song. You want me to interpret that? 'Hiding Out In Lake Louise.' Is it a true story? It can or can't be a true story. It's obviously about somebody I know who is in Lake Louise hiding out, or, am I hiding out in Lake Louise? Something has happened. Something has gone down. There might've been a split, like a personal relationship."

As for the seemingly incongruous "April in Toledo" title, the postal code for Lake Louise turns out to be T0L 1E0. That's some nice wordplay, as is the use of the name April, which could refer to the month or the female protagonist of the story.

"Let me see, I think that one was older," reflects Kim. "I think a lot of this stuff was written and was laying around. We'd bring it to rehearsal and it wouldn't work a certain way. With this new band I thought, well, this could be nice. The 'April in Toledo' guitar solo I remember was with a really crappy Electro Harmonix. It was an early synth guitar, and it was just a pedal you plugged into, and you'd move these things, and it would just like go all stupid and wouldn't work. You had to be really touchy with it. You'd get a sting to it, and you couldn't even go near the pedal, with a cord moving or anything. So, I remember that being fun. I loved the lyric, and I loved the chorus lyric in that. That was one of my favourite Max Webster lyrics: 'I'll run, I'll run to Niagara, I'll cry, I'll cry in the dark.' Yeah, I always remember singing that and going, geez, this is nice singing it."

Next is "Juveniles Don't Stop," which turned out to be the closest thing to a title track, after "Chalkers" got renamed from its working title, "Universal Juveniles." After the "April in Toledo" respite, the band is back to a wall of hard rock sound. However, with this production picture and the song's synthesizer shadings, not to mention a nod to boogie, what we end up with instead is a slightly oppressive party rocker—yes, that would be a contradiction in terms.

Closing side one of the original vinyl is one of the great Max classics, "Battle Scar," a monster epic that is the band's slow—62 beats-per-minute slow—and steamy panorama, much like Rush and their "Tom Sawyer" set piece. Look who's along for the doomful slog underneath Sahara stars—why it's Rush, with every bit of Geddy, Alex and Neil on board to jam the song out with the Max pack.

"That was actually hard to set up technically," begins Kim, on a demanding track that is a concert highlight to this day, as part of the man's solo set. "It was a case of getting enough microphones, getting a console large enough, enough channels; all the logistics of that were kind of hard to work out technically. But the idea was that Neil would play drums, every night, to our set. He would be behind a scrim and playing drums. He said, 'Man, we really gotta record "Battle Scar" together; we should do something like that.' We always thought, okay, yeah, right, whatever. So, when we went in to do the album, they were like, 'Are you guys recording "Battle Scar?"' We said 'yeah.' 'Well, can we join you?' So, it was holy fuck, okay. So, we did it all live off the floor, two bands just fuckin' ploughing, two drummers; man, it was fun. No headphones, nothing, just amps in the room, bleahhh! Let's go (laughs). It was pretty powerful. It sounded like six Harley Davidsons in the studio all revving up. It was just like, man oh man."

Rodney Bowes, adds to Kim's comment about Neil shadowing Gary in concert... "I loved Neil Peart. Those guys are really the nicest men in the world. There's another example of a band where there's just a real brotherhood there, between those three guys. They're all absolutely lovely, lovely people, like U2 are—they're real. So, what they would do is they would have Max Webster on the stage and they would have the black curtain with all the huge Rush set-up behind it. Neil used to warm up, not amplified, but right behind Gary, right behind the fucking black curtain. What he would do is fuck with Gary, right? So, he'd speed up the beat and he'd double-time it and he would play along. But he would just do all of what Gary does. It was like, he used to have to go into this like Gary McCracken world and count out loud, because... and then afterwards, Neil would have a huge smile and he goes, 'Hey, good, I only made you fall twice.' Gary says, 'You gotta stop doing that!' He goes, 'Nope. It's good for you.'"

"To this day I'm always correcting people about that song we did with Rush," continues Kim. "It's like, no, Rush wanted to do it with us. They asked us—they came down to our studio. There is a lot to be said about the creative process, and how some of it came from Rush, and how a lot of their ideas came from us. There was a point when we were on the road with Rush and they started dressing like us, and their manager flew down and gave them shit. But really, Alex started going on stage with helmets on and big flight suits; it was getting crazy. They took a lot of their attitude from Pye and I."

"Oh yeah, I was there for almost everything in a recording situation, and that one was pretty wonderful," laughs Pye, who, if you know Pye, wouldn't miss a rock summit like this for anything in the world. "What can you say? Max was playing this song live. I think that's why Rush said absolutely, 'What do you think about "Battle Scar?"' 'Yeah!' Because they loved the song. You technically don't want to put 24 tracks together, and the electricians did that. A great tune. You know it's going to be heavy, it's going to be loud. I have a vague memory of how they set up, on the soundstage. They played together. There wasn't a lot of, 'Okay, Geddy, you go do your part,' and the band would sit there waiting for Geddy to do his part. It was like, set up, 'Okay guys, play the song.' Live off the floor."

"Battle Scar" was definitely an early Max number, but then again, concerning *Universal Juveniles* as a whole, "These songs weren't just written," says Pye, "and then the next week we would go into the studio and record them. Some of these songs had been around awhile before. It wasn't, 'Oh, Kim, we have to do an album. Let's start to write.' We were always writing. We weren't for want of material. 'Oh, we gotta sit down; we need songs.' No, we had songs. We just always had songs."

"It's just a very simple anti-American song," answers Pye, asked about the lyric. "Uncle Sam's time is only to grease the wheel. I think that's self-explanatory. Okay, forgive me—for me it's self-explanatory. Uncle Sam is the United States, and 'Uncle Sam's time is only a greased wheel...' I don't know how you used the term, a greased wheel, but you've heard people say grease the wheel? You grease the palm, yeah, grease the wheels of commerce—it's blatantly anti-American. 'Bust the busters, screw the feeders,' well, why bust me if I have dope? Let's go bust them. You know? You know, the people that feeds me this cultural crap, they're the ones that need to be fed. etc. I mean, don't be busting me!"

"I had pretty much equal opportunity on all of them to blow," says Gary, asked about most active drum performances through the catalogue, "but when you look at 'Battle Scar,' right, you look at doing that thing with Neil, that's a good drum show right there (laughs). If you're going to consider anything a drum tour de force, there it is. That was exciting and it was historical, for the most part, more than exciting. Because nobody else has ever sat down and double drummed with Neil, on a song. He's only considered the best guy on the planet. So, I feel pretty good being the one guy that did jam with him, and we got it on a record, right? First time two bands ever tried to record with two 24-track machines, ever. Jack Richardson brought in two 24-track recording machines and linked them up so they would be in sync. Then they recorded one band on the one machine, and they recorded the other band on the other, and it was unbelievable. We recorded 'Battle Scar' all day. We did fifteen or sixteen takes. It was live. That's another big thing—all our stuff was done live. It's all live off the floor. So, it wasn't like Pro Tools or all computerised. It's all real stuff. I think that's one of the charming parts of the band. But Jack was a great guy. His whole thing was trying to make us big-sounding. He was known for that wall-of-sound kind of thing. It turned out good. We needed a producer and we were in good hands with Jack."

Prompted to indulge in a little comparison with Neil along the lines of Max Webster = baby Rush or Gary = baby Neil, McCracken figures, "Yep, it's pretty funny that way. Just being in the same sentence as Neil, that's insane. Let alone somebody thinking that maybe you play better than him. It wouldn't be me saying that, but there are people that really like my style. People tell me that I'm a musical drummer, I'm a musical guy. Again, when you're in Rush, you've got three people. So, you're going to have more room with the drums. When you're in a band like Max Webster, you have to always remember that there is that fourth guy who has quite a lot to do with it. There's the keys and the guitar but there's always that extra, just that fourth dimension. So, when you're playing drums you have to click to that format. As opposed to with the trio, you've got more freedom to go loony. Like Neil couldn't play the way he plays on some of those tunes... he couldn't play like that in a normal band. Normal bands, you just have guys play normal drums (laughs), with a good singer. But when you play like Neil, it's that environment in Rush, you have to be in Rush to play that way. Max Webster was quite similar in that way, that there's a certain way to play."

To prepare for the "Battle Scar" session, two weeks prior, Gary had driven out to Neil's rural home in Beamsville, Ontario where, in Neil's drum room over his garage, they worked out some of the parts that they would unleash upon their unsuspecting bandmates, some parts unison, some diverging. Neil recalls driving to the session days later in his black Ferrari 308 GTS and pulling up to Phase One just as an epic thunderstorm struck.

Dave Myles has fond memories of the "Battle Scar" session as well. "You know, here I am, I travelled with Geddy, we come into the studio, and from like previous terrors of the tape, I thought I'm not going to get into a bass lick shootout with Geddy Lee. I'm just not gonna do it. I know when to pick my battles. So, I thought, I'm gonna do the background thing and I'll let Geddy blow. That was a good thing."

"'Battle Scar,' the thing with Rush was genius," comments Mike Tilka, Myles' predecessor. "It was wonderful that the guys in Rush did it. It became a huge FM hit. I personally don't think it's much of a song, but it's neat. But the recording is amazing."

"We had the tune together already, without Rush coming in," continues Myles, asked if for such an occasion, the guys figured that they would turn it into a party atmosphere. "No, when you're recording like that, you don't party. You're straight and you're clean and you're there to get the best you can get down on tape. Of course, those guys are confident professionals too. There wasn't a party, with that tune. Man, I remember when we were listening to the playback, after putting the backing tracks down, came back in and listened to Geddy wailing, wow, like really great."

From a business standpoint, it was pretty easy getting the bands together, says Deane Cameron. "That was all done at the Anthem/ SRO level, because both bands were there for management. So, my recollection was that it almost popped up out of nowhere (laughs). I heard what was going to happen. But it's really handy when you have both acts with the same management company."

Capitol was breathing a collective sigh of relief that there was a "Battle Scar." After all, no one felt there was much of a single otherwise buried within the murk of *Universal Juveniles*. "Yep. Let's just say we used that as much as we absolutely could at the time," laughs Deane. "When the record was delivered, there were opinions from the US. For here, everybody pretty well felt, we could probably get by with this. Everyone has one of those creative albums that aren't extraordinarily commercial. But I was concerned all around, and I certainly had a healthy round of scepticism and disappointment from the US. Even though at that point there wasn't necessarily a full commitment to release it. But I was living in hope."

Even in the hiring of Jack Richardson to produce the album, there was a hint of international politics to contend with. "I think there was some suggestions from the American label," says Deane. "Ray and I talked about it. Jack had a track record, and there was the influence that he had produced a lot of big records. Plus, he had a great studio—that was always one of the great attractions. And it just seemed like a good, creative idea. Oddly enough, you'd get from our American label, well geez, he's Australian and you're an Australian band. Or he's Canadian and you're a Canadian band. I think the actual suggestion came on the record company side, from my boss, Rupert Perry. But I knew Jack, and shortly after that, I tried getting him to do an Alfie Zappacosta record, and then he got very sick."

Geddy Lee would, not long after "Battle Scar," find himself a conduit once again for a Pye Dubois lyric. Rush's *Moving Pictures* album, issued February 12, 1981, would open with what would become a huge Rush classic called "Tom Sawyer," music by Lee and Lifeson, lyrics by Dubois and Peart, who—credit where credit is due—got to learn all too well what Kim went through wrestling Pye's wonderwall of words into songful form.

"Oh, I think that we do the song injustice if we started to pick it apart," demurs Pye. "It doesn't make any sense. It was just two people painting a picture, wasn't it? The original was 'Louie the Lawyer' (note: I clarified with Pye that it was not, as often reported, 'Louie the Warrior'), 60, 70 lines or something, very typical of what you see here (shows journals). I would start writing and I had ten pages of foolscap. I liked this line, and I would write it a different way, very modular. That was when we were in the studio doing 'Battle Scar,' and setting up all the equipment, 24 tracks and all that.

It was Rush and Max just hanging out, doing some recording."

"So typically, there was some down time," continues Pye, "and Neil goes, 'What are you doing?' 'I'm writing this "Louie the Lawyer."' 'What's that?' I read him some of it. There was a lot of editing before I gave Neil a new 'Louie the Lawyer' version. I didn't just give him the pages. If memory serves me correct, I scanned the pages I had and just took out lines that I liked and put them in one poem."

At that juncture, "It never came back to me," says Pye. "Originally it was 'Louie the Lawyer,' when I gave those pages to Neil, and then it was 'Tom Sawyer' all of a sudden (laughs). He didn't like 'Louie the Lawyer.' It was completely different; well, not completely. It was the same with respect to some of these lines I had written. I had just grabbed lines from the original that I thought were nice. I don't remember putting them in any kind of order either. In some respects, that's how we wrote songs subsequently to that too. I would have the general idea, but I would have it very modular. I would just change the syntax or the verb, and it shows up in a new form. But the original was, I'm sure, 80 lines. Four or five pieces of foolscap. Those 80 lines didn't go to Neil. I might've given him 25 or 30 lines, and two or three versions of the one line. Then it came back to me in finished form."

As for Pye's assessment of the finished classic lyric, "There is a wonderful steely Rush sense to it. It's a bit ambiguous but hard-edged. You get a sense of… if you use the word government in a song, you open up the door to feedback, in that you're making a comment, a political statement. Or a comment about politics. I think the lyric really speaks for itself. Today's Tom Sawyer, today's warrior. Tom Sawyer had his own battles back then, probably just the waves in the river and the marsh. I was young enough then to have people in my life that were lost and confused with things in our culture, or with the way their life was going. It was a fight or flight kind of experience growing up at that age. How do you not buy into the system, or how could you be different from the system? That's all."

To reiterate, the handing over of "Louie the Lawyer" to Neil the drummer... this is all happening during "Battle Scar?"

"Yes, that's where it started with Neil. But that's not where 'Louie the Lawyer' started. It started a year or two earlier. I was just writing. I just had this idea, had 'Louie the Lawyer' at the top of the page, and I was just writing these lines. Here was 'Louie the Lawyer' and over here was maybe 'All We Are' or something else. But I generally kept these ideas together. The ideas for one I'd keep together—or apart. Anyway, I had no intention that this 'Louie the Lawyer' was anything. I maybe just read a couple things aloud. 'Oh, that's neat.' It was all very innocent. It wasn't, 'Oh my God, I hope he'll wants to read this.' It was never that (laughs). No one thought at that moment of 'Louie the Lawyer,' or even to work together. We were just in the studio hanging out. Typically in that kind of scenario, I would be writing something down on paper, as much as someone would be over in the corner practicing guitar. I remember me introducing that to Neil, but it was completely innocent. It may have just been a simple social situation of Neil saying to me, 'What are you writing there?' Or me saying, 'Hey Neil, wanna hear this line?' It was very innocent. It was never meant to be a song. All I can say is there were four or five minutes of, 'What are you writing?' 'Well, I'm writing "Louie the Lawyer."' Neil said, 'Well, that's nice.' He probably didn't mean all of it's nice (laughs). There were probably just a couple of ideas in there he liked."

"Pye's method is that he just sends me pages of scribbles and I impose order on them," Neil Peart told me back in 2004. "So, it's a perfect meeting of personalities, in that he dwells in an imagistic universe and an impressionistic universe and expresses it as such, whereas I live in a much more ordered universe and impose that structure and rhythm and parallel construction on it. I think right from that foundation, it's a collaboration of personalities, as much as it is of words. Because I'll tend to... for example, I'll start with the way he set up the framework for a song like 'Force Ten,' and I'll respond to that. I'll start creating images in his voice, as it were, just because that's the character of the piece. I adapt it like a language. I translate my thoughts into his images or his images into my kind of language, and it becomes a very kind of interwoven, interpersonal collaboration."

It is of note that Kim at times has offered a significantly different version of the "Louie the Lawyer"/"Tom Sawyer" story, implying a little more forethought. Whatever discussions did indeed go down between Pye and Kim, Neil recalls the situation much the way Pye explains it.

"I saw just real love and respect," recalls Tom Berry, on the interaction between Rush and Max. "The 'Tom Sawyer' thing, I remember when that went down. I know that Neil always respected what Pye did with lyrics. I think actually, the band wanted at one point or another, just wanted to work out a tune with Pye, and there you go, they did, and it's one of Rush's biggest songs. It was respect, and there was the room to move in on that."

"I wish he had kept going and writing for other people," muses Deane Cameron, on Pye's situation post-Max, even though it's always easy to forget the huge run Dubois had as word-spinner for Kim as a solo artist, throughout the rest of the '80s. "A lot of early Max Webster was in Pye code. So, I think Pye had a lot to say. But a little too much of it was obscure. It sounded great, it was great wordsmithing, but not a lot of it was understandable. You weren't even sure of those messages and what you were hearing. The other person I worked with who was probably one of the finest lyricists this country has ever seen is Paul Hyde. He didn't really want to write with other people, except for Bob Rock, or his own stuff. But he is a monster, monster poet. I always felt that Pye could've been that. But with Max, he developed himself a specific flavour, and as I say, spoke in code. Maybe he wanted that duality of meaning that kept people guessing. But I always felt he had the talent to be much more prolific, much more of a direct poet/lyricist."

Back to Max world, *Universal Juveniles* next coughs up "Chalkers," a loping, funky, progressive atmospheric tune that is quite dark, and significantly quieter than the rest of the album, but every bit as challenging of norms.

Notes Dave Stone on his chance to blow (and frankly "key into" the psyche of Kim), "One of the nicer things that I think I ever did was that little synth solo on the *Universal Juveniles* album, on 'Chalkers.' A lot of the guitar is doubled with the Oberheim. And then I take a little Jan Hammer-type solo in the middle of that. I thought that was kinda cute."

"Chalkers" is a co-write between Pye and Dave Myles, a nod to the idea of Kim trying to get the other guys more involved at the creative end. "The lyric is actually 'Universal Juveniles,' and it was going to be titled that, but at one point, Pye decided it was going to be called 'Chalkers,' right? That's what was so crazy about Max, especially in the last year. People would just interject things and you could tell it was a power-play. In this case it was Pye going, well, it's going to be this. Okay, fine."

"Pye is an island unto himself," reflects Dave. "Pye would often come forward, he would be, I think he would be mysterious just for the sake of being mysterious (laughs). Just because he wanted to create some buzz and take on something, I don't know. But I tell you, at the end of that, a psychiatrist would've said you guys are all fucked (laughs). But of course, that's what the music business is like.

It is. It's just crazy stuff. But Pye was, he was Pye. I just have no idea what he's doing now. Probably living off of 'Tom Sawyer,' I think. I guess at the time, bands had lyricists that were doing that kind of thing. Just because Pye didn't play an instrument, he was integral to that band, and Max's persona. The lyrics were as quirky as the music sometimes, if not all the time. Sometimes Pye would come in with stuff and we'd look at it and go, how are you supposed to… I'd look at Kim, how are you going to use this? How does this make sense? Recording with Max, it was like, this is too conventional. Some of the stuff that we'd do… and I know fully why Kim finally broke away. Because I can't get into doing these tunes anymore. I can't get into doing some of the straight-ahead rock stuff that we did—it was too lollipop. Kim wanted to get out there and still rock—it still had to kick. But I could tell, when certain things started to come up through Max in music, Kim would go, 'I'm not there; I'm not into that.' But we did it."

Says Pye, "'Chalkers' is an unusual song because it's Dave Myles and not Kim Mitchell. That's a Dave Myles song that we wrote together. I didn't just put lyrics to music; we just worked through it together. I like the bass line he came up with. That intrigued me; it felt a bit like the momentum of a horse. Chalk is a catchphrase in gambling for the favourite. If you are the chalk, you are the favourite in the race. So 'Chalkers' is, well, in my mind, the audience, our fans—the people in the audience are chalkers. That's how I like to nickname them, as chalkers. 'Like a thirsty horse going for the water.' Yeah, like coming into our town, our time, underdogs, the audience. I was talking about us as well, people in the music business: 'Long shot in the music morning line.' Line, what's the line? That's the line on the horse. The gambler would say, 'What's the line on the horse?' 'It's eight to one.' We might have been talking about us too. Being long shots."

Summing up Pye's point, "Chalkers" on the lyric sleeve is the only track with an extra subtitle or comment, including just below the title "(the favourite in any race!)," with the US spelling of favourite. For more wordplay, the first, er, line of the album's next song, "Drive and Desire," includes the word "line" as well, whereas "Chalkers" includes the words desire and drive(s). Additionally, both tracks could be interpreted as songs about the band and its interaction with the audience, a concept always on Pye's mind, given how much he dug live rock 'n' roll, and in particular—weirdly, coincidentally almost—the live rock 'n' roll of this band of broke hosers that would have to be the most demystified band in Pye's life, given that he wrote the words and he saw them live constantly.

"That might have been a line or a phrase or something that I had around for a couple of years," wonders Dubois, on the idea behind "Drive and Desire," a groovy, riffy rocker full up with stadium rock drama. "I have a feeling this is from Heath Street, St. Clair and Yonge; all the Websters were in one house, because after that we moved just down back of here, a one-way street leading onto Logan. We lived there for four or five years. But this was long before that. So, I think this was Heath Street. 'Drive and Desire,' I know I had the title written down somewhere, and I ticked the page, oh, drive and desire, that's cool. 'Standing in a line with angels;' that's a line... it didn't take me long. There was an instant connection, where I came up with standing in a line with angels; it's just a great sounding line. 'Standing in a line with angels.' There was a sense about me back then that I could almost automatically hear Kim singing that, hear his vocal, even though he'd never sung it before. It's just a great opening line."

Moving on, "Blue River Liquor Shine" is the closest thing we get to a ballad on the hard-hitting *Universal Juveniles* album. Sure, it is one, after the heavy rock fake-out that opens the song. "Blue River Liquor Shine" is wondrously odd of construction, like "Paradise Skies," although one supposes less odd. Still, it's novel in the way the gorgeous and quite loud and energetic chorus drops out to acoustic for the verse, acoustic strumming without drums, in fact. It features a starry chorus of pop magic. Kim's soloing and isolated licks throughout, as well as Doug Riley's clean, clear piano, reach for similar altitudes that the full-band chorus so elegantly achieves.

"That's just a song about sadness, isn't it?" reflects Pye. "I'm not a drinker, wasn't a drinker, so blue liquor might be more of an alliteration or a rhyme, emotional sadness rather than liquor hangover. I think it's fairly simple, isn't it? Just the sense of being lost, like a hangover, not quite with it."

"'Blue River Liquor Shine' has interesting joyful chorus moments, but it just felt dark," muses Tom, who says that with Pye's words in general, "There's a lot of joy, but there is a significant amount of darker edge as well, that you don't find in, say, April Wine or Streetheart etc. He was actually dark a lot of the time. Sure, you had your 'Diamonds Diamonds' but there was also 'Lily.'"

Then it's back to more of the strangely Viking-proud hard rock of songs like "Drive and Desire," through the riffy and rhythmic

"What Do You Do with the Urge," "which, by the way, was mine, although that's a non-commercial song," says Gary McCracken—indeed the track features a Dubois/McCracken credit. "Not like 'A Million Vacations,' I put this one together for the album. At the time, Kim says, 'Look, anybody got something we can use? Let's give it a listen,' right? He's quite open about it. He hadn't totally abandoned that idea, right? And I said, well, I've got this demo of this tune and what do you think? And he ended up going, okay, I think we can make that sound like something. And I think Doug Riley played piano on that one. Dave's not on that one, but Dave was great, very creative. He did a really good job on that album. And at the time he had an Oberheim synthesizer, which was really cool, an OB-X."

As for the boogie woogie of the verse, well, you can hear that in "A Million Vacations" as well. "Yeah, yeah. That's just the formula I use. Even I have a formula (laughs)."

"That's McCracken and me," confirms Pye. "I don't think you have to go beyond the title of that one, do you? I don't know what urges you have. Gary had two lines, and he asked me, what can you do with these? I wrote an entire set of lyrics. I know what urges a lot of humans have. I can't speak for your urges. But you can speak for what you do with them."

McCracken is all over this track, as he is everywhere on this quite percussive album. I asked him how his kit had evolved over the years to this point.

"Well, all I did was, at one point, added a few more toms to the equation. That's when I started using the big Milestone kit, and that was in '79. Up until then, my drum kit was always three toms and the two floor toms and the double bass. With, I don't know, five or six cymbals. Back in the '70s, you almost couldn't be in a band unless you had a big monster drum set. It just didn't look right, a little four-piece. It just didn't seem right. The whole tom thing... it was important to let people know that you've got eight toms. It was important to me to let people know that I could play then. That I could play what was in my picture. So, I'm going, well, I'm a Canadian guy, Canadian all the way, and I'm going to buy Canadian-made Milestones. I loved the sound of them, and as it turned out, so did everybody else. But that was my progression into, I'm not going to get any more drums than this ever. I've got enough now. But the Milestone drums, they were just so well made and they just sounded unique and different, and yet just as good as everything else."

Universal Juveniles closes with a progressive metal epic that is part "Battle Scar," part "21st Century Schizoid Man." "Cry Out for Your Life" lopes to a complicated beat, with Kim emoting at times toward quite the bellow, as he does on the previous track as well.

"I had that line around for years," reckons Pye. "I love it. This is the first time I've heard that in twenty years and I still love it. That flow, that inner rhythm and rhyme, that's very poetic to me. This gives me the sense that I'm starting to grow as a writer. I can't explain it. Because that's a little more poetry. But there's something about the way I'm writing that, that I like, even now. There is this sense of, yeah, when I read that, I just keep going. Some of the other ones are not quite like that. They're a little bit more staccato-like, musical or metered."

With "Cry Out for Your Life," there's jamming, there's top-shelf musicianship, there's arguably an uneasy realization that the goose is cooked and sod any brass ring of commercial success. As postulated at the beginning of this chapter, like Rush, Max was going to go out on its own terms, burning the house down. Only unlike Rush, who fabulously turned the corner with their last stand *2112*, "Cry Out for Your Life" would stand as Max Webster's last song.

Nonetheless, *Universal Juveniles* got to No.41 on the Canadian charts and certified gold within a couple of weeks. There's conjecture that it might be unofficially platinum by this point, and when one starts to do the computation of how streaming numbers add to the tallies, there may be some validity to that, with "Battle Scar" doing the heavy lifting.

As well, US sales were estimated at 60,000, which is enough on its own for a gold record in Canada. The album spawned one Canadian single, a picture sleeve affair, pairing "Blue River Liquor Shine" (shortened by a minute) with "Check." Also picture sleeve was "Battle Scar"/"April in Toledo," issued in the UK.

Summed up an underwhelmed Keith Sharp in *Music Express*, "Despite the fact that Max Webster has undergone more changes than a traffic light, Kim Mitchell has managed to pull his assorted troops together for a solid if unspectacular vinyl effort. The album's main weakness is Pye Dubois' offbeat lyrics. Dubois' esoteric poetry may be considered brilliant prose, but this writer still finds a lot of his offerings difficult to digest when taken in the context of rock music material. At times, it's difficult to figure out what Dubois is trying to say."

In the same issue of *Music Express*, it was the inscrutable lyricist who was doing the artful job of spinning the new album in a positive light, specifically addressing the personnel changes. "I've watched Max for seven years now. I've seen all the changes. I don't want to put my foot into my mouth, 'cause I did a year and a half ago. I said, 'I think this band has just peaked.' But then all of a sudden there was these crumblings. Terry Watkinson, our keyboard player left, then Dave Myles, our bass player left, and all of a sudden I see this five-piece band and I said, 'My God, it's a new band in my life.' To do that to me, they've got to be pretty good, because I'm too critical. There's more meat to it, more stage presence, and the tunes are coming alive. There's a challenge, once again. If anything, they're just stronger and more mature. I guess a good word for it is succinct. They're more refined, and have more of an edge to them. I don't want to bad-mouth other groups, but Max isn't your Triumph, straight-laced, 'we go this way'-type of band. Max is like a wild African bush. Depending on the weather or the water, it can go anywhere. This last year has been just the power, the rock 'n' roll juvenile approach. It just flared right up on the album."

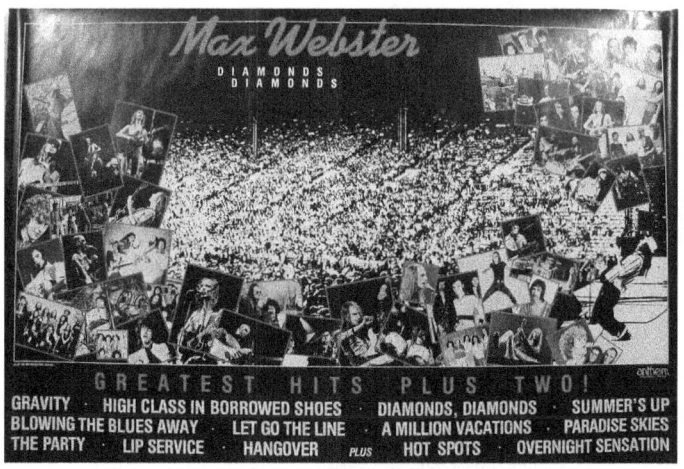

MAXED OUT –
"Everything's yellow"

Max Webster entered 1981 with yet another hopeful and extensive tour with Rush, the same way they had started 1980. They supported Canada's "progressive metal" heroes in February through May of 1981, anchored in the US rust belt, after beginning the year headlining in Canada, followed by the aforementioned two shows in the UK supporting Black Sabbath.

But perhaps the band's last glorious stand would be represented by the last show of 1980, proving that they were still a major live draw, headlining Maple Leaf Gardens, supported by Goddo and B.B. Gabor.

An estimated 19,000 Canuck punters saw the band that night, as did *Music Express*'s Keith Sharp, who wrote, "Max Webster has rejuvenated itself now that all the personnel hassles have been ironed out. Capitalising on new guitarist Steve McMurray, Kim Mitchell used his newfound freedom to bound around the stage, delivering his trademark leaps without the weight of carrying the lead guitar attack. The band as a whole sounded tighter and more filled out than in previous appearances, an added bonus being the appearance of Rush front man Geddy Lee for a dual vocal attack with Mitchell on 'Battle Scar.' If there's one complaint, it's that

Mitchell seemed to be playing over the top of his audience. There was little direct communication between Mitchell and the crowd. It was a master and servant relationship which lacked the spontaneity of Goddo's set."

Pye remained constantly amused by the Max Webster fan base, telling *Music Express*, "They come up and start talking in Max jargonisms: references to themselves in reference to the tunes. 'All this lip service is happening.' They're trying to show off to me. But I know damn well that they use it with their friends too. That's their doughnut shop rapport. That's the way they communicate. And then you have someone who's older, who asks you an important question about the lyrics. It goes on and on." As for "Max-lobsters," "It's a nickname everybody calls us. The Max-lobsters. It started in Kitchener, when Kim was singing 'Waterline:' 'rising slowly to meet the waterline,' and he started hooking his hands into claws and then everyone in the audience started doing that. So all of a sudden, a week later, there were Max Webster lobster T-shirts, a real snowball."

Already at this massive homegrown rock show, the membership of the band that had made the loud and valiant *Universal Juveniles* record had been compromised. Since then, there was the aforementioned Steve McMurray, ex-of Wireless on second guitar, plus keyboardist Greg Chadd, who was already replaced by the time of the New Year's Eve show by a returning Terry Watkinson. Bassist of choice was one Mike Gingrich, a new character to the story—and replacement for Dave Myles—who will take us towards the final flame-out of the band up into April of 1981, down south in Tennessee.

"In the mid '70s, I put a progressive trio together called Zing Dingo with Gary McCracken and Dave Myles," explains Chadd, beginning with a much earlier connection to the band. "We played mainly in the Windsor/Detroit area. They were all friends from Sarnia, so Kim came down and jammed with us at our rehearsal studio/home. We talked about playing together sometime but nothing really serious. After we broke up, we all found other gigs. Then it was funny. First Gary, then Dave, then myself ended up playing in Max. Dave left just as I was coming in, and Mike Gingrich from the group Toronto joined with another guitarist Steve McMurray from Wireless."

"We did some headline gigs across Canada," continues Chadd, "and then joined up with some major US groups and opened for them in the US for some exposure where the band was unknown. We did quite well for a bunch of unknown 'frozen' Canadian boys. I even remember the road manager of one of the headliners giving us time for an encore, which is not usually the case. The few months that I played with them was extremely busy. I think there was one stretch when we played 27 dates in 31 days. I really enjoyed our gigs with Kansas, as I was a big fan of their music. Another time I got food poisoning—fortunately on one of those few nights off—and some of the crew guys, who I had never met, came in and gave me some moral support and some ideas to expedite my recovery. We had a lot of fun and I will remember those good times. At that time there were a lot things going on with Kim and outside pressures as well. I was replaced when Terry came back, and then Kim disbanded the group a couple of months later. Max will be remembered for the quirky music and on-stage antics as well as the strong musicianship and songs they performed. I only wish we could have written some material together."

"We replaced Dave in one day," noted Kim, to *Music Express*, addressing the bass position. "We knew he would be hard to replace, especially on record where he was really great, but his replacement, Mike Gingrich, more than fills the shoes. He's always loved Max, so it was a fan coming into the band. He's on stage and he's singing the tunes. It's a nice feeling to look over and see him there."

Reflected Kim on the loss of Dave, "Pye and myself are idealists, so I guess it's easy for us. But when Dave left because his wife needed him at home, I thought, well, if he feels he has to, it's best to split. I just had to say something though. I said, 'Look, I respect you for making a decision on your life; I just think it's a waste of a good musician. You're going home to sell plastic forks for the Kentucky Fried Chicken business—I think you could have held that off for a while. That would have always been there.' I've seen that happen too many times."

"Dave didn't come to management meetings ever," recalls Mike Tilka, who was working at SRO during Dave's last days, and for a few more years in fact. "I knew Dave before he was in the band. He was a friend of Terry's and he was a guitar player in Sarnia. But he quit the band or whatever, and he had no problems going home, because his wife's dad was a grocer or something, or had owned food franchises. Anyway, he went back to Sarnia into a job."

"I came out of a band called Nightwinds," begins Mike Gingrich. "We were playing the bars in Toronto, and it was a Genesis clone band, basically. We actually opened for Max one time, and I guess

Kim, talking with Kim a little bit, when the band split up, it was right around just after *Universal Juveniles* was made, just a week or two after, and basically Kim called me at home to see if I wanted to audition. They had briefly broken up and reformed, and they hired another guitar player too, Steve. We hit the road. Terry Watkinson rejoined the band. So, with Gary McCracken we had three of the originals."

Kim was pretty fired up by the new, tougher band, telling Greg Quill, "We've decided the next album will be more democratic. Tunes will be welcomed from everyone in the band and given a fair hearing. I haven't been enjoying the role that seems to have been thrust on me, to tell you the truth. You know, my picture on the cover, Kim Mitchell as Max Webster—I feel uncomfortable with that. I want to feel part of a band again. This business is so crazy that one person can't do it by himself. You can't compromise if you're a genuine artist. Eventually it comes down to the fact that you've got to do what you've got to do. When you're delivering something you really love, that's been a part of you, it comes out so much stronger than anything that may involve compromises based on commercial potential or money considerations. So, anything written by members of this band will get recorded as long as we're all into it. If it's not comfortable, we won't do it. Even if it's one of my tunes."

Additionally, Mitchell was still generating ideas for the continuation of the band, musing about making the next record at Le Studio with Terry Brown presiding, and then heading straight to the UK for initial tour dates, to rectify all the false starts with that hopeful fan base. A proposed swing back to Brown might have been because of regrets over *Universal Juveniles*' "west coast smoothness," with Kim telling Quill, "It works fine. It's very even from bottom to top, and everyone likes it, but to me, after all the times I've listened to it, it's not hard enough. When I put my earphones on and crank it up, I like to feel my head pop on snare and bass drumbeats—that doesn't happen with this album."

Mike Gingrich would have joined in October 1980. "Yes, I think it was fall, because it wasn't too long after that... the first major gig I did with them was New Year's Eve at Maple Leaf Gardens, 1980. Which, I have a picture of Geddy and myself—it's pretty rough, but it's a picture."

By the time Kim would hang it up for good, Mike says, "We were very close to pre-production on the next record, finishing touring. We opened about three tours with Rush through the States. We went to England, opened for Sabbath. We were over there for about a week. But yeah, we were there, we did three or four Canadian tours, most of the time with Rush. A lot of really good memories. I really got on with Neil. The guys that I was playing with earlier in that Nightwinds band, they were from St. Catharines, and some of them actually went to school with Neil, so I had a connection there, and Neil was just the greatest guy. He invited me to sit up behind his kit; he had a little monitor system set up behind his kit, and during the show, I was allowed a few times to come up and sit behind the kit and watch him play."

"Yeah, actually, quite a bit," answers Mike, on whether he ever talked bass shop with Geddy. "Geddy was a great guy. We played hockey in a few places. He let me use his equipment (laughs), once. He got to the point where I can remember three or four times doing the sound check with Rush, where Geddy wanted to go out into the stadium and listen. So, I was actually playing Geddy's gear while he was out listening, jamming with Alex and Neil. That was a thrill."

Pressed for a little more detail and clarity on those last Max dates, Gingrich explains, "First I think it was Canada. We did Ontario, a bunch of gigs, and then we did Maple Leaf Gardens. I think we went on an American and Canadian tour, across Canada, and we were on a Rush tour. The States, right to the Midwest, down to Texas, and all the time we were writing new stuff. I think just again, a Canadian tour, did a Rush tour again, and went over to England for that week with Sabbath."

"The schedule was London, Leeds and Newcastle," continues Mike. In reality, the show at the Hammersmith Odeon in London and at Newcastle City Hall in Newcastle were cancelled due to low ticket sales, although, according to Mike below, something might have been put together during the day in Newcastle. Two shows were confirmed to have taken place: Leeds on January 24th, 1981, and Stafford the following night. On both occasions, Max Webster played first, followed by New Wave of British Heavy Metal band AIIZ and then Black Sabbath.

Amusingly, Gingrich remembers Black Sabbath's crowds much the way Kim did. "We played Leeds, where they recorded The Who *Live at Leeds*. It's basically a bus garage, an underground garage. The concerts, as I remember them, were mostly 18- to 19-year-old guys, blue jean jackets and construction boots. That's what I remember, shag haircuts. We did Newcastle. We went up and did an outdoor thing in Newcastle, during the day and that was spooky. Scary metal crowd, but by the end of our set they had accepted us and had got off on this very strange band from Canada. But I remember a sea of blue jean jackets, mullets and construction boots, exclusively young males, swaying in unison, but no projectiles or nasty comments. Still, you look out in a sea of faces of all these guys, and I remember we started the set and we were worried. We thought we were going to get our asses kicked."

Max Webster indeed had got their asses kicked—by the business. The plan had been for the English swing to be a triumphant Max Webster headline tour. Fond memories of 1979 had lingered. "Paradise Skies" had been a much-loved song in England. With the UK in the throes of the New Wave of British Heavy Metal, Max had crafted a heavy record which on paper should have had the British headbangers air-guitarin' up a storm. Iron Maiden was on Capitol and Max was on Capitol (although, significantly, back on Mercury in the US).

Instead, ticket sales were anaemic, the tour was yanked, and Kim was described in press releases as having a throat infection. Ten dates went down to four, and somewhere along the line it was switched to a support slot with Black Sabbath. In the end, two nights were notched, along with a loss of $23,000. Indeed, as alluded to, notices appeared in the UK music newspapers for headlining dates over Angel Witch, scheduled for the Hammersmith Odeon on January 22nd and Newcastle City Hall the following night. The next week, one notice informed of the two Black Sabbath shows, with support from Max Webster and AIIZ, accurately for January 25th in Leeds and January 26th in Stafford.

Lurching toward the end, says Mike, "It was on a Rush tour, I think the third one, when we were down in Texas or somewhere down that way, when the band split up. That was heartbreaking for me. We were two weeks away from pre-production going in and coming back after that tour. We supposed to start serious production on the next record, which never happened of course."

"We were having some very good shows opening for Rush. We opened for Molly Hatchet, we did some side gigs while we were touring, and we would go over to a university somewhere to open for different bands or do our own thing. We had some pretty good bar shows, things like that. It was a real shock to me. I was looking forward, very much, to working on and releasing that record. Max has always been one of my favourite bands. I was thrilled to be part of it for that short time."

The last show took place on April 16th, 1981, at the Mid-South Coliseum in Memphis, Tennessee, with Kim informing the band at soundcheck that he was heading home after the band did their rock 'n' roll duty later that night.

"Basically nil," answers Mike on the subject of drinking and drugging in the band. "Other than drinking, there was always beer around. Of course everybody smoked cigarettes. But the drug thing didn't really enter into it too much. I guess everybody had seen too much of that. But everybody smoked. I remember rooming with Kim many, many times, and we would have our cigarettes and ashtrays out. Smoking in the room, oh yeah. It was just before that went by the wayside."

Mike says he, "always liked Terry. He's a very quiet guy, very artistic, very, very humorous. But yeah. I really liked hanging with Terry. Very, very creative. And Gary too; I was really close with Gary. I think I hung out with him more than any of the other guys. While we were off, Gary ended up buying a cottage up by where I live now, in the Kawarthas. I just bought a place in the Peterborough area and I have been here for quite a while. We used to hang together at his cottage and that. I taught him how to fish. We used to go fishing all the time, like the fishing musicians from Second City (laughs). But I did spend a lot of time with Gary, and we did that Klaatu tour together as well. They called us the heavy metal twins. Gary was very steady, very, like right in the pocket, very powerful. He kind of amazed me with the power that he has. He's a big guy, heavy guy, and boy when he wants to, he could really put it across. He could really lay it down."

Mike, like pretty much everybody else, come to think of it, dispels the stories of Kim being a taskmaster on the road. "I don't remember him being too domineering that way. But he had an idea. He would always contribute ideas to what he thought we should look like. We put together a few solo things where we would trade off lyrics and stuff like that. But I don't remember him ever being domineering. He was definitely the front man and he was throwing in advice every now and then. Which I was grateful for. I sang back-ups, harmonies. Like I say, there was another guitar player, Steve. He was from Australia. Very good slide player. But he was basically playing a lot of rhythm stuff, augmenting what Kim was doing. Kim wanted to have another guitar in the band, for rhythm."

Asked what sorts of fresh songs might have been available for a new Max album, Mike contradicts Kim's assertion that there was a clean break between thoughts of Max material and solo material.

"Yeah, there was stuff that Kim eventually put on his first solo album. It naturally would become that. Kim called me and asked me to do some work with him on his solo stuff. I actually did some pre-production with him on his first solo record. But at that point, Kim didn't have a record contract, I was basically a starving musician, and I got an opportunity to tour with Klaatu, who decided to go out on the road for the very first time. Actually Gary McCracken played drums, and I had to take it just because of the money situation. By the time I got back from that tour, Kim had got a friend of his to fill in and do bass for him. Not Peter Fredette; Peter came in a little bit later. Right around the same time... well, he had his eye on Peter for a while. I can't remember the name of the band he was in, but they played gigs around town, and he was playing bass, keyboards and singing a lot. You'd see him perform. Kim really liked his voice—it was his voice that Kim really wanted to have."

As for this pre-production session, Mike says the drummer was the immensely talented Paul Delong, soon to be seminal, early-years drummer for Kim as a solo artist. "We just started briefly in a rehearsal space in Mississauga, and it didn't get much further than that. Now, I didn't actually... we did some really rough demos, just recording off the floor of the rehearsal hall. They are around somewhere."

Apparently next door at this space, I reminded Mike, there was a band that would annoy Kim to no end, with their needling renditions of Max Webster songs. "Probably, could've been (laughs). I probably remember that. There were actually a couple bands in the building. It was pretty rough at that point, but a lot of it did show up on his first solo album. We were just putting together songs at that point. It was pretty much right at the very beginning. I lost touch at that point. I did see him a couple of times after that. I ended up joining Toronto as well and did an album with them. Actually, a Holly Woods solo album as well. But we had a good... I'm sure there were six or seven songs there that were looking or sounding pretty good."

Reconciling this with Kim's assertion, it's plausible that Mike is remembering these as sessions somehow linked to Max, but that in Kim's mind, he had already moved on to a solo career. Supporting that concept, Mike says that they had never done any of them live on the last Max dates. "No, we weren't quite at that point. Terry Watkinson was working on stuff that he wanted to contribute, and Kim of course had his stuff going. I think Kim was pretty happy with the sound. As far as I know, we were going ahead, gung ho, to do this next album. Again, I was kind of shocked. I think everybody was. It just came out of the blue."

Back to that fateful day, in the middle of a tour, that Kim called it quits, Gingrich figures, "I think he'd just gotten to the point where... maybe it was just the frustration. The lack of support in the US. I remember doing, in Texas, somewhere in Texas, an in-store at a record store. It was a pretty good turnout, but they didn't have any albums to sell. It was that bad. The kind of support he was getting from his company just wasn't there. I think the frustration had gotten to the point where he just wanted to step back and regroup and rethink everything. As for the road, he could handle it, but all of us were the same way. It does get boring. It's not as glamorous as it might sound."

"I think that was maybe in the back of his mind, that that's what he should be doing," reflects Mike, about Kim going solo. "I think it was just a combination of being too long on the road and too little support from people who were supposed to be supporting him. It was a very frustrating thing. In Canada, he was a big name, still is, but in the US, it was like pulling teeth. Although the crowds were always fairly very receptive. Even in England we were accepted quite well. Although the worst place for crowd abuse was England. Because at that point that was when the punk scene was switching over, so they're over there with the Mods and Rockers kind of thing. But for walking out cold with such a different kind of act, we'd usually go over pretty good."

But of course Max was wilfully stepping in it by virtue of their pomp and circus pants stage get-ups. "It was fairly wacky. I've got an actual studio group shot that we did the morning or the afternoon of the Junos. We won best new group, which was a joke. I think we were with SRO still, The Agency. But yeah, laughably, we won the Juno for best new band. I have a certificate somewhere."

"I heard about it when he left the tour," says Mike with a wry laugh, literally, as discussed, having been on the road when Kim pulled the plug with no advance warning. "We were, again, like I said, on tour. We got up one morning and the road manager came to us and said, 'Kim got on a plane and went home last night.' There was no event. I think it was brewing. It was brewing in him for a long time, and whether or not it was a little bit of a breakdown or what went on, I really don't know. But I think he had thought about it a long time. When it happened, it was a total surprise and shock to me. I didn't see it coming, and I don't think a lot of people saw it coming."

As for how Gary and Terry were taking it, "Actually, yeah, we were all blown away. We ended up doing some recording when we got back, just as an instrumental act. I can't remember what the hell we were even called. But we were going to make an attempt to do a recording, instrumentally, or maybe look for singer. We did that for quite a while. We ended up recording a few things that I still like."

"It was quite good actually," reflects Mike. "We actually got another guitar player. The other guitar player from Wireless, Mike Crawford, came in, and we just started writing a bunch of instrumental stuff. See, we didn't know whether Kim was going to come back at that point or what was going on. Then Kim called me and asked me, and he said, 'I'm working on some solo stuff. Do you want to come in and work on it with me?' I didn't ask. I wasn't about to ostracise everybody. He knew he had let people down, in a way. It wasn't a happy time, but I admired Kim so much that I... if he called me today, I'd probably quit my job and go play with him. I really admired the guy, and still do."

Relates Terry Watkinson on Kim's departure, "I think a lot of it was fatigue, because we had been playing so much together, even before the albums started coming out. You know how it is when a band is struggling to make it, and they are on the road all the time. In the early days it was like two of us to a room in a seedy hotel, and eventually you just feel like you've got to get out of that situation and take a new approach to music and your life. Kim tended to be pretty private sometimes. But no, he was fine, I thought. Actually, I was the first one to quit, and then I came back for a few months, and then Kim pulled the plug. There was no animosity, really. There were some regrets, but I think we all knew that we just couldn't face going through the United States with Rush again. That was a big factor too, is that we never did really break the market in the States. We made a dent, but not much of a dent."

Backing up a bit, Terry qualifies that on *Universal Juveniles*, he, "was only on one song, 'Battle Scar.' So that was when I left and they got a couple of keyboards players in, including David Stone. Then I'm not sure why he left, and then they had another keyboard player. Then they were looking at doing Maple Leaf Gardens on New Year's Eve and Kim said, 'I can't do it with this keyboard player.' So, somebody called me and said, 'Do you want to do some more dates with Max?' I said okay, so there I was again. It wasn't very long after that when the band broke up. There was no talk about going solo. I suppose he was thinking about it quite a bit. It all happened pretty suddenly, really, as far as we were concerned. I'm not sure what was going through his mind in the last year or so."

Once Terry was gone from the band he was essentially gone from rock and back into the art world, as alluded to by his daughter Chloe. "My dad is a very confusing guy, in the best sense of the word. He never let anyone tell him what life should be, or how he should act. Although he has always been very good at exploring the intricacies of life, he seems to believe that life is pretty simple. Surround yourself with company you enjoy, have a good time, unless it makes you feel like shit, and learn about the world. Growing up with him, the fridge was constantly blocked by a giant easel, usually with a painting drying on it. There were pictures of surgical openings around the house, and I was fascinated by my dad's illustrations of veins, arteries, and especially eyes, and their layers. My dad was very caring, and nurturing, and I couldn't have asked for a funnier guy."

Chloe's mother and Terry's girlfriend at the time, Carla, says that directly post-Max, the only musical thing he attempted to get off the ground was the previously described band, which was called Espresso. There were no high-profile auditions or anything, and it was quite quickly decided that he would go back to school and become a medical illustrator.

"It was just time to stop playing for a while," said Kim back in 1982 to Greg Quill, as he was turning the corner toward what would become a productive solo run. "I wanted to see life from some other perspective than a Holiday Inn or camper or backstage. It's not that I couldn't handle playing live—I can. Everyone was devastated because it happened pretty fast. I'd been thinking about it for a long time, for a few months, then it just happened one day and I was off tour the next. I just walked into the dressing room and said, 'That's it. I'm going home after Memphis.' There are a few reasons I don't want to talk about it, but the main one was, like I said before, I just wanted to write. I wanted to take some time off. I was losing contact with reality, is what it was. I was dealing all the time with concert promoters, hotel rooms, concertgoers, the camper—not too much of the real world in there. Reality, for me, is sitting at home with the tape recorder and creating. Going out to play—I do enjoy that. I wasn't in control of anything at the end of Max Webster—people were dictating to me and I had no say. If anyone knew how to market himself, you'd think it'd be the individual involved. I went off the road, I didn't talk to anyone, and eventually I went in and told them, 'This is the way it has to be for me. Are you still in?' They saw that as a positive move on my part, as Mitchell taking the bull by the horns—to their credit. I don't mind a bit of compromise. I enjoy those confrontations with people. Not to get cosmic, but I'm a Cancer, and when too much starts happening, too much provocation, the crab just walks backwards into his hole and stays there 'til it's gone away."

During the same interview, Kim expressed his dissatisfaction with the way his old label handled *Diamonds Diamonds*, the 1981 compilation that included Max rarities "Hot Spots" and "Overnight Sensation." "Six or eight years ago, when Max Webster was recording their first album, there were two outtakes of the 12 or 13 songs which, way back in our musical naïveté, when we didn't even know what an overdub was, were deemed to be not good enough—by everyone, by ourselves and the record company. However good or bad that first album was, we all decided those two songs didn't make the standard. Seven years down the line, the record company put those tracks on a ridiculous package they called the greatest hits—two outtakes! That pissed me off royally. If they weren't good enough for seven years before, what makes them good enough now?"

The *Diamonds Diamonds* album sold gold as well, making every Max album at least gold, even though a point of contention and puzzlement is the fact that the catalogue hasn't been examined for further certifications since the early '80s. It must have driven Kim further around the bend when he saw the full-page ads for the album. Calling the record "Greatest Hits Plus Two," additional text read "featuring the previously unreleased track 'Hot Spots' as the first single."

Other than the two archival tracks, there wasn't much to the album besides the hits and, on the jacket, a bevy of small black-and-white shots. Recalls photographer Patrick Harbron, "When I became a music photographer in Toronto, Rush and Max were some of the first groups I worked with. My favourite shoot with Max was for *Roxy* magazine in Toronto, March 30th, 1978. Kim, shared a house on Grandview Avenue, a couple of blocks from my home in Riverdale, east Toronto. The magazine was pretty loose about what the shoot should entail but we did expect the entire band. When I arrived at the house, I was dismayed to find that Terry Watkinson had bailed at the last minute—flu or something. Pye Dubois was there and his presence was vital. As I recall, there hadn't been a print shoot with

Pye who was considered the 'silent' member of Max Webster. This was early in my career as a working photographer. I owned little camera equipment and a small hand-flash for lighting, but I had no shortage of ideas."

"Obviously fans were drawn to the band because of the music, but Pye's lyrics took the group to another level of mischievousness and cynicism. That was my cue for photographing the band. We shot all afternoon, in the house and on the street, eventually piling them onto a chesterfield from the front room, then in the middle of the road in front of their house. Later as they packed their band van with gear for the gig, I took final photographs of Kim through the driver's window before they pulled away."

"Over the years, I continued to photograph Max Webster and Kim's later bands. The main photograph for the cover of their 'best of' album, *Diamonds Diamonds* was taken July 10th, 1978 at the CNE Stadium, when they opened for Genesis during that band's *...And Then Were Three* tour. It was early in the day for a rock concert, but Max was well received by the Toronto audience in the half-filled venue. Opening bands often suffer rough handling from the headliners and are not allowed to do their regular sets but Genesis was a class act, as they say. While Max left the stage after their set, I asked their manager Tom Berry, if they were going back for an encore. He looked at me as if I had just swallowed broken glass and said, 'Fuck, yeah!' The *Diamonds Diamonds* cover includes 24 additional photographs, half of which are mine from live gigs at Massey Hall, Maple Leaf Gardens (opening for Rush), and other situations including the *Roxy* magazine shoot. It serves as a visual history for me as well as Max Webster."

Very interesting how different stakeholders in the band can harbour different motivations for pushing out product like this. Read between the lines of Deane Cameron's comments below, and one can almost envision the issuing of *Diamonds Diamonds* as a love note, as an overture to see if the Max brand still had legs, enough so that the band could be reconvened.

"Is this too early?" was one thought, says Cameron. "Could there be more? That record was really just for Canada, and we were just a distributor. So, we were certainly expecting one, and the advances we paid for the label contemplated that. But it never got down to you owe us a hits record because you owe us a record. Yeah, it wouldn't have been that. Greatest hits records can be something to kick something back in the butt and get it going, or it can be a bit of a closer. So, you have to be somewhat strategic. Sometimes it can just be, we've got this incredible track but we're not coming up with enough for an album. This could be called our sixth album, and maybe it's an album or two early, but if anything, it always felt like, should we do maybe an album or two more?"

"I was living in hope that things like the US not happening... that some of that stuff would wear off," continues Deane. "People would come back together. Because I've seen that many, many times. Now, maybe Anthem or SRO had a different opinion. They were closer to a lot of the conversations with Kim, obviously. But I always thought, maybe somebody will see that this is a good idea to get back together."

But back to the demise of the band that came instead, "I know Kim was very tired," reflects Dave Myles, "because he wasn't doing what he wanted to do. I knew this thing was going to blow up. After I left, I think they toured for maybe another couple months and then he just said I'm done, I'm going home. It didn't surprise me at all. Because it's very tough to do that, especially if you're not traveling first class and you're the opening act. If you're headlining you can do lots of stuff. But if you're opening, it's a tough call."

Reflects Tom Berry, who would shortly thereafter take Kim solo, and to much greater success than Mitchell ever had with Max, "At that point, I just think that all of the frustrations, the artistic, creative frustrations that were there in the band, the Kim/Pye, the Pye/Kim, the Pye/band, the Kim/Pye/band, artistic band versus management, management really feeling like they knew the way because look at what we're doing with Rush etc., and you can't just cookie-cutter or cookie-cut Max into that. Although they did support Max greatly, by giving them the opening slots, which gave Max a huge step up. There was real love from Rush to Max, as people and back-and-forth. But there were these management tensions, and tensions within the band. The other band members not really getting the Pye thing. So, there was all that going on, and then Kim on the road, and I just think Kim finally went, 'Fuck it, I've had it.' It wasn't, 'Fuck it. I've had it. I've been thinking about this for six months and I'm gonna go have a solo career.' It was just, 'Fuck it, I've had it.' That was hard on Kim, because he took the heat."

Heat indeed—packing up and going home in the middle of a tour is a major no-no, and more than a few people have speculated Kim as a solo artist was held back due to long memories of the way he went about quitting Max.

"They were horrible contracts," continues Tom, intimating that there was a kernel of truth to the idea that given what they'd signed, the band was never going to make any money as Max Webster, and that it was best to crudely blow the whole thing up. "They were typical of the day. Yeah, they were contracts that just... it's pretty hard on a band when you have to recoup everything; everything was cross-collateralised, publishing against recording, etc. etc. Yeah, they were tough deals. Ray was probably one of the best dealmakers for and against a band that I've ever seen. He's just a brilliant dealmaker. So at that point, four albums in, and you're looking at your unrecouped balance being who knows what. Yeah, it's tough to see the way forward to ever making a penny, for sure."

Tom chuckles in confirming that Pye was indeed the one raising concerns around the money, causing no end of consternation at the office. "Yeah, Pye didn't hesitate to ask questions, because that was his artistic license to— he was the artsiest artist, right? So, he could always pose everything and anything. At that point, there was absolutely no relationship between him and the management company. Because, yeah, because he asked questions, and because he just couldn't be contained."

"I know, that was always a problem," laughs Tom, at the idea that Pye could be just as inscrutable in this type of day-to-day stuff as he could in his legendary, highly dense and poetic lyrics. "Jesus, man. Like, have you just seen any of what's going on around here? It's like living in a totally red world, and Pye would come in and say—without even commenting on the red world— 'Everything's yellow.' It's like, 'What?! Dude, you missed *everything*! Really?!' Anyway, awfully interesting. There's no doubt about it."

"It wasn't an absolute surprise," notes Deane Cameron, "because of the frustration of doing a lot of international promotion and work and it not happening. So, it didn't completely surprise me. Obviously, it was a disappointment and sad and it gave the American market the excuse to back off of something that was already a difficult project to get going. Yeah, I wasn't totally surprised, but I've seen that before. Where bands have some success locally and they start on the international trail and it doesn't work, or it doesn't work right away. So, people say, well, we're gonna make a big change. Maybe I just need to get out on my own."

Gary offers a recap to the end of the band as well, while pushing forward a little. "For *Universal Juveniles*, Terry had quit. Watkinson wasn't with the band by then, and the bass player Dave Myles had quit the band, but he did the album and then moved on. But all of a sudden, after Kim decided to let the band offer material, it wasn't a year later that he decided, well, I'm not going to do that anymore. He wanted material, but at the same time... this was all when he was getting ready to quit. He was getting all set up to move on with Tom Berry and Alert Records and all that stuff. This was all getting set up during that period. By then, everyone had quit except me (laughs). There's quite a web of intrigue there, and again, a lot of times, I don't know if Kim knows that a lot of the stuff even happened, or he just doesn't want to talk about it or what. I don't think you've got a problem talking about Max in a general way, but when it gets to specifics, everyone says, why does a band break up? No one ever really knows. Other than Kim says, I'm done. We were in Memphis, Tennessee and he says, 'That's it. We play tonight and then we're going home.' That was it."

"We certainly weren't particularly disillusioned," laughs Gary, on the process of getting over it. "We always were disillusioned right out of the gate (laughs). It was like aw shit! It's at the point now where it's pretty much 'Who cares?' for me. It's like any reasons why we did break up is certainly water under the bridge at this point for everybody. But we had fun. We had our fun. Kim went on to do his own thing, and right on! We carried on and did our things and no problem. It's like everything else. Max Webster is not the only band to break up. A lot of bands do it. You'd like to think the band would stay together forever, but it almost seems inevitable. There's a few bands that do it but most don't (laughs)."

"I'd say one of the lowest points was finding out that we were never going to make any money," laughs Gary ruefully. "I'd say that would be a key point as a downer. It was funny, but when the band broke up, I wasn't particularly upset. We had done a lot of work, but I wasn't particularly unhappy about it at the time. It just seemed like it was bound to happen anyways. So, it was a low point, but not a big shock."

"It was a shitty deal," continued Gary, on why there was no hope of making any money. "Like low points, right? You ever hear the story about... like we had better points than The Beatles' first album. Did you ever hear the stories where The Beatles said they want the same deal Elvis gets, and they'd be happy? Well, they got four points. Four points. That's not considered good. And in our case, I can't remember, I think it was ten or 11, or 12, maybe. But it wasn't really good. Because you have to split that up with everybody. Not just one guy gets it. So, to get a good record deal when you're a young band—you hear it all the time—you just don't get that kind of situation. You work into it. You develop to where you get maybe some money out of the deal, because you've learned how to deal with it all. But in our case, by the time everybody learned how to deal with it, we were so burnt-out, and Kim, he was so fried with it all, that he says, 'I'm taking a year off and I'm gonna start a new thing, and thanks a lot.' That was it."

I guess the time to renegotiate, if that was at all possible, would have been after the success of *A Million Vacations*...

"Well, again, we had one year to go with our current contract. And again, bands that were stabilised and knew what they were doing, we weren't quite that stable, because of everybody coming and going at one point there. It was really just me and Kim, and I even had the conversation with him at one point that I wanted to quit. He talked me out of it. He goes, 'Well, don't quit yet; stick with me and we'll do *Universal Juveniles*. We'll do the album, and then we'll see how it goes from there.' And I thought well, okay, that's a good deal."

"We signed a three-hat deal, they call it, which is now illegal. You can't even do that now. Unbelievable. So, us, it's like, once we realised what was happening, that's the real reason Kim quit. There's a few other ones. But the main one was, I'm not working my ass off for you anymore. This is insane what we're doing. The bigger we get, the less money we make, and the more money everybody else is making—the typical story. Kim just had had enough of that. He realised that the only way that he was going to do anything—and he did it right—was no more partners, no more third owners with anybody. None of that. New record company, new record label, new management, which was Tom Berry. Which, previously, he was the A&R guy at Anthem. Tom Berry, for years. All of a sudden Tom learns how to run a record company. Kim says, okay, you're going to be my new manager, my new record company and I want this kind of deal where you get a nice, tasty deal, because Tom is going, I got the biggest rock star in Canada, and he wants me to manage him, and be on my new record label."

Then there's Mike Tilka, still back at headquarters, upholding the business of being in the music business. Ticking off the boxes, he figures, "Oh, Kim got divorced, they weren't as successful as they thought, Kim wasn't happy, he was tired of being on the road. I wasn't out there with him at that time. I went to a gig in Detroit, at Joe Louis Arena, and I went backstage, and Kim pulled me aside and he asked me a bunch of questions, most of which I can't even remember. But I couldn't answer any of them. He said, 'Don't you work in the office?' I said to him, 'All I do is look at your bank account. I don't look at your dates, I don't negotiate your tours, I'm not invited to your meetings, I had nothing to do with your last two records. You're asking me questions I don't know anything about!' He understood that. I could tell he was extremely unhappy. I wasn't out on the road with them because he wanted Pye in the band. He was an expense to the band which I thought was silly. Again, that was my only opinion there. Because I was the money guy. But I really don't know. Terry told me some story the other day I didn't even know about. He and I were having a beer, and he told some stories of being on the road, and I didn't even know that stuff."

Speaking of Watkinson, what was Mike's view of the mad professor's state of mind at that juncture? "Well, he quit. He had had it. You know, when a band starts to have a certain modicum of success, even headlining at Maple Leaf Gardens, that's one market. You know, you're not rich, you're not buying a Mercedes, unless you have the forward momentum that makes sense. Really, there was no momentum. Kim broke up the band before the tour was over. Which is too bad, because you make your money at the end of the tour. All your expenses are at the front end of the tour, when you book the vehicles and book the hotels and book everything. But if you don't make the income, it's not as if you can come back to Toronto and make five, six grand a night. You just don't. So anyway, I really don't know. It's not as if we sat around and had beers and talked."

There's no more poignant a close that can be had to this specific topic than a written missive received by the author from Pye. There's a major irony embedded in this treatise, namely that for all the talk of the pointlessness of having Pye on the road, well, maybe this would have been a good time to have had Pye on the road.

"Alarming—you need to ask me! Disbanding. Crime report. Point: Max would not have disbanded if I had been on tour when Kim pulled the plug—yeah! He might have made the decision, but he would have had to go through me first! The decision (his decision) was secondary to reasons why and the anxiety encapsulating his reasons. I would have diffused his anxiety quickly and early (like I had many times in the past). Me, the garde malade. Acute ambivalence was okay—it was what he was going to do with it. That was the problem; nothing wrong with being angry, it's what you do with it!"

"Actually, it was one of the first times I wasn't on tour with the band. I didn't mind. Yeah, I would miss the stimuli and the opportunity to write, but at that time, expenses for the band had to be considered. I think KJ Mitchell pulled the plug in Chicago. I don't remember where I was when the word got back to me, but I do remember what I said: 'throwing the baby out with the bathwater... cut off the nose to spite the face.' Clichés ad infinitum, walking/breathing."

"I don't remember being preoccupied about the demise of the band. I had writings ready for music, so my horizontal elevator moved the creativeness onward regardless. Max would not have disbanded if I was on that tour. Disbanded over my dead body! I guarantee the band would not have been dissolved. Yeah, maybe at the end of that tour, or in a year, the band was gone. But not in the middle of that tour, and not with me being there. I guarantee it!"

"I had an edge; I had one up on Kim. Sagacity, not wrath would've been in his face—he would back down (for the tour, at least). I had an arsenal of skills and techniques (supportive and otherwise) to dissipate his anger, anxiety, angst, animosities, assholeness. I guarantee. Not on my watch. I would've prevailed. I know what needed to be said, I knew what needed to be done. It was not as simple as saying, 'Give that baby a drink from the water it was thrown out with.'"

In any event, what we surely have come to understand is that the reasons for the break-up of Max Webster are varied and numerous (and as I alluded to in the introduction, we've left out one that is just too, too personal—sorry).

"Max was huge in Ontario," continues Tom, adding to the postmortem, "but we would go from selling out Massey Hall, and at one point Maple Leaf Gardens, to Vancouver, and we'd be playing in a Commodore-type of situation. Montréal, we'd be in a club, almost. Ottawa was big but that's because Ontario was big. In Cleveland, it would be back to little rooms."

Throwing on another wet blanket of psychology, it couldn't be fun watching your buddies in Rush go from strength to stratospheric strength, while you sputtered, *High Class* to the bad vibes and middling reception of *Mutiny*, (regional) hit record in *A Million Vacations* and then back to the bad vibes and middling reception afforded *Universal Juveniles*.

Opines Tom, "Rush was allowed to be, and do, most exactly whatever it wanted to be. So, to be a little brother in that situation puts you in that mind space too, right? Well Rush is doing it; they can do whatever they want. So, Max was within that same thing. But was all of a sudden being told, no, you can't be like that, you gotta be more like this. You can't ever... You might have a writer like Neil Peart, but... What?! He's outside of the band?! So, it created interesting tensions, when your big brother is successful and doing everything he wants, and you somehow can't all the time. So, it really was like Rush were the big brothers and very successful, and Max were the younger brothers with lots of potential, but just at times a little too weird for even a Rush audience."

"We continued to gig, but you could just feel it slowly falling apart," continues Tom, counting the last days. "At the same time, I was starting to think that I should be doing something else myself. I had Bob and Doug McKenzie and that went through the fucking roof! That record cost eight grand and sold platinum in America and four times platinum in Canada. I basically had done the marketing with my team, and just thought, hmm, I don't know, maybe it's time for me to move on. Then I could see the Kim thing happening, and then it happened, and then I decided to do the same thing. It was a significant time of change and turmoil."

Offering a reflection, a post-mortem, on what could have been, Dave Myles qualifies that, "All those records went gold, including *Universal Juveniles*. They all did—except gold in Canada is 50,000 and gold in America is 500,000. And yeah, we got all the records and all that shit. One of them was platinum, *A Million Vacations*. Again, here I was, I slipped into the band right after *High Class* really starts to do well for the band. So, it was like, 'I'm not on this.' 'Well, which one are you?' I'm going, 'I'm the guy with the white toga. The bald head' (laughs). But yeah, it was a wonderful time, a magical time. Really magic."

"We really did not know what was going to happen. Anything could happen. We were out there playing our hand. We're out there and we would go and do it. We would talk to anybody who would want to listen to us. We'd take pictures, we'd do the shows, and we'd go out and go anywhere. It's this simple? You'd go out on a show, and you'd go to play something, and you'd go, this is it, okay, this is the stage. Okay, here's the people. Do your thing. I'll tell you when I knew it was time for me to leave. When I felt we sounded like a polka band. Sometimes 'The Party' sounded like a polka (laughs). Really, some of the lines were, they were just hilarious. Hilarious lines. Kim would deliver one of Pye's gems, and you'd just go, this is crazy. If people figure out what we're doing here, it's going to be... the jig is up (laughs)."

"You've got to look at the stable we were in," continues Dave. "Here we were with Rush; they are a totally uncompromising band, but very dark. Here's Max Webster, who is like, what, are you kidding me? Are you kidding me?! So, we said, 'Oh you want more of that? Okay, we'll give you more.' That's where I think at one point, that started to... even though we wanted to make the move to being more heavy and more serious and tough, people still wanted to hear 'Hangover.'"

"I've often wondered what would've happened if we had started off when there were music videos. I wonder what effect a video would have had on Max's longevity. If we would've done a music video and if it would have been after 'I want my MTV.' A lot of bands that we played with, they'd say, 'I really dig what you're doing. It's really different.' I think it's better to be doing that than looking like a lot of other people."

I asked Dave if indeed, Max were Canada's answer to Cheap Trick. "No, because they had well-crafted songs. When they put together their tunes, like 'I Want You To Want Me,' they are full of hooks. You can see why they were so big. Of course when you went to see them live, it was as much humour as it was music. The whole thing was over the top. You couldn't take your eyes off some of these people. Kim was always like that. Kim, even when I played with him in high school, he had an awesome stage presence. He really did. You just could not take your eyes off the guy. He just drew you in. That was the thing in Max too. Even though we were all trying to support and do our parts, it was really about Kim. That's why it didn't surprise me at all that he went solo. It became apparent that Kim was not willing to do anybody else's scene. He had his own thing he wanted to do, and that's where he was going."

"There were tunes that Kim would sometimes give us just glimpses of, that, I went, 'Wow, that's really good,' and he goes, 'Well, yeah, that's for another time though.' So, he had a bunch of stuff banging around in his head that would've been appropriate on certain albums, and they just didn't get on the album. They ended up... some of those ideas came up on a solo album for Kim. He kept everything. I tell you, Kim is just an amazing, amazing musician. It was really just a pleasure to work with him."

Terry Watkinson's eulogy for Max is typically succinct. "The concept of the band in general was to–how shall I put this?—be successful to a wide audience while playing alternative music. Not being a commercial band but having elements of that in there but also elements of bizarreness and musical experimentation. We achieved that in Canada, and what we were doing during those last couple of years was to try break through in the United States. We had some success there, but not enough to get a big ball rolling internationally. Probably why we never did that is that we didn't produce radio play singles."

"I don't know what sound we were trying to achieve," reflects Gary McCracken. "I guess at the time we wanted to be heavy, and we wanted to be progressive, and we wanted to be different, and we wanted to challenge certain things about the music. Other bands weren't doing this kind of stuff and I don't think anybody's done it since. Kim was writing the tunes mostly, and as time went on, we contributed a bit. I guess the whole idea was to be different and not too commercial. I think we certainly were different. We only got as big as we did because we played all the time. We built our audience where we sold those records to people because they liked the band, right? There was never any particular promo. For anybody. Certainly not individually, until way after the fact, and then Kim went on to be Kim Mitchell. But we sold over a half-million albums. Which, okay, it's not ten million, but it's a half a million (laughs)."

"That was just a unique thing, that last album, compared to the other material. Kim has never been known to be radio-friendly. Certainly, Max Webster was never considered to be really radio-friendly. We just ended up forcing our way in there. Because people like this, and so it ended up there. So, we were always trying to be not commercial, and yet still have people like us. We weren't trying to be so bad or weird that nobody liked us. But we thought we have something to offer with our approach. Kim's music always had that outside thing, and yet it rocks. But when we went through all that, like all the guys leaving and coming and going. Kim actually realised that if he was going to keep going, he would have to split and start up from scratch, and just hire side guys. It's just, in Kim Mitchell's universe, anyone who is going to be in it is going to be employed."

"You're not winning anything," sighs Gary, disagreeing that in some manner, at least creatively, Max was a winning proposition. "Yeah, a lot of it was that, and again, we had the crappiest record deal—that you could ever have. But we had it, and one of the things back then was, bands would say, well, you always sign a crappy deal. If you do well, you renegotiate. Well, we never got the chance to renegotiate, right? We never got a chance to renegotiate. That's when Kim said, well, if I'm going to renegotiate, I'm just gonna start up my whole thing and Tom Berry is going to look after everything and be my manager. So, Kim's already laughing. Then in the meantime, I don't know what Ray even thinks anymore. I don't know what Ray thinks about it all. Ray and I were always quite friendly. We got along good. He'd come and pick me up at midnight in his Rolls-Royce and we'd go for French fries on the Danforth. Right? Eat fries and shoot the shit about stuff. That was our band meeting. A lot of times he'd just have a chauffeur come by. Funny thing. Actually, Vic Wilson had the Rolls, I'm sorry—a white one (laughs)."

"I just look back at it, and quite frankly, I'm just happy to be part of the fabric of Canadian music," says Gary, in closing. "Because again, every kid grows up, when you're ten or eleven, everyone wants to make a record and be on the radio. To have that happen is really neat. Whether it cost you a fortune or not, it doesn't matter. The money is just, that's another experience. But to be sitting around when I'm sixty listening to something I did thirty years ago, and it's on the radio as if it was a new band or something, it's like looking at somebody else almost. It's really a trip."

Is it a trip worth writing a book about?

"Nothing overly unique there," answers Kim, when I asked him this very question thirty years ago. "Most artists are the same; most rock bands are the same. We may come from different unique places but that's it. But on the creative stuff, sure, some of the pain of making records, some of the hot spots... yeah, it doesn't sound like a horrible idea. I don't know if it would be worth your while. I'd have to think about it. It wouldn't cost me anything to talk about the whole thing. It's a nice idea: this is your story. Everybody has a story, and everybody's is equally interesting and important to hear."

EPILOGUE

As discussed in the introduction, the original plan with this book was to include two long epilogues. One would have the catchy title Akimbo and would be centred on Kim's hugely worthy solo career. The other would be called Alogo and would focus on the brief reunion in the '90s and a "Where are they now?" on everybody.

That material will now be shelved, in the interest of some sense of brevity for this book as well as the possibility of a second book, in which all of that would be covered. Or, more accurately, there could be a book on Kim as a solo artist, in which an early chapter would be a dip back into the waters of Max.

But, in the spirit of some semblance of epilogue, here are the facts, ma'am. Perhaps pointing to the magic of Max, or the fragility thereof, or... any number of reasons positive and negative, no one from Max besides Kim stayed in the business to any appreciable level beyond the odd indie release. Hard to believe, but very much Terry, Gary, Paul, Dave, Mike... they all wound up in a combination of non-music jobs and/or pretty much part-time dabblings in music, at a level under the radar to anyone except the deepest digger. But everybody's alive. That's good, right?

Kim, on the other hand, became a Canadian rock icon over and above anything Max Webster would achieve. His record of records, at the time of writing (and for the foreseeable future), comprises eight studio albums, a live record, a greatest hits, and the greatest EP ever issued in all of rock across all time and however many planets we have today in our solar system, based on how you feel about Pluto. Amongst the lot, there are five platinum albums, one of them double and one of them, *Shakin' Like a Human Being*, triple. Then for eleven years he was a top DJ on Toronto's classic rock station, Q107, ending his residency there in August of 2015. As well, despite slowing down on making records, Kim is still regularly hot-clockin' some of the greatest displays of power trio mania you'll ever witness.

But you may have noticed I haven't mentioned Canada's only lyricist head and shoulders floated above (yes, picture a bare-foot an' horizontal Rick Rubin or Jerry on the cover of *Go to Heaven*) the likes of Joni Mitchell, Leonard Cohen and Neil Peart. Yes, Sir Pye Dubois—who you'd figure to be the greatest recluse of all the Maxers, and about whom I get the most questions surrounding his mysterious sightings—well, let's just say that the accurate answer to the above is that Pye, like Kim, continued in the business.

How so? Well, Pye remained Kim's wise wordsmith through Kim's glory years, which, in a little more detail than above, included *Kim Mitchell* (1982), *Akimbo Alogo* (1984), *Shakin' Like A Human Being* (1986) and *Rockland* (1989). And then after two records away, he returned for 1994's *Itch*, and with relations at an impasse, did not return for Kim's last three albums.

Really, the only other important epilogue bit would be the reunion of Max for a handful of hugely magical live dates between December 30th of 1995 and early '96. At these Pye recited some poetry, the bass player was Kim solo legend Peter Fredette, but otherwise, you also got Terry and you got Gary. As I wrote at the time, as I've said in interviews, the concert sound was so good in Hamilton, January 26th, 1996, it was like strapping on a pair of headphones.

Then it was poof again until May 24th of 2007, when the band played a special one-off Q107 gig in Toronto—a private party, big Canuck bill to a bunch of hosers that were all highly indebted to the magnificence of Max.

DISCOGRAPHY

A. Studio Albums

Max Webster
(Taurus/Anthem, May 3, 1976)
Side 1: 1. Hangover 4:36; 2. Here Among the Cats 3:07; 3. Blowing the Blues Away 3:33; 4. Summer Turning Blue 3:05; 5. Toronto Tontos 3:40
Side 2: 1. Coming Off the Moon 3:38; 2. Only Your Nose Knows 4:16; 3. Summer's Up 2:45; 4. Lily 7:42
Notes: Band personnel is Kim Mitchell: guitar and lead vocals, Mike Tilka: bass and vocals, Terry Watkinson: keyboards and vocals, Paul Kersey: drums and percussion and Pye Dubois: lyrics. Produced by Max Webster and Terry Brown. US issue is on Mercury/Polygram and features different cover art and different title, *Hangover*.

High Class in Borrowed Shoes
(Anthem, May 16, 1977)
Side 1: 1. High Class in Borrowed Shoes 4:00; 2. Diamonds Diamonds 3:18; 3. Gravity 4:53; 4. Words to Words 3:34; 5. America's Veins 4:08
Side 2: 1. Oh War! 4:25; 2. On the Road 3:25; 3. Rain Child 4:22; 9. In Context of the Moon 5:13
Notes: Gary McCracken replaces Paul Kersey on drums. Produced by Max Webster and Terry Brown.

Mutiny Up My Sleeve
(Anthem, April 17, 1978)
Side 1: 1. Lip Service 4:02; 2. Astonish Me 4:49; 3. Let Your Man Fly 2:46; 4. Water Me Down 3:13; 5. Distressed 4:12
Side 2: 1. The Party 4:46; 2. Waterline 4:08 3. Hawaii 4:08 4. Beyond the Moon 6:17
Notes: Dave Myles replaces Mike Tilka on bass. Produced by Max Webster, Mike Tilka and Terry Brown.

A Million Vacations
(Anthem, March 5, 1979)
Side 1: 1. Paradise Skies 3:15; 2. Charmonium 4:15; 3. Night Flights 3:02; 4. Sun Voices 4:50; 5. Moon Voices 3:05
Side 2: 1. A Million Vacations 3:10; 2. Look Out 4:53; 3. Let Go the Line 3:25; 4. Rascal Houdi 3:28; 5. Research (At Beach Resorts) 4:45
Notes: Produced by John de Nottbeck and Max Webster.

Discography

Universal Juveniles
(Anthem, October 3, 1980)
Side 1: 1. In the World of Giants 4:18; 2. Check 2:37; 3. April in Toledo 3:40; 4. Juveniles Don't Stop 3:32; 5. Battle Scar 5:48
Side 2: 1. Chalkers 3:45; 2. Drive and Desire 3:53 3. Blue River Liquor Shine 4:15; 4. What Do You Do with the Urge 3:20; 5. Cry Out for Your Life 5:33
Notes: Keyboards performed by Terry Watkinson, Doug Riley and David Stone. The three members of Rush join Max Webster for "Battle Scar." Produced by Jack Richardson.

B. Live Albums

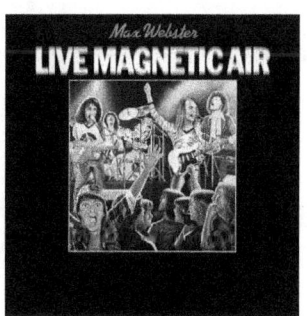

Live Magnetic Air
(Anthem, October 22, 1979)
Side 1: 1. America's Veins 3:56; 2. Paradise Skies 3:12; 3. In Context of the Moon 4:57; 4. Night Flights 3:03; 5. Lip Service 4:10; 6. Sarniatown Reggae 1:21
Side 2: 1. Here Among the Cats 3:25; 2. Gravity 4:31; 3. Waterline 4:26; 4. Charmonium 4:16; 5. Hangover 5:24
Notes: Produced by Max Webster and Terry Brown.

C. Compilations

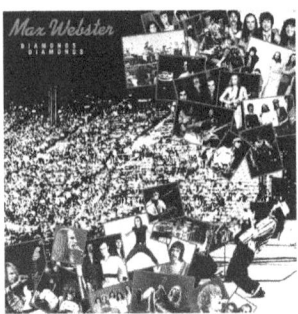

Diamonds Diamonds
(Anthem, August 7, 1981)
Side 1: 1. Gravity 4:53; 2. High Class in Borrowed Shoes 4:00; 3. Diamonds Diamonds 3:18; 4. Summer's Up 2:45; 5. Blowing the Blues Away 3:33; 6. A Million Vacations 3:10; 7. Let Go the Line 3:25
Side 2: 1. The Party 4:46; 2. Hot Spots 2:39; 3. Paradise Skies 3:15; 4. Overnight Sensation 2:52; 5. Lip Service 4:02; 13. Hangover 4:36
Notes: Posthumous LP compilation. Includes two previously unreleased tracks, "Hot Spots" and "Overnight Sensation."

The Best Of
(Anthem, 1989)
1. Check 2:36; 2. High Class in Borrowed Shoes 3:59; 3. A Million Vacations 3:13; 4. Diamonds Diamonds 3:17; 5. Let Go the Line 3:32; 6. Night Flights 3:04; 7. The Party 4:46; 8. Hangover (live) 5:36; 9. Kids in Action 4:29; 10. Gravity 4:52; 11. Paradise Skies 3:26; 12. Words to Words 3:35; 13. Oh War! 4:26; 14. Here Among the Cats 3:02; 15. Waterline (live) 4:37; 16. Battle Scar 5:50
Notes: Posthumous CD compilation. Includes Kim Mitchell solo song "Kids in Action."

Discography

The Party
(Anthem, 2017)
Notes: This is a box set, available in LP or CD format, consisting of the five studio albums, the live album, eight additional rarities under the umbrella name Limited Edition Bootleg, along with the five-track *Kim Mitchell* EP. Liner notes by the author.

INTERVIEWS WITH THE AUTHOR

Berry, Tom. June 11, 2014.
Bowes, Rodney. June 19, 2014.
Brown, Terry. December 13, 2007.
Brown, Terry. March 24, 2014.
Cameron, Deane. June 20, 2014.
Chadd, Greg. July 13, 2014.
Dubois, Pye. 1996.
Dubois, Pye. February 17, 2004.
Dubois, Pye. October 15, 2013.
Dubois, Pye. October 17, 2013.
Dubois, Pye. October 18, 2013.
Gingrich, Mike. July 3, 2013.
Harbron, Patrick. March 18, 2014.
Kersey, Paul. May 3, 2013.
McCracken, Gary. 1996.
McCracken, Gary. April 29, 2013.
McCracken, Gary. May 2, 2013.
Mitchell, Kim. June 9, 1994.
Mitchell, Kim. March 3, 2004.
Mitchell, Kim. July 2007.
Mitchell, Kim. June 10, 2014.
Moore, Gil. November 26, 2013.
Myles, Dave. April 26, 2013.
Peart, Neil. April 25, 2004.
Sheehan, Billy. April 18, 2009.
Tilka, Mike. April 24, 2013.
Watkinson, Terry. 1996.
Watkinson, Terry. May 23, 2007.
Watkinson, Terry. June 25, 2013.

ADDITIONAL SOURCES

Canadian Musician. Max Webster by Mad Stone. December, 1979.
Canadian Musician. Kim Mitchell of Max Webster. by Greg Quill. June 1981.
Cheap Thrills. *Max Webster* record review by Michael Raceway. Volume 3, Number 1. May 1976.
Cheap Thrills. Max by Sam Charters. Volume 3, Number 11. March 1977.
CHUM FM 104.5. Report by Larry Wilson. February 18, 1974.
Georgia Straight. Mutiny "Beyond the Moon" by Tom Harrison. April 21-28, 1978.
Globe And Mail, The. Neighborhood flavor at free park concert by Paul Koring. July 15, 1974.
Keyboard. *A Million Vacations* record review by Robbie Gennet. June 2004.
Lethbridge Herald, The. Slim crowd turns out to listen to Rush by Mike Rogers. October 25, 1976.
Montreal Gazette, The. Heavy rockers hype local fans by Juan Rodriguez. July 21, 1976.
Music Express. *High Class in Borrowed Shoes* record review. Vol. 1, No. 8. August 1977.
Music Express. High Class in Borrowed Shoes by Boyd Tattrie. September, 1977.
Music Express. *Live Magnetic Air* record review. Vol. 3, No. 10. Christmas 1979.
Music Express. Universal Juveniles stretching their claws by Elliott Lefko. Vol. 5, No. 1. Issue No.41.
Music Express. *Universal Juveniles* record review by Keith Sharp. Vol. 5, No. 1. Issue No.41.
Music Express. Max Webster/Goddo/B.B. Gabor concert review by Keith Sharp. Vol. 5, No. 3. Issue No.43. 1981.
Music Express. No Worries: Kim Mitchell Returns by Greg Quill. Vol. 7. Issue No.63. Nov./Dec. '82.
New Music, The. Max Goes to Europe by Roman Mintz. August 1979.
New Musical Express, The. Who is Max Webster? by Harry George. April 28, 1979.
Nightout. Max Webster: Max-imum Music by Stan Lepka. August 16, 1976.
Record Review. Bewitched by Max Webster by Boni Johnson. June, 1980.
Roxy. Max Webster: Zen Archery for the Well-Rippled Mind by John Lamont. Vol. 1, No. 1. June 1978.
Sarnia Observer. Their Roots Are in Sarnia by Gary Lamphier. March 22, 1978.
Sounds. The Max Factor by Geoff Barton. May 12, 1979.
Sounds. *A Million Vacations* record review by Geoff Barton. 1979.
Stone Cold Crazy. A Very Candid Conversation with Dave Stone by Jeff Cramer. May 18, 2013.
Toronto Sun, The. Short Riffs by Bruce Blackadar. August 1, 1974.
Vancouver Sun, The. And now, for something completely different by Vaughn Palmer. April 24, 1978.
Windsor Star. Freaky Friends by John Laycock. May 27, 1976.
Winnipeg Free Press. Youthscene by Andy Mellen. June 5, 1976.
Winnipeg Free Press. Canadian LPs get some scrutiny by Jim Millican. 1976.

IMAGE CREDITS

Thanks to the following for graciously providing shots for the book. If we've missed anybody, we would be pleased to correct in future editions.

Bill Baran, Jack in Buffalo, Jim Chapman, Don Dale, Scott Feeney, Mike Gingrich, Philip Kamin, Carla Jensen, Paul Kersey, Brian Petruk and Brian Smolik.

ACKNOWLEDGEMENTS

A special hearty hail to universal juveniles Brian Smolik and Adrian Orso for making the original edition of this project happen. Also, lovely people are Juan Alemparte, Scott Feeney, Philip Kamin, Tim Rempel and Bob Wegner, who not only has created a masterpiece of a Max Webster book called *High Class: The Definitive History*, but he's quite the guitar-picker as well. Thanks as well to Agustin Garcia de Paredes, who found and flagged many of the typos and other gremlins that were there in the first, cursed edition of this book.

ABOUT THE AUTHOR

At approximately 7900 (with over 7000 appearing in his books), Martin has unofficially written more record reviews than anybody in the history of music writing across all genres. Additionally, Martin has penned approximately 135 books on hard rock, heavy metal, classic rock, progressive rock, punk and record collecting. He was Editor-in-Chief of the now retired *Brave Words & Bloody Knuckles*, Canada's foremost heavy metal publication for 14 years, and has also contributed to *Revolver*, *Guitar World*, *Goldmine*, *Record Collector*, bravewords.com, lollipop.com and hardradio.com, with many record label band bios and liner notes to his credit as well.

Additionally, Martin has been a regular contractor to Banger Films, having worked for two years as researcher on the award-winning documentary *Rush: Beyond the Lighted Stage*, on the writing and research team for the 11-episode *Metal Evolution* and on the ten-episode *Rock Icons*, both for VH1 Classic. Additionally, Martin is the writer of the original metal genre chart used in *Metal: A Headbanger's Journey* and throughout the *Metal Evolution* episodes.

Then there's his audio podcast, *History in Five Songs with Martin Popoff* and the YouTube channel he runs with Marco D'Auria and Grant Arthur, called *The Contrarians*. Martin currently resides in Toronto and can be reached through martinp@inforamp.net or martinpopoff.com.

A MARTIN POPOFF BIBLIOGRAPHY

2025: A Million Vacations: The Max Webster Story, The Unholy Scriptures: The Complete Unofficial Chronicle of Ronnie James Dio's Solo Canon, A Dangerous Meeting: In the Shadows with Mercyful Fate, Guns N' Roses at 40, Hallowed by Their Name: The Unofficial Iron Maiden Bible, Blockbuster! The Sweet Story

2024: Judas Priest: Album by Album, Behind the Lines: Genesis on Record: 1978 – 1997, Entangled: Genesis on Record 1969 - 1976, Run with the Wolf: Rainbow on Record, Van Halen at 50, Honesty Is No Excuse: Thin Lizzy on Record, Pictures at Eleven: Robert Plant Album by Album, Perfect Water: The Rebel Imaginos

2023: Kiss at 50, The Electric Church: The Biography, Dominance and Submission: The Blue Öyster Cult Canon, The Who and Quadrophenia, Wild Mood Swings: Disintegrating The Cure Album by Album, AC/DC at 50

2022: Pink Floyd and The Dark Side of the Moon: 50 Years, Killing the Dragon: Dio in the '90s and 2000s, Feed My Frankenstein: Alice Cooper, the Solo Years, Easy Action: The Original Alice Cooper Band, Lively Arts: The Damned Deconstructed, Yes: A Visual Biography II: 1982 – 2022, Bowie @ 75, Dream Evil: Dio in the '80s, Judas Priest: A Visual Biography, UFO: A Visual Biography

2021: Hawkwind: A Visual Biography, Loud 'n' Proud: Fifty Years of Nazareth, Yes: A Visual Biography, Uriah Heep: A Visual Biography, Driven: Rush in the '90s and "In the End," Flaming Telepaths: Imaginos Expanded and Specified, Rebel Rouser: A Sweet User Manual

2020: The Fortune: On the Rocks with Angel, Van Halen: A Visual Biography, Limelight: Rush in the '80s, Thin Lizzy: A Visual Biography, Empire of the Clouds: Iron Maiden in the 2000s, Blue Öyster Cult: A Visual Biography, Anthem: Rush in the '70s, Denim and Leather: Saxon's First Ten Years, Black Funeral: Into the Coven with Mercyful Fate

2019: Satisfaction: 10 Albums That Changed My Life, Holy Smoke: Iron Maiden in the '90s, Sensitive to Light: The Rainbow Story, Where Eagles Dare: Iron Maiden in the '80s, Aces High: The Top 250 Heavy Metal Songs of the '80s, Judas Priest: Turbo 'til Now, Born Again! Black Sabbath in the Eighties and Nineties

2018: Riff Raff: The Top 250 Heavy Metal Songs of the '70s, Lettin' Go: UFO in the '80s and '90s, Queen: Album by Album, Unchained: A Van Halen User Manual, Iron Maiden: Album by Album, Sabotage! Black Sabbath in the Seventies, Welcome to My Nightmare: 50 Years of Alice Cooper, Judas Priest: Decade of Domination, Popoff Archive – 6: American Power Metal, Popoff Archive – 5: European Power Metal, The Clash: All the Albums, All the Songs

2017: Led Zeppelin: All the Albums, All the Songs, AC/DC: Album by Album, Lights Out: Surviving the '70s with UFO, Tornado of Souls: Thrash's Titanic Clash, Caught in a Mosh: The Golden Era of Thrash, Rush: Album by Album, Beer Drinkers and Hell Raisers: The Rise of Motörhead, Metal Collector: Gathered Tales from Headbangers, Hit the Lights: The Birth of Thrash, Popoff Archive – 4: Classic Rock, Popoff Archive – 3: Hair Metal

2016: Popoff Archive – 2: Progressive Rock, Popoff Archive – 1: Doom Metal, Rock the Nation: Montrose, Gamma and Ronnie Redefined, Punk Tees: The Punk Revolution in 125 T-Shirts, Metal Heart: Aiming High with Accept, Ramones at 40, Time and a Word: The Yes Story

2015: Kickstart My Heart: A Mötley Crüe Day-by-Day, This Means War: The Sunset Years of the NWOBHM, Wheels of Steel: The Explosive Early Years of the NWOBHM, Swords and Tequila: Riot's Classic First Decade, Who Invented Heavy Metal?, Sail Away: Whitesnake's Fantastic Voyage

2014: Live Magnetic Air: The Unlikely Saga of the Superlative Max Webster, Steal Away the Night: An Ozzy Osbourne Day-by-Day, The Big Book of Hair Metal, Sweating Bullets: The Deth and Rebirth of Megadeth, Smokin' Valves: A Headbanger's Guide to 900 NWOBHM Records

2013: The Art of Metal (co-edit with Malcolm Dome), 2 Minutes to Midnight: An Iron Maiden Day-by-Day, Metallica: The Complete Illustrated History, Rush: The Illustrated History, Ye Olde Metal: 1979, Scorpions: Top of the Bill - updated and reissued as Wind of Change: The Scorpions Story in 2016

2012: Epic Ted Nugent, Fade To Black: Hard Rock Cover Art of the Vinyl Age, It's Getting Dangerous: Thin Lizzy 81-12, We Will Be Strong: Thin Lizzy 76-81, Fighting My Way Back: Thin Lizzy 69-76, The Deep Purple Royal Family: Chain of Events '80 – '11, The Deep Purple Royal Family: Chain of Events Through '79 - reissued as The Deep Purple Family Year by Year books

2011: Black Sabbath FAQ, The Collector's Guide to Heavy Metal: Volume 4: The '00s (co-authored with David Perri)

2010: Goldmine Standard Catalog of American Records 1948 – 1991, 7th Edition

2009: Goldmine Record Album Price Guide, 6th Edition, Goldmine 45 RPM Price Guide, 7th Edition, A Castle Full of Rascals: Deep Purple '83 – '09, Worlds Away: Voivod and the Art of Michel Langevin, Ye Olde Metal: 1978

2008: Gettin' Tighter: Deep Purple '68 – '76, All Access: The Art of the Backstage Pass, Ye Olde Metal: 1977, Ye Olde Metal: 1976

2007: Judas Priest: Heavy Metal Painkillers, Ye Olde Metal: 1973 to 1975, The Collector's Guide to Heavy Metal: Volume 3: The Nineties, Ye Olde Metal: 1968 to 1972

2006: Run for Cover: The Art of Derek Riggs, Black Sabbath: Doom Let Loose, Dio: Light Beyond the Black

2005: The Collector's Guide to Heavy Metal: Volume 2: The Eighties, Rainbow: English Castle Magic, UFO: Shoot Out the Lights, The New Wave of British Heavy Metal Singles

2004: Blue Öyster Cult: Secrets Revealed! (updated and reissued in 2009 with the same title; updated and reissued as Agents of Fortune: The Blue Öyster Cult Story in 2016), Contents Under Pressure: 30 Years of Rush at Home & Away, The Top 500 Heavy Metal Albums of All Time

2003: The Collector's Guide to Heavy Metal: Volume 1: The Seventies, The Top 500 Heavy Metal Songs of All Time

2001: Southern Rock Review

2000: Heavy Metal: 20th Century Rock and Roll, The Goldmine Price Guide to Heavy Metal Records

1997: The Collector's Guide to Heavy Metal

1993: Riff Kills Man! 25 Years of Recorded Hard Rock & Heavy Metal

www.ingramcontent.com/pod-product-compliance
Lightning Source LLC
Chambersburg PA
CBHW070639160426
43194CB00009B/1508